To WSC

Hoping for a Great Revie

From a Great Magazine

Kind Regards

Yours Sincerely

Jan 2006

TALES FROM THE RIVERBANK

TALES FROM
THE RIVERBANK

**The match by match story of
FULHAM FOOTBALL CLUB**

Part 1

Seasons 1965–66 and 1966–67

MARTIN PLUMB

*A*SHWATER
PRESS

Rene Belloq to Indiana Jones:

You want to see it opened as well as I. Indiana, we are simply passing through history—this, this **is** history.

Raiders of the Lost Ark, 1979

First published in October 2005

Copyright © Martin Plumb 2005

The right of Martin Plumb to be identified as the author of this work has been asserted by him in accordance with the Copyright, Designs and Patent Act 1988.

Designed and published by
Ashwater Press
68 Tranmere Road, Whitton, Twickenham, Middlesex, TW2 7JB

Printed and bound by Butler and Tanner, Frome, Somerset

10 digit ISBN 0 9548938 2 4

13 digit ISBN 978-0-9548938-2-8

FULHAM FOOTBALL CLUB

The coat of arms of the former Borough of Fulham carried the motto PRO CIVIBUS ET CIVITATE—For Citizen and State—*and appeared on the front of Fulham FC programmes during the 1950s and part of the 60s. Over subsequent years it was changed and adapted, but retained the feature of the River Thames, which formed the boundary of the borough for approximately 3½ miles. The crossed swords and mitre were taken from the arms of the See of London, the borough's most ancient association with history. The ship represents the wintering of the Danes on Thames side in 879*

MARTIN PLUMB

Author Martin Plumb has been a regular at Craven Cottage since 1963. He was trained in accountancy, but has subsequently spent thirty years in I.T. consultancy, working with many leading software houses. He is a teacher of mathematics and a professional guitarist and keyboards player with a long career in music. He is a respected author, a school governor and a devotee of heritage railways. He has been with his partner Jean for almost 40 years, has three daughters, and lives in Ascot in Berkshire.

Acknowledgments

WHEN FULHAM left the First Division in 1968, I hoped that one day, before the good Lord brandished the red card and I ascended to the great Craven Cottage in the Sky, I would, once again, see my beloved team compete regularly against the best clubs in the land in the top flight. In the dark days of the early 1990s that hope was just a distant dream, but after five remarkable years, and finally in 2001, the dream became a glorious reality.

I saw the last Fulham goal scored at Craven Cottage in the top flight, netted by Joe Gilroy against Southampton in 1968 and I witnessed Barry Hayles score the first goal for Fulham against Sunderland back in top flight in 2001—a span of thirty-three years.

I have written this book not for any self-aggrandizement, but because when like-minded, life-long football supporters get together, it isn't long before someone pipes up, 'Remember that time when …' or 'Do you recall when Fulham played so and so in the Cup and…' and a whole raft of opinions, emotions and maudlin recollections arises. The work here is the first in a series of factual summaries of those times gone by. The content should answer a number of the questions that appear regularly on the club's messageboards.

Although I had been following Fulham for two seasons before 1965–66 and attending sporadically, I had few match reports, scrapbook material or detailed recollections of those seasons. I chose the season 1965–66 to start the history because of its drama and because of my regular attendance. I hope that another Fulham supporter will write some of the history prior to 1965.

My thanks, if I included everyone, would be longer than a Jessica Sarah Parker award acceptance speech, but here goes:

With apologies to the great Bard, I often think of my own, very bastardised, version of a quote from *Twelfth Night:* 'Some people are born Fulham, others become Fulham and some have Fulham thrust upon them.' I am certainly one who falls into the second group and have been clearly given a 'life sentence', whilst my long-suffering wife Jean and my three daughters clearly fall into the third category, I thank them all for their understanding, patience and support whilst writing this.

Mostly, I would like to sincerely thank Bill Frith and his lovely late wife Betty for freely taking me so often to the club and around the country in their car during my years as an impecunious student. If it hadn't been for their companionship and support during those times, none of this would have been written. They were great times, even breaking down on the M4 on a cold evening returning from Bristol City!

A big thank you to the representatives of all the major national newspaper groups who raised no objection to me extracting sentences from their match reports to be included in the book: Solo Syndication Limited, Express Syndication, NI Syndication Limited, Mirror Syndication International, IPC Media and the Fulham Chronicle.

Also many thanks to the members of the British Library Newspapers in Colindale who helped in obtaining the relevant reels of microfiche information very quickly, and allowed me to 'fast track' straight to the photocopy area as I knew exactly what I was looking for! Thanks to Vic and the other staff at the Colindale library who took an interest in the work.

Similar thanks must go to Anne and the helpful staff at the Hammersmith and Fulham archives, for rapidly providing microfiche information from the *Fulham Chronicle*. Many thanks too must go to Sarah Brookes and Fulham Football Club for permitting me to use extracts from the club's official programmes and handbooks.

Professional thanks go to Sarah Price at Sprite Documentation Services in Binfield for her meticulous proof-reading and helpful suggestions. At least it was a change from the usual 'technical writing' she did, and it helped that she was actually interested in football, even though her allegiance lay with a team called United that played somewhere in Manchester! Also super thanks to my teacher daughter Jessica for religiously going through the text paragraph by paragraph and picking up a number of points. Thank you too to 'guinea pig' and long-time Fulham supporter Andy Cox for reading the books and adding his own slant.

Very many thanks go to the 'master lensman' Ken Coton, for his friendly nature, his undying enthusiasm for the project and all-round know-how in getting books like this published. It would still all be somewhere in my head if it hadn't been for him. Also thanks to Ken for access to his collection of Fulham pictures and for the usage of much new material. I owe him a great deal, as he kept encouraging me—even when the black dog of depression was sitting firmly on my shoulder. In terms of pictures, a great deal of thanks must also go to my photographer daughter Joanna for her many hours of diligent work with Photoshop and her Mac, bringing forty year-old football pictures back to life.

Thank you to David Lloyd and all at TOOFIF for actively supporting the book.

Finally a great big thank you to the players—it is really their book after all. Top marks go to Steve Earle, John Dempsey and Johnny Haynes for their comments, insights and ripping yarns, most of which could be published—although a couple of tales couldn't!

I am always keen to be contacted by Fulham supporters with material, ideas or any errata. I am contactable via: Martin_Plumb@talk21.com

Finally, this book is dedicated to the memory of Mary Doughty—Mrs Fulham, a lady with a most appropriate surname, the mother duck ensuring that all her ducklings got across the road and back onto the supporters' club coaches safely. She was the embodiment of everything that is Fulham Football Club. She would, I trust, have enjoyed this history, and she will be forever missed at the club.

Despite what I had originally anticipated, writing up these recollections has not been easy. The investigation and research has re-opened a number of wounds from that Fulham era, some of which are as raw today as they were all those years ago. However, I felt there were experiences that needed to be documented, and steps that just had to be re-traced. I hope you enjoy the start of this epic journey as much as I did.

Martin Plumb – Ascot, July 2005

Picture Credits

THE PHOTOGRAPHS on the following pages are by Ken Coton and are his copyright: 12, 30, 33, 35, 37, 39, 42, 43, 46, 47, 49, 50, 51, 53, 55 (RIGHT), 58, 60, 63 (TOP), 65, 67, 69, 71, 75, 78, 81 (TOP), 82, 87 (BOTH), 93, 95 (BOTH), 102, 106, 107, 109, 111, 113, 114, 117 (LEFT), 118, 119, 121 (BOTTOM), 125, 127, 128, 130, 131, 132, 137, 138, 140, 142, 143, 144, 146, 151, 152, 154, 155, 157, 159, 160, 161, 164, 167, 170, 172 (BOTH), 174, BACK COVER. Those on pages 25, 48, 72 and 135 are copyright Empics. Some photographs are from the author's own collection. Whilst best efforts have been made to trace the owners of the other photographs used, this has sometimes proved impossible. Such copyright owners are invited to contact the author.

READ ALL ABOUT IT!

Season 1965–66

- ☐ *The brand new Hammersmith End Stand.*
- ☐ *Fulham's five-goal start against Blackburn.*
- ☐ *Fulham's first-ever substitute.*
- ☐ *Graham Leggat hitting a hat trick but Fulham still losing.*
- ☐ *The West Ham egg shampoo.*
- ☐ *Everton's Colin Harvey being dismissed at the Cottage.*
- ☐ *Fulham's centre half John Dempsey scoring a hat trick.*
- ☐ *Fulham's first-ever Sunday TV coverage.*
- ☐ *Forward Rodney Marsh playing in goal.*
- ☐ *Pancho Pearson being sent off for swearing against Burnley.*
- ☐ *Goalkeeper Tony Macedo asking for his cards.*
- ☐ *The arrival of Dave Sexton.*
- ☐ *Vic Buckingham teaching the players to dance.*
- ☐ *Defender Bobby Keetch playing his last game—in the forward line.*
- ☐ *The return of Steve Earle and the arrival of Les Barrett.*
- ☐ *The seven-goal first half at Tottenham.*
- ☐ *The victory over league champions elect Liverpool.*
- ☐ *Ian St John being sent off for knocking out Pancho.*
- ☐ *The first Fulham away win in thirty-one attempts with five goals at Aston Villa.*
- ☐ *Five straight league wins in a row.*
- ☐ *The acrimonious departure of Rodney Marsh.*
- ☐ *The arrival of record signing Allan Clarke.*
- ☐ *Steve Earle's hat trick at Northampton.*
- ☐ *The Stoke City crunch game.*
- ☐ *Allan Clarke's first goal—and Fulham's safety from relegation.*
- ☐ *George Cohen's injury—threatening his World Cup hopes.*
- ☐ *The sponsored close season tour of Asia.*

READ ALL ABOUT IT!

Season 1966-67

- ☐ *The shock departure of Dave Sexton.*
- ☐ *The arrival of Gordon Jago.*
- ☐ *Fulham winning in the last ten seconds at Stoke, and the papers get it wrong.*
- ☐ *Fulham travelling without a substitute to West Bromwich Albion.*
- ☐ *The second consecutive seven-goal thriller with Spurs.*
- ☐ *Spurs directors getting upset at Fulham's VD advert.*
- ☐ *The arrival of Jimmy Conway.*
- ☐ *Wolves getting a five-goal hammering at the Cottage.*
- ☐ *Allan Clarke hitting four goals on his England debut.*
- ☐ *Tony Hateley proving to be a knockout in more ways than one for Chelsea.*
- ☐ *Fulham conceding six at Upton Park after leading West Ham.*
- ☐ *Fulham scoring five in one half against Aston Villa.*
- ☐ *George Cohen's last goal for Fulham.*
- ☐ *Graham Leggat returning with five goals in two games.*
- ☐ *Fulham on the rise with six league wins in seven matches by Christmas.*
- ☐ *Graham Leggat's shock departure from the Cottage.*
- ☐ *Out go the floodlights against West Bromwich Albion.*
- ☐ *Newcastle United turning up at the Cottage with the wrong kit.*
- ☐ *Allan Clarke's first Fulham hat trick.*
- ☐ *Fred Callaghan's punch-up with Terry Venables at White Hart Lane.*
- ☐ *The amazing Sheffield United Cup tie.*
- ☐ *The Sheffield United replay farces and Ol' Bill Punton.*
- ☐ *Fulham's best ever post-war attendance, against Manchester United.*
- ☐ *Fulham being foiled twice by Nobby Stiles on consecutive days.*
- ☐ *Goalkeeper Ian Seymour's debut in front of 60,000 at Old Trafford.*
- ☐ *Fulham's first goalscoring substitute.*
- ☐ *Allan Clarke's brawl with Arsenal's Ian Ure.*
- ☐ *The quick trip to America for £5,000.*
- ☐ *Bobby Robson's retirement.*

IN REMEMBRANCE

BOBBY KEETCH
(1941–1996)

RON BURGESS
(1917–2005)

Introduction

Fulham Football Club were once considered to rival *The Mousetrap* as London's longest running show! They were colloquially known as the 'Houdini' Club, or the perennial escapologists, because of their amazing dogfights with relegation and an uncanny ability to cheat the executioner's relegation trapdoor at the very last moment. It was a tightrope act that had been going on for several years.

Fulham were also known affectionately as 'The Cinderella Club'—a title they were not particularly ashamed of. They were the club that swept up behind the other giants, the club that lived under the suzerainty of at least one big ugly sister in London SW6, and admitted honestly and publicly that they did not have the finances of some of the other First Division (Premiership) giants. This particular Cinderella always aspired to better things, but for so many years it often looked like she would remain amongst the cinders and rags of the lower divisions. Then, between 1996 and 1998, encouraged by the faith of a certain Prince Charming in Mickey Adams, and subsequently bolstered and underpinned by an extremely benevolent Fairy Godfather in Mohammed Al Fayed, after a thirty-three year absence, this particular Cinderella finally got her chance, once again, to go to the Premiership ball.

Having sampled the 'new' football, it is time to re-examine and re-create this Fulham past, and to document a 'then and now' account, highlighting both the footballing similarities and differences. The result is a purely historical account of those times, and although many supporters may not have been born when these matches took place, there is certainly enough here for Fulham followers to read and understand that similar goals, incidents, decisions, controversies and injuries occurred just as much then as now; same game, same club, often the same opponents—just different players in a different time.

In this 'age of information', there is a frequent complaint that, even with the coming of the Internet, there is very little detailed information anywhere relating to football from the Sixties and Seventies generally, let alone an individual club's history. Most of the information readily available on the web is at a high level, repeated or fragmented over several web sites. This work addresses those issues.

There have been many excellent books written about Fulham Football Club, most of them statistical or at a summary level, but this volume drills down to the lowest level. You know from the summaries, for example, that Fulham drew a match 3-3, but this will tell you nothing of the game's character. Did Fulham throw away a three-goal lead? Did they roar back from being three behind? Did they have the lead three times, each time to be pegged back? Or did the lead change hands several times throughout the game. The recollections in this book will tell you.

The highs and the lows are charted, as well as the in-betweens. They focus on the incidents that changed the direction of matches and Fulham's future: the controversial penalties, the major injuries, the bizarre refereeing decisions, the woodwork, the dismissals and even the weather! It's a 'warts and all' account of the day-to-day life of Fulham Football Club, its players, managers, directors and supporters. It is a blow-by-blow account: the laughter and the tears, the joy and the sadness. Around a hundred Fulham matches are covered in this first book.

Although the writing is predominantly focussed on Fulham FC, it is just as much a statement about the 'soccer scene' of the Sixties; the text pays particular attention to the First Division table, and the fluctuating changes in fortune of the clubs that inhabited the First Division throughout that time. The book will interest a wider audience seeking information on the 'stars' of the time. It includes all the star teams, their managers and the superstar players that turned out regularly at Craven Cottage, from Law and Best, Greaves and Gilzean to Hurst and Peters. It is written in a style taken from the Sixties, *exactly* as the national and local media saw and recorded it.

The book also utilises, where possible, terminology relevant to that time. All references to the *First Division* are equivalent to today's *Premiership*, and references to the *Second Division* are equivalent to the current *Coca Cola Championship*. The book refers to a time when just two points were awarded for a win instead of three. There were twenty-two clubs contained in the top division as opposed to the current twenty. League positions were decided by goal *average* rather than goal *difference*. At this time only two teams were promoted from the Second Division, and only two teams were relegated from the First Division each season. There were also no 'play off' matches; the champions and the runners-up from the Second Division were automatically promoted. Where appropriate, the book details team formations from the starting point in the Sixties of the standard 2–3–5 formation, evolving into the 4–2–4 or the 4–3–3 formations. Fulham's score is given *first* in each report. There are references to full backs, wing halves and inside forwards, and very few references to the 'lone' striker, wingback, sweeper or the defensive midfielder sitting just in front of the back four!

Although it is almost impossible to look backwards without some sort of nostalgia, the Sixties was an era with a very distinctive character. Association football was certainly a workingman's game, a time of Woodbines and 6d-bag (2.5p today) peanut sellers, muddy grassless pitches, cold November days, and foggy February afternoons. It was an age of heavy brown footballs, rattles and rosettes; players with 'Brylcreem' hairstyles and the heavy pervading smell of 'wintergreen'. An age where you could immediately read about your team's afternoon exploits in the Saturday *Evening Standard* or *Pink'un* brought round the streets by a young lad on a bicycle early in the evening. An era of loyal players that often walked to the ground with the supporters. A time when the referees all seemed to be either policemen, or come from Norfolk or Suffolk!

Although it is commonly accepted that football was certainly more physical (some would even say 'dirty') in the Sixties, bookings and dismissals were a relative rarity, and such events would cast rather a dark stain over the player and bring a certain amount of disgrace to the club. There were few football politics, no agents or middle-men, no FA investigations and, for the most part, a healthy respect amongst all the players, no diving, little overt cheating and certainly very few deliberate attempts to get an opposition player sent off. This was a time when any tough talking, either within the club or between clubs, remained for the most part behind closed doors, and was not conducted on a vulgar escalating basis through the back pages of the national press. It was a time when the supporters' only opportunity to argue about decisions made on the pitch was in the pub after the match, and the 'was the ball over the line' or 'was the tackle inside the penalty area' debate would *never* be proven one way or the other–which probably made the game more interesting. There was little football on television, let alone slow motion 'action replays'. There were no analyses of 'incidents' shown from dozens of different angles, or referees living in goldfish bowls having every decision scrutinised by television 'pundits' not to mention millions of cross-examining TV viewers.

This book covers two seasons and begins in August 1965 with Vic Buckingham as the new man appointed at the helm. After an average start, Fulham fall away badly and are rock bottom by January 1966. The appointment of Dave Sexton, coupled with some inspired performances by

Tommy Trinder.

young players brought in as a last resort, see Fulham produce championship winning form to claw themselves free of relegation. It is the season rightly known as 'The Great Escape'. The following season starts in August 1966, with Fulham in up and down form, but the team improve significantly, particularly at home, to be in a good position by New Year. With supporters expecting a top eight finish and a good FA Cup run, this season then goes totally the other way, and Fulham slip slowly down the league to finish once again in the lower reaches. In May 1967, with Graham Leggat gone, and Bobby Robson now retired, Fulham are definitely a club at the crossroads.

This was the Sixties—the true 'Tales From The Riverbank'. Those of you who witnessed it all may or may not choose to debate with chairman Tommy Trinder's interpretation of the time: "You *lucky* people!"

Setting the Scene

A council estate in the mid-Sixties

The council estate where all the teenage boys (hereafter called the lads) lived and were brought up was built just outside the boundaries of west London, six years after the war was over. Families lived in identical tidy three-bedroom terraced 'Pete Seeger—little box' houses, similar to those so well portrayed by Sir John Betjeman in his documentary *Metroland*. All kinds of interesting people lived on the estate, and there was always a plethora of different accents to be heard— Yorkshire, Lancashire, Scottish and, of course, east London. Money was always tight, and when the estate was built rationing was still in force, but there was at least healthy employment thanks to the burgeoning London Airport being built in the hamlet of Heath Row.

There was not a lot of luxury around in the Sixties, but most never really thought that they were particularly 'going without'. Initially most houses had 'bare boards' upstairs, and later perhaps posh linoleum; one of the principal producers of 'Lino' manufactured locally at Staines. The thought of carpets, especially upstairs, would have been unthinkable. There was also no upstairs heating, and to keep out the winter cold it was thick pyjamas, bed socks, a hot water bottle, winceyette sheets and extras thrown on top of the bed, There was regularly frost on the inside of the windows, and occasionally small icicles hung from the inside window sill. The only thing to warm your clothes on was an electric upright 'Belling' heater.

To try and get the upstairs heated, most houses possessed a paraffin heater, usually a bit of a death trap that wobbled worryingly on any sort of physical contact, left dark marks on the ceiling and gave off quite a sickening smell. When the paraffin couldn't be delivered due to the severe winter weather, it was not uncommon to trudge precariously to the shopping parade in over a foot of snow to buy your gallon of 'Esso blue' or 'Esso pink' from the now long-gone local ironmonger shop.

In the early years of the Sixties, obtaining hot water involved assisting in a number of exciting activities such as clearing out the grate, neatly wrapping all the dregs and ashes in paper, chopping up sticks, expertly placing the nuggets of coal, folding and twisting paper and then using a combination of Zip firelighters, matches, spills and a hint of good fortune to get the fire going. It was absolute luxury later in the decade to be able to receive instant hot water from a wall mounted 'Ascot' heater. The annual visit from the chimney sweep was one of the most exciting days of the year, and the whole job was quite an exercise, covering up the house furniture and floor with sheets, watching him put all his kit together, and giving him the nod as the sweeping tool emerged triumphant from the top of the chimney.

Most families had just enough food (although some families didn't), usually having porridge for breakfast most winter mornings with milk and syrup. There were copious amounts of shepherd's pies, corned beef hash, and minced up meat pies; some also ate rabbit, as turkey and chicken were, at that time, really 'once a year' dishes. Luxury was a slice of toast, cooked on a toasting fork by the open fire, with beef dripping spread upon it, which was kept in an enamel dish. There was always a regular supply of egg and bacon pie, bread pudding and fruitcake.

Rice pudding was also a weekly dish, enhanced with copious quantities of strawberry or raspberry jam. A real treat would be a small Hovis loaf on a Sunday. Most gardens were used for planting potatoes, runner beans, peas and other associated vegetables to keep the household bills down.

Cars were a real luxury; occasionally someone in the street would have a Riley Elf, Humber Hawk, or Wolesley 1500 or even a modern Vauxhall Cresta. Most people drove Morris Minors or Morris Travellers. The cars all seemed to have leather seats and real walnut fascias. Most children were not really used to travelling in cars, and the peculiar combination of the smells of leather, petrol and tobacco smoke usually induced a particular effect—that of an emetic!

Most fathers cycled to work, or possessed a peculiar 'pop pop' bike, which was half bicycle and half small-moped. From the sidelines, it looked like quite a pantomime as the adults pedalled like fury in an attempt to bring the stuttering engine to life. If you didn't cycle, you walked or used the bus. The bus service was as poor if not worse in the Sixties than it is today, despite the introduction of the new state-of-the-art Routemaster bus in 1962.

The height of luxury would be to travel somewhere on the Greenline bus. These buses, which travelled long distances to exotic places like Gravesend, were always immaculately clean, quiet and comfortable and the conductors wore smart, dark racing-green uniforms, but the fares were often prohibitively expensive.

There also seemed to be a reassuring regularity about everything: the coalman (not Chris) delivered regularly into the 'bunker' at the back of the house, the 'Provident man' came round for your clothing book money regularly, and the grocer still delivered your weekly order to your home in cardboard boxes, including fresh bacon and cheese, with prices marked in pencil. Families filled up hundreds of books of Green Shield Stamps, licking the little rectangles until their tongues lost all ability to taste anything, hoping to save enough for an electric blanket or a toaster. The milkman delivered regularly, and in the summer brought round those lovely third-of-a-pint bottles of orange juice with a green top. In the summer, the 'Toni' man came round in an old blue and cream van with the ice creams. He would sometimes let you ride in the van (something that the EU would prevent today for sure), and you could buy an ice cream for as little as 1d (about 0.5p). If you had no money, he would sometimes give you just an empty cone, but if you were really lucky, a bit of ice cream on top too. He was a lovely, benign fellow who always had time for the lads.

At this time there was still a 'rag and bone' man who travelled around the streets in a horse-drawn cart, collecting all kinds of junk and scrap metal, and a regular road sweeper cheerily going about his duties in a diligent way. Most families owned pets, usually cats or dogs. A kitten could be bought from Staines market for 5/- (25p). Most people on the estate owned a tortoise (or two), usually with their names painted on the shells in white gloss paint, for ease of identification when they escaped!

Children whose parents worked for BOAC or BEA (before the merged entity British Airways came into being) could obtain discounted flights, and although most could only afford an inexpensive Scottish guesthouse with its obligatory pea soup and dragon-like landlady, it did enable families to leave the confines of the estate and become acquainted with Prestwick, the Ayrshire countryside and the Scottish west coastline. If you couldn't fly, a holiday would probably be a week in Bournemouth on the chilly, stony beach with a blanket. You could then have the transistor on, lean against the seawall and listen to Boycott, Barrington, Graveney and Cowdrey being skittled out by the West Indies in the form of Hall, Griffiths and Gibbs. This would subsequently be followed by the delights of Brown, Snow and Higgs being belted all round the ground by Kanhai, Sobers & Co; some things hardly change!

For entertainment, it was still a time of black and white television, powered by valves that used to glow bright orange, and needed time to 'warm up', and when you switched the set off, a little white dot remained on the screen for what seemed an eternity. The choice was also a little limited, as there were just the two channels (BBC and ATV). Progressing from *The Army Game* and *The Rag Trade* the viewing diet on offer included such gems as: *Mogul, Not Only But Also, 'United', How!, It's a Knockout, Softly-Softly, Callan, The Golden Shot, Magpie, Please Sir* and the first *Dad's Army*. Sunday evening fare was either *The Saint* or *The Prisoner*, which was followed by *Val Parnell's Sunday Night at the London Palladium*, with Bruce Forsyth—and he's still going!

Being at school, the lads didn't listen to the radio during the day (except furtively in the school toilets awaiting the Monday lunchtime FA Cup draw). During the holidays there were the hideous *Workers' Playtime* or *Parade of the Pops* programmes, which were swiftly turned off. Radio listening was usually limited to Sunday lunchtime, the jelly and custard dessert complemented by *Two-way Family Favourites* with Jean Metcalfe, *The Navy Lark, The Clitheroe Kid* and then *'Wakey Wakey'—The Billy Cotton Band Show*.

When the teenagers ought to have been soundly sleeping, it was time instead for Radio Luxembourg–'Your station of the stars', your only real access to continual pop music. The reception could vary enormously from excellent to virtually non-existent, and could sometimes vanish completely for minutes on end. In the end, you would begin to mis-trust the dial, and make the fatal mistake of trying to re-tune your trusty transistor. Here, again, the whole concept of regularity kicked in as these Luxembourg DJs were there for you every night during every week; these people were *your* friends. Amongst the favourites were: The Deep River Boys, Pete Murray (Fulham supporter) and the DECCA label, Sam Costa, Muriel Young and Shaw Taylor (of *Police Five* fame) with the *Friday Spectacular* and, believe it or not, sometimes even the art of whistling from Ronnie Ronalde!

The one aspect of Radio Luxembourg that everyone remembers, of course, is Horace Bachelor and his famous football pools busting scheme the 'Infra-Draw method'. From his voice, I always had a vision of him looking like Alfred Hitchcock. Nearly everyone still remembers his address nearly forty years on, 'Keynsham, spelt K-E-Y-N-S-H-A-M, Bristol'; the advert must have been one of the earliest forms of brainwashing. Most teenagers lost count of the admonishments that they received from their parents who usually barged in at about 11pm, only to hear muffled sounds still emanating from under the pillow. Listening was rather an expensive habit too, as often teenagers fell asleep with the radio left on and woke the next morning to yet another set of dud batteries.

Sixties reading (non-football), was still *very* British, and regular reading was *The Eagle,* with Dan Dare, Digby and the Mekon, PC Forty-Nine, Harris Tweed and Jeff Arnold. Also included in *The Eagle* were a considerable number of educational topics that spawned an interest in: electricity, photography, television, gas turbines and even atomic power! For further 'educational' reading, the lads were beginning to get urges to look at pictures of Sabrina in *Parade*, and were starting to become inquisitive about what was *really* behind the cover pages of *Health and Efficiency*!

Bonfire night was another great communal event in the Sixties, and the parents probably enjoyed the evening as much as the children. The night was always a great excuse to dispose of some old unwanted furniture (bonfire), some old clothes (guy), and voluminous amounts of paper; preparations were often made weeks in advance. The evening was usually bitterly cold, and every family in the road put on their own individual display. Many recall watching parents and uncles ignite, and retreat very quickly from, Golden Rain, Chrysanthemum Fountains, Shimmering Cascades and Catherine Wheels along with the dangerous, and now illegal Jumping Jacks, Air Bombs and the big (3d, about 1.5p) red 'cannon' Bangers. The main task next day was to collect the soggy, smelly, black burnt out rockets and other projectiles that had landed in your immediate vicinity.

Setting The Scene

Holidays on the estate in the mid-Sixties

By the time the mid-Sixties had arrived, the era of seeing Zorro and Marvelman for 6d at 'The Regal' during 'Saturday Morning Pictures' was over, along with Sunday School, Scouts and using your impressive Hornby Doublo set. The estate lads were now at senior school attempting to hone their limited ball skills with a battered tennis ball, playing one versus one during the school lunchtime, protecting, and trying to score into, an open entrance to the school bike sheds. Early adolescence was a major transition period, dumping your old hard-toe Stanley Matthews Continental boots and replacing them with sleek Adidas Santiago or Adidas Le Paz. If you couldn't afford these, you would probably have to settle for Gola boots.

Summertime

The school summer holidays always seemed to contain wall-to-wall sunshine, although, in truth, it probably wasn't so; but there was always something to do. The six weeks always appeared to pass by in a flash, and all too soon the lads were checking their protractors and compasses ready for the new September term. If it ever did rain during that time, the lads would retreat inside for a game of Totopoly or Monopoly, or a group would play a game of brag. If you felt like exercising both hand and brain, there was the trusty Meccano set. Lads made simple cranes or vehicles, dreaming of the day they would be able afford to buy an electric motor to augment it.

If it was too hot for sport, there was the Ashford Swimming Pool, a classic open-air summer pool. Although it wasn't that classy, everyone learned to swim there. Mind you, the temperature of the water could be as low as 52 degrees F (11 degrees C), and never reached anything above 68 degrees F (20 degrees C), so sometimes it was hard to catch your breath, let alone swim. The pool possessed a small kiosk where you could stand shivering, shaking and dripping while you waited to buy sweets, drink and single Woodbines (under the counter!). The princely sum of 7/6d (37.5p) entitled you to a monthly blue season ticket, which was date stamped every time you visited. This entitled you to have up to ninety swimming 'sessions' in that month if you wished. This worked out at 1d each time you swam, and so was pretty good value. Sadly, like most good things for the children of the time, the open-air pool eventually disappeared under a new housing complex.

A small river (the River Ash) ran behind the pool, and was again a place of wonderment. The stream was full of lampreys, minnows and sticklebacks and it provided a place for younger children to properly use their wind-up clockwork boats. In the summers, many would try to cross the river ford on their bicycles, even though the streambed was slippery, rocky and quite deep in places, and many came to grief!

Some lads built track bikes for riding over the remains of the Feltham goods yard that had just been dismantled as part of Dr. Beeching's railway purge. These bikes were, of course, death traps, with 'cow horn' handlebars (with the obligatory Esso Tiger Tails hanging from them), fixed wheels and, naturally, no brakes. Some clever dick would stand on the fixed wheel in a display of bravado and go up and down, which was fine until the gearing gave way, bringing the rider's privates into swift and painful contact with the crossbar.

The lads built 'go-karts', made from old pram wheels, orange boxes and some reclaimed timber. Some of these even possessed crude brakes, a rudimentary light and a Pifco horn. These karts would be pushed around the pavements of the estate for hours, with lads taking it in turns to ride or push. The rope steering mechanism was never that sophisticated, and a 'ninety-degree right' would nearly always see the kart flip over, tipping the incumbent driver into the road.

Most of the lads owned a bicycle, usually a basic BSA, Triumph, Raleigh or equivalent, complete with copious saddlebag, dynamo and three Sturmey Archer gears, essential for school and holidays;

if you were a bit flash you had *four* speed gears. There was always one spoilt kid, however, and bringing out *his* racing bike would leave us all salivating. He owned a Claude Butler racer with double clanger, ten metal Campagnolo gears, Mafac brakes and water bottle.

There would also be mini 'camps' built in the back garden out of corrugated iron and chicken wire, and miniature 'ovens' were created with bits of old brick. Fires would then be started, water boiled, potatoes and chestnuts cooked. The more intelligent and adventurous lads also used heat, but as part of their chemistry 'sets'. The 'safe' chemicals these sets contained were augmented with a few dangerous household product 'bits and pieces', to cook up some real fun. One trick was to mix liquid and powder bleach together to create a gas certain to kill any unwanted insects, or best of all to mix weed killer and sugar and make dangerous and unstable 'bombs', which you could then take to Shortwood Common in Staines, place in a cow pat and blow semi solid bovine excrement over a very wide range.

The lads rarely ventured very far, and if they did it would be trips to Staines 'Arcade' to either play on the early Sixties wood and metal Gottlieb pinball machines, or illegally play the slot machines. The stake was 1d a go, and you could win a 'jackpot' of twelve heavy old pennies (5p).

As money was tight, and as a treat, a few sometimes took a trip to Staines to travel on the small, pretty Great Western branch line between Staines West—a station complete with classic GWR gas lamps, semaphore signals and wooden station awning—and West Drayton and Yiewsley; the lads usually alighted at Poyle or Colnbrook. The motive power was usually a ramshackle single diesel railcar unit operating over a rickety single track. Little did we know then that within a couple of years the passenger station and the branch line would all be swept away.

If the branch line journey was too expensive, you could lazily wile away the afternoons for free at the Shortwood common crossing, watching the Southern Region electric trains all in green, powering their way to Waterloo. There was a semaphore signal that used to clunk noisily up and down near to the crossing signalling the impending arrival of the next train. This signal was controlled by a signal box, situated just outside Staines (Central) station; the box controller always kept a safe, watchful eye on us. This period coincided with the last days of steam, but occasionally a steam freighter would pass impressively through Staines, and the drivers would blast the whistle, smile and wave at you as they passed. These freighters would often pull eighty to a hundred freight wagons, and you could make yourself giddy trying to accurately count them all. If you felt really brave, you would furtively place an old penny on the line, and watch the next train flatten the disc into three times its original size.

The lads were also a lot closer to nature in the Sixties. There would be the walk to the Spinney at rural Laleham, with its treacherous 'swamps'. There were numerous tales and folklore that abounded relating to lads that had been sucked in and drowned there, but most thought that these had been invented by anxious parents as a deterrent to ever visiting there. For all its dangers, there was interesting flora and fauna there. Further along the quiet, rustic road was the 'Attested Cattle Field'. This too possessed a lake, but was a safer environment. The lads would all watch the frogs mating, and come back a little while later to 'pond dip'. The lads collected their spawn and other pond samples, took them home and placed them in an old, chipped enamel bowl. They would then watch them all 'progress' over the summer days. With the spawn, several other strange organisms were brought back home: microscopic things, wriggling things, floating things, red, green and black things, all spellbindingly interesting. Depressingly, the 'Attested Cattle Field' has now also disappeared under another yet another housing development.

Before the era of nationally induced pesticides, the garden was always alive with butterflies: red admirals, peacocks, painted ladies and yellow brimstone. The butterflies would appear to smother the buddleia and lavender, and the blackbirds would nest annually in the honeysuckle. To relieve any potential boredom, and to rid your garden of annoying pests, there were always basic wasp traps to make with jam, a jam jar, some water, a piece of paper and an elastic band— simple but effective. Alternatively, you could incinerate a few red ants with the aid of the summer sun and a magnifying glass.

Most of the lads had a fascination for water, and a number loved coarse fishing. The copy of *Mr Crabtree Goes Fishing* by the late Bernard Venables was so well thumbed that many were forced to purchase a second copy as the first one usually fell to pieces. The lads owned very rudimentary tackle, but it was good enough. Fishing on the Thames meant cycling down to Laleham with the split-cane rods strapped to the crossbars, and the reels, floats and bait rattling around in the copious saddlebags. The baits would be some maggots, dug-up garden worms, and leftover stale bread. When the bait ran out, the keener fishermen would resort to using 'spoons and spinners'.

The clean Thames usually gave up excellent perch, roach, dace, bleak, the occasional eel and a few 'nuisance' pope/ruff! If the fish weren't biting, then it would be time to pack up and visit the lock-keeper at Penton Hook at Laleham. If we lads behaved, he would allow us to help operate the locks, open and close the lock gates and let the boats through. He was a nice old fella who seemed genuinely pleased to see us throughout those summer days. The lock gates were all manually operated by 'wheel' in those days, there being few automatic hydraulic systems around.

Occasionally, the more intrepid anglers amongst us would fish off the weir at Penton Hook, which meant rolling up our trousers, and walking barefoot into the freezing, flowing, shallow weir with its slippery, green, silt covered rocks. As it was free, we would use silt weed as bait, tied directly to the hook. This was then floated along and over the weir, and you watched the float 'dip' as the roach took the offering as it emerged on the other side. The roaring sound of the water and the fresh ozone smell was intoxicating. Worn out fishing, it was a real treat to stop off at The Feathers in Laleham for a bottle (glass, of course) of 7-UP with a straw, and either a 2d packet of salted peanuts, or a packet of Smith's Crisps, complete with blue bag (not sachet) of salt. A number of these meandering rivers and streams that formed our adolescent fishing pleasure are now sadly out of reach of today's children; no longer free, but snapped up to become expensive 'private' angling stretches.

Wintertime

After the summer was over, September arrived, and the lads were back in school, just as the new football season was underway. There was a brief period of falling leaves, fogs and, of course, conkers either fresh or soaked in vinegar and baked in an oven. There was always someone with a 'fifty-niner', who would ultimately sink crestfallen as his pride and joy was eventually pulverised. After that, the weather became just—cold. By the time Bonfire Night came round, it was so cold that you could hardly push a garden fork into the ground.

It was then back to smogs, scarves over your mouth, balaclavas under your cap, and five, long, freezing months ahead. During the snow and frost, when the weather became too dangerous to ride or even walk to school, some school chums' Dads would take 'passengers' to school in their noisy motorbike sidecars; that was really living the high life. In the depths of winter, most would string up food for the birds—peanuts in their shells, bits of bacon fat and, if they were lucky, half a coconut; there weren't, however, too many scraps around!

During the long, dark winter evenings there was still plenty to do; some would retreat to their British Commonwealth or European stamp collections, and immerse themselves in colour charts, watermarks, perforation gauges, overprints and their *Stanley Gibbons Catalogue*, whilst others would retreat to their tropical fish tanks, and literally immerse themselves in guppies, gouramis, fin rot and white spot cures.

Returning to chemistry, using a potassium nitrate solution and a brush you could 'paint' a 'saltpetre drawing' or 'trail' on a piece of paper. These drawings once dry could then be 'ignited' with a match, and you could watch as they fizzled away down the paper, and magically created your drawings. It was also possible to make moving 'mini-tanks' out of a notched cotton reel, a matchstick (spent of course), an elastic band, a small pencil and half an inch of candle—a good way to learn about elementary physics!

The Tiger comic at the start of the football season would issue a slotted 'wallchart' containing the clubs from all four divisions, and the two Scottish Leagues. Each team would have a small piece of cardboard in appropriate team colours. On winter nights the team's league position could be updated on the board following the Saturday or mid-week results.

All the time

Whatever season it was, music was always high on most lads' agenda; some lads already owned their first cheap guitars. Fledgling bands were formed that used to 'rehearse' at a friend's garage at the weekend. Living in Staines, the teenagers were all close to the Station Hotel and the Crawdaddy Club in Richmond, where the Rolling Stones had cut their teeth, and also the Rikki Tik club. The venue The Attic was nearby in Hounslow, and the Staines Town Hall was surprisingly also a major music venue. The Slough Adelphi was a venue where you could see a 'Package Tour' with about six famous acts for about 7/- (35p) all on the same bill. On one particular bill were: Joe Brown, The Crystals, Manfred Mann, Johnny Kidd and the Pirates, Heinz Burt and the Tornadoes and others! At our ages, it shouldn't have been possible to get into some of the venues, but younger lads often accompanied older teenagers with the same musical inclinations, and somehow, with their help, we blagged our way in.

Most importantly, the teenagers were in close proximity to Eel Pie Island near Twickenham. With this influence so close to our doorsteps, it was hardly surprising that most of the locals turned their noses up at the 'Mersey Sound' and most of the 'chart' music, and were instead magnetically drawn more to the Stones, the Animals and the Small Faces.

The youth culture was raised on a diet of 'English/Chicago' Rhythm and Blues. Our heroes were the likes of John Mayall's Bluesbreakers (with Clapton, John McVie and later Peter Green), the Graham Bond Organisation, Zoot Money's Big Roll Band, The Downliners Sect, Long John Baldry, The Yardbirds and, of course, the legendary Alexis Korner's Blues Incorporated.

It may seem crazy now, but it was possible to witness The Who, all dressed in Union Jack suits, with mad Keith Moon propelling drumsticks everywhere, at Staines Town Hall for 4/- (20p), and then later John Mayall with Eric Clapton for 3/- (15p). The stars stood literally feet away, and occasionally some of the band members would come down to the side of the stage at the interval, chat freely with the crowd and share a drink. It was possible to observe, from *very* close quarters, the young Jeff Beck and Jimmy Page (Led Zeppelin) take their first fledgling steps to fame with the Yardbirds—events that could never occur today.

This period saw the teenagers caught up in the first phases of the 'teenage revolution': long hair, Chelsea boots, (where the height of the boots was *all* important), Cuban heeled shoes, chisel toe shoes, collarless Beatle jackets, parkas with fur and studded leather jackets. It was a time of Lambrettas, where your ranking depended to a great degree on the numbers of mirrors or headlights you possessed, and shiny, powerful motorcycles.

Television-wise, it was the time of programmes such as *Juke Box Jury*, *Thank your Lucky Stars* and *Ready, Steady, Go*. A 7-inch single (45rpm) was 6/8d (33p) or three for £1. The principal labels were Columbia, Parlophone, Decca, Philips and Pye. A 12-inch vinyl long playing (LP) album (33rpm) (10–12 tracks) was 28/4d (£1.42p); this took some saving for. Any lad not being able to afford the top prices, sometimes bought, but would rarely admit to owning, a 'cover' version of a chart single by an unknown artist on the brown Embassy label from Woolworths for around 3/6d (17.5p); this label is apparently where Elton John started!

The lads seldom watched any television during the day, and only listened to the radio in the evening for the pop music. It is uncertain whether we would have found time to use a Playstation or a Gameboy, but despite all the other holiday 'distractions', there was, indeed, *plenty of time for football.*

Setting the Scene

Sport on the estate in the mid-Sixties

For a short period during the summer holidays (during the football close season), the estate lads would all consider it 'proper' to stop playing football for a minute to play a bit of cricket. The spoilt kid owned a bat, ball and stumps with real bails; the games didn't usually last too long. The spoilt kid was older than most of us, and by the time he had slogged his way to seventy not out, with the help of some cafeteria bowling (i.e. help yourself), everyone had lost interest. Certainly there were never any successful lbw appeals made against him.

The format demanded was 'tip must run' (if the ball touches the bat in delivery, you have to attempt to achieve at least one run). This was necessary in order to get people out, and to involve others in the game a bit more. Although three or four took the cricket seriously, for the rest of us it was just a quick laugh in between the serious bouts of football. A couple of cricket balls were quickly lost to neighbouring gardens and the adjoining canal, and that was cricket finished really, so, of course, it was back to football.

On the council estate there was one particularly long road with almost one hundred houses on it. If there were other teenage lads living at the other 'half' of the road, it seemed like a universe away. Even taking only half the road length, those houses contained at least *thirty* teenage footballing lads, and a couple more used to cycle over regularly from neighbouring areas to join in. The football clubs supported by the lads were also fairly wide-ranging: Chelsea, Manchester United, Tottenham, as well as lads with allegiances to Celtic, Crystal Palace and Cardiff City. There were also, of course, numerous Fulham supporters. Also living in the road were men playing first team football at a high level for Staines Town and Egham Town in the Spartan League as well as for Ashford Town. There was also one particularly gifted teenager, destined to play for QPR, West Bromwich Albion and Orient.

Our estate was very fortunate in that it possessed a very good local 'rec' (recreation ground) in which to play football. The 'rec' possessed decent grass, but some of the surrounding fences were ridiculously low, and often footballs were lost temporarily because they had been booted over-enthusiastically onto neighbouring properties. On the whole, most homeowners were pretty co-operative when it came to 'lost balls', most having lads of a similar age themselves, but one or two were certainly more tetchy, often denying there was a ball on their property, whilst others saw fit to admit to the presence of the ball by promptly confiscating it!

The lads played football morning, noon and night, often eight hours a day or more. It was naturally the classic 'jumpers for goalposts' stuff, although not many could afford decent jumpers! The lads were a tatterdemalion bunch, with plimsolls and baseball boots, badly fitting jeans with obligatory two-tone 'S' snake belt, topped off with a T-shirt or roll-neck, hidden underneath a raddled, shapeless V-necked jumper complete with mandatory hole.

Was it just wide or did it go over the jumper? Was it in, or did it go over the imaginary crossbar? Games of nine or ten a side were normal; games finishing with scores of 17–13 were also commonplace. Football was a good way of keeping fit, a method of burning off any excess energy and aggression and a means of keeping us out of any serious mischief. Occasionally, the games became a bit niggly if the sides picked were grossly unfair and the score was 11-1 or similar, but, by and large, everybody got on reasonably well. Indeed, so well organised were the estate lads that sometimes friendly games were arranged with other streets or other estate teams.

The popular lads were the ones that owned a football. Very few lads owned a real *leather* ball; any such ball was often out of shape, anyway. The plastic balls varied enormously in quality from excellent heavy balls to cheap flyaway spheres that seemed to have a will of their own irrespective of where you tried to place them. Due to the spiked railings on one side of the 'rec', balls often burst, had slow punctures or sometimes maybe faulty valves. If a ball needed to be replaced, then sometimes all of the street would 'club together' with 6d each. With the large number of lads contributing, the amount collected was sufficient for the purchase of a new communal 'Frido' or 'Mettoy'. The lads continued to play football until one of three conditions occurred: either it was too dark to see any more, or the midges were so abundant that every intake of breath sucked in more insects than air, or some of the more 'stricter' parents came over to the 'rec' to call their lads in, often to their embarrassment.

As the years passed, motorcars became a more common sight and parking locally became 'a problem'. The council's solution, in their infinite wisdom, was to turn our 'rec' into garages. There were howls of protest, even from parents. The lads even offered to cut the grass, mark out a pitch, put up proper goals and nets, even to help put meshing up to protect neighbours' gardens. However, all arguments fell on deaf ears, and within a year of the scheme being mooted, the dirty deed was done, and our 'rec' became just another shapeless lump of tarmac, concrete and corrugated iron.

To add insult to injury, the council also slapped a 'No Ball Games' sign on the only other possible place to play locally, known as 'the green'. There was one other site, but it meant a long trek on foot, and crossing the very busy A308 main road; the council never did manage to build a footbridge over the road. It was a shame, as 'the big field', as it was known locally, was ideal and almost the size of a real pitch, but due to its location was rarely used. 'The big field' has also now disappeared, and is currently a bowling-green and pitch and putt facility. At least the area retains *some* use for the local community, sadly, however, not for football crazy lads. This shortsighted approach has been perpetuated over the years, and has given rise to a lack of local usable outdoor facilities, and has denied free exercise and sporting fun to future generations.

To try and circumvent the 'no ball games' on 'the green', the lads played in the road, a fairly safe option in those days, given the volume of cars. Using just one goal, which was a lamppost and a jumper, the game was 'three pots and in'. The lads also incorporated an interesting variation—there was one 'keeper' (who obviously could handle), who was assisted by one 'defender on the line' (who couldn't handle). The rest tried to score goals against the two of them. You had to try and keep the ball in the air, but even if you didn't, you were allowed a maximum of three touches, the third of which had to be an attempted header at the goal. If, you took more than three touches, or your headed attempt was wide or over, it was a point to the keeper and his assistant. If the effort was on target but was saved by the keeper or kept out by the defender, then no point was awarded to anyone, but if it was on target and beat the keeper and defender, then it was a point to the 'attackers'. The first one to ten points was the winner, when the keeper and defender were changed. That type of footballing practice used and honed a wide range of skills, and was a great deal of fun. The perpetual noise resulting from the bouncing of the ball on the tarmac road often proved too much for nearby parents in the end, and the gathering were asked politely to 'move on' (or a similar phrase!).

During the short break for lunch, some would nip in for a sandwich, whilst others would 'go up the shops', a time having been set for re-convening for the afternoon football session. If you didn't have a real lunch, then it was a case of buying the usual sweets: shrimps, blackjacks, liquorice sticks, palm tree toffee bars, everlasting strips, jamboree bags and sherbet dabs, washed down by frozen Jubblies or Jungle Juices. If you were really flush, you bought a 2d bar of Cadbury's chocolate. If money ran out, a few sweets were furtively purloined whilst other miscreants distracted the shop assistant.

Lunchtime was also the time for searching out and perusing the latest monthly supply of *Superman* and *Legion of Super Heroes* comics from American DC magazines in the papers shop. These were quite expensive at 9d each, and four comics would almost eat up a whole week's pocket money. Another major source of income for lunch was of course the '3d back on the Corona bottles' (lemonade, limeade, etc). Often neighbours would be asked if they possessed any bottles that we could take back to supplement our own bagful. If the group were 'down on numbers', then bottles would be 'borrowed' (i.e. those already returned) from the rear of the newspaper shop, and re-presented to the owner as our own. This practice was very successful for a while, until some became over-greedy and suspicions became aroused!

At the end of the evening football session, around ten o'clock, the tribe would all depart the 'rec' and cycle to the local shops to devour the evening's chips. The chip shop was run by a jolly Lancastrian and his wife who came from, and supported, Blackpool. He had wispy hair, a bulbous red nose and a very strong accent. Almost every night he heard the standard joke from the lads, as they rushed in red faced, sweaty, flustered and hungry: 'Hey mister, have you got any chips left?' He would always reply 'Yes', to be met with our normal retort: 'Serves you right for cooking too many.' If the joke wore thin, he never showed it; he enjoyed feeding us. There were always some free or cheap 'extras' going, plus free batter.

If the estate lads ever got up to any day or evening mischief, the deeds were probably confined to: some scrumping, letting off bangers in milk bottles, putting foreign coins (similar in size and weight to a sixpence) in the chocolate machine and putting our phone 'tapping' skills into practice in the old button 'A' / button 'B' phone boxes to order an unwanted hundredweight of coal for one of the neighbours who had confiscated our football.

There were quite a few elderly people around, most of the pensioners used to wave to us on our way up to the shops, and we respected them. Even though money was short, the idea of breaking into their houses, assaulting them and stealing their pensions would *never* have crossed our minds. There were strict codes of conduct even amongst the estate lads, and the members of the group were very self-regulating. If any lad had even harboured or mentioned such ideas, he would have been rendered an instant pariah.

If outdoor football was not possible due to a rare episode of bad weather, then there was always indoor football instead. Most lads possessed the customary 'flick and shoot' Subbuteo set (with a black and white painted Fulham team of course), or there was 'magnetic football', played on a table with legs, where you controlled the players from underneath with a magnet on a stick. These games probably provoked more arguments and aggression than the real ones played in the 'rec'!

The gravitation of some of us towards Fulham FC came about due to four totally separate and unrelated events. Firstly, some of the lads were, like many others, captivated by the news reports of Fulham's 10–1 victory over Ipswich Town on Boxing Day 1963 (Graham Leggat had scored four, and Bobby Howfield three). The papers had been full of it. Secondly, the lad in the road who supported Cardiff City had thrown to us a tatty Fulham v Cardiff matchday programme. Cardiff City had been a First Division side until relegated with Chelsea at the end of the 1961–62 season. The small programme gave us the first glimpse of the Fulham ground, as the cover showed an aerial shot of the Cottage and stands, and we devoured the contents avidly. Thirdly, some spoke to the talented lad who was then with QPR juniors. His family were Fulham supporters, and had wanted him to join Fulham. However, Fulham were then a First Division side and pretty awash with forward talent, and Johnny Haynes had advised him to join QPR (then in the old Third Division), as he would probably reach the first team more quickly there. He had plenty of good words to say about Fulham. Finally, from a personal perspective, a school friend of mine asked me if I would like to accompany his father and himself to a Fulham home game. 'Just get yourself to Feltham station,' he said. I did, and the rest is history.

Setting the Scene

Watching Fulham in the mid-Sixties

Despite the prevalence of crowd trouble in the Sixties, parents were prepared to let their sons travel to Fulham for home matches, even at twelve and thirteen years of age, unaccompanied. A basic weekly pocket money of about 4/- (20p), supplemented by a 'willingness' to assist with the housework drudgery, was just about enough to enable us to watch Fulham every fortnight.

A breakdown of the costs for our day out would have been as follows:

A half return to Putney (BR)	2s 10d	(14p)
U-16 Ground Admission (Half price)	2s 0d	(10p)
Matchday Programme	6d	(2.5p)
Chocolate (outbound) & chips (inbound)	1s 2d	(6p)
Evening Standard	4d	(2p)
Total	6s 10d	(34.5p)

Not bad value for a 'Premiership' level match.

The lads were soon all bitten with the bug of catching the same train, wearing the same scarf, same clothes, even underwear and socks, walking the same route, crossing Putney High Street at the same place and even going through the same Cottage turnstile in order to perpetuate a lucky streak.

If there were a number of home games scheduled close together and money was really tight, many would try and 'skip the train fare'. In those days, the return rail ticket was an 'Edmundson' type of stiff, pink card with your destination station printed on it, which you tore in half, one segment given up on the outward journey, and one part retained for the home leg. Our journey involved a change at Richmond, and you could always pick up bits of ticket on the platform there, and also on the floor at Putney station. There was always a swirling, rampaging mass of people passing through Putney station on match days, and usually thrusting any piece of pink card into the hands of the inspectors and staff would suffice.

On one particular day, the ruse didn't work. As I passed through, I heard the dreaded 'Just a minute', and felt the heavy arm of the inspector on my shoulder. I hadn't even *looked* at the ticket stub; the ticket was a single from Barnes to Putney, and our train hadn't even stopped there! I was in trouble. After the inspector had read the riot act, and the police had threatened me with court action, I had to hand over the full train fare. Having done so, I trudged mournfully back towards the down platform for Ashford. A voice said, 'And where are you off to now?'

I explained that paying the full train fare had left me about a shilling short for the match so I would have to go back home. On hearing this, he called me back, looked furtively around, took a shilling out of his own pocket and gave it to me, and said, smiling, 'Now get off with you.' He was either a Fulham supporter, or someone who had soccer crazy lads of his own. I not sure if that would still happen today.

Our rabble soon learned the regular course to the Cottage: dodging the weekend shoppers in the High Street using body swerves that would have done George Best proud, pacing over Putney Bridge, the first sight of the floodlights, the bracing wind, watching the District Line tube trains and observing the various stages of the tide and the birdlife traversing the shores.

Then it was time for a quick pee in the now defunct toilets on Putney Bridge, and off for our own personal walk to the Paradise Gardens (apologies to Frederick Delius)—through Bishops Park. We admired the characteristics of the park long before it was ever associated with Senator Thorn—Gregory Peck, Father Brennan—Patrick Troughton and the evil 'Omen' Damien Thorn—Sam Neill!

The church (All Saints) on the entrance to the park always appeared to have weddings taking place in the late summer and early autumn, and the official photographs were sometimes being taken as the boisterous, footballing hordes passed by. Many a bride and official photographer ended up with some extra bodies and splashes of extra colour in their photographs. Once in the park, there were a number of routes through to Stevenage Road—a walk by the river when it was fine, taking some time to soak up the sun on one of the benches, or a perambulation through the main central route, where people sunbathed and dozed on the grass, small children swam and played in the Lido, and the youngsters played football.

In the earlier days, Bishops Park possessed no bandstand, but later there was a period when an impressive structure was built to accommodate the music. Now, once again, however, the Park falls silent on match days, and the area that the bandstand occupied echoes only to the sound of skateboards. The Salvation Army band that made its home within the bandstand were indeed very talented, and, if you arrived early for matches during the summer and autumn months, you could sit on a little 'director's' chair, eat an ice cream purchased from the little kiosk adjacent to the bandstand and just listen to the brass band! It was just like an early version of *Ground Force*. Everyone seemed to have a particular or favourite route through the park, and a 'lucky' exit gate from the park onto the Stevenage Road.

Inside the Fulham ground with its three open terraces, the era of rattles and rosettes was beginning to draw to a close, and there were few signs of either remaining. What was intriguing was the flat-cap brigade, and the pervading smell of roll-up cigarettes. It was really easy to be drawn to the waspish wit and repartee of the 'wags' in the crowd, and, all in all, it was a humorous family atmosphere. In the naivety of our youth, it was difficult to fully understand how the partisan home crowd could give their Fulham heroes a piece of their mind peppered with expletives, or why they would 'target' certain players (usually Johnny 'Daisy' Key and Maurice Cook) for criticism. However, we soon got the hang of these fervent perorations and were soon cussing along with the rest of them! Obviously all of us had heard such 'barrack room' language before from older lads on the estate and at school, but it was probably the first time we had actually heard it from adults—directed at other adults!

Placed above the Stevenage Road stand, was the impressive epithet defining the club. The team was Fulham, but they 'traded' under the grand title of 'The Fulham Football and Athletic Company Limited – Craven Cottage'. This would probably have been a rather taxing mouthful for James Alexander Gordon when he read the classified results.

The flagpoles were also striking, and the white 'masts' ran the entire length of the then open riverside terrace. There was a pole and a corresponding flag for each team that was currently occupying a place in the First Division. There were therefore twenty-two poles and flags spaced evenly along the terrace. The flags flapped in the breeze, and the rope that tethered the flag rattled against the staff. If you closed your eyes, it was easy to imagine yourself at a regatta in a yachting marina, especially with the sights, sounds and smells of the river so close by, rather than at a football match.

The river Thames in itself was quite interesting, as you were literally right on top of it on the terrace, and, at half time, you could review all the interesting flotsam and jetsam that lapped regularly at the foot of the stand. During the seasons that a Fulham home fixture coincided with the annual Oxford v Cambridge Boat Race, there was the surreal spectacle of almost a quarter of the crowd with its back turned to the game 'boycotting' Fulham and the match, and cheering on another totally separate sporting event. In those days it seemed that your preference for Oxford or Cambridge was almost as important as your political leanings, or the football club you followed!

Fulham were usually the last football club to take advantage of *any* particular innovation; for example the club were the last in the First Division to install floodlights. Yet, they possessed the most comprehensive electronic half time scoreboard in the division, years ahead of its time. The structure was positioned on top of what almost looked like a Martello tower, positioned halfway along the open riverside terrace. It looked as if it could have been constructed as a fort to defend Fulham FC from any wartime invasion. Whilst most First Division sides of the period employed

Sitting at a ramshackle desk, well past its best days, club manager Vic Buckingham goes about his administrative duties in a corner of the boardroom, converted temporarily into an office. The drawers of the desk appear to be held up by several telephone directories, whilst the desk contents reveal necessary tools for getting through the day: a 'two-tone' telephone, a bottle opener and several tins of Three Nuns tobacco! So shambolic, so Sixties—so Fulham!

a gentleman trotting round the sides of the pitch at half time putting a few cards with scores on them next to alphabetic letters embedded into the advertising hoardings, Fulham's electronic scoreboard would give you thirty half time scores, by way of a matrix of five colours each, with six match scores within each colour. This meant that two-thirds of all the football league matches being played that afternoon would be included. The lights were coloured red, amber, green, pink and white; the letters were 'A' through to 'F'. There was a 'key' to the matches on the back page of the official programme. The scores were shown in a bright, orange colour, and in the depths of winter the scores seemed to shine out almost as brightly as the floodlights. The structure was also three sided, so that the scores could be viewed easily from any position within the ground. As thirty matches could be accommodated, the set-up would allow half time scores relating to matches from even the old Third Division to be included as well. This was usually limited to the local London interest, sides like Brentford, QPR and Leyton Orient.

The Cottage from which the ground got its name, with its attractive ornate balcony, sat snugly tucked in between the Stevenage Road stand and the Putney terrace. The little house wasn't really that conspicuous, but it was symbolic of the club, and it was its image. It was almost as if the building was an artefact of a bygone age, seemingly in line with the argument for a 'steady state universe'. Something that had always been there, was here now, and would always be there in the future.

Following a game, one of the most amusing sights would be to observe supporters making a beeline for the few fans holding transistor radios tightly to their ears getting the full-time results. This 'line' would then follow these poor people just like a group of hens or geese following a farmer with feed. Every time the 'victim' changed pace, deviated in direction or crossed the road, the others would react immediately and do the same. He would also have to be a great memory man. Fans followed him like disciples asking questions of this Messiah:

'How did Chelsea get on mate?'
'Won 2−1.'
'Heard the Hammers result mate?'
'Lost 2−0.'
This was fine until someone would come up with a ridiculous question like:
'Sorry, but you don't by any chance know the Wrexham score do you?'
*'NO, I ******* don't!!!'*

It was easy to be enthusiastic about football in the Sixties, as there was no blanket television coverage like today. One of the big events after dinner on a Saturday evening was to venture out into the foggy evening, and listen out for the faint cries in the distance of 'Standard'. It was imperative to search out that dim voice, get hold of your paper and check all the match facts. In order to meet printing deadlines, the first hour of the Fulham game was usually covered in great detail, but the last half hour was covered by virtual footnotes: *Leggat second for Fulham 74 mins*, and suchlike—absolutely no detail at all.

There wasn't *any* televised football league coverage at all during our early times at Craven Cottage. It wasn't until August 1964 (the start of the 1964–65 season) that the nation witnessed the start of the fledgling *Match of the Day* programme. The chosen single game was televised for about thirty to forty minutes on BBC2, and screened at a ridiculous time like 6.30 in the evening. If you had been to see a game, either home or away, then there was precious little chance of actually seeing the chosen televised match, unless you lived very near to the ground.

There was no independent television (ATV) coverage of football until the first season covered by this volume (the 1965–66 season) with the birth of *Star Soccer*. This sported match commentary from Peter Lorenzo, backed up in later years by 'expert opinion' from ex-Wolves and England captain Billy Wright. The highlights were shown on Sunday afternoons and the programme was again about thirty minutes long. Without the aid of videos or repeats, some lads were a bit ahead of the time, and would set up their tape recorders, dangling a microphone in front of the telly. It was then possible to 'sound record' the whole Fulham ATV broadcast, then sit back replaying the commentary over and over again, rewinding the half-inch brown tape time and time again to re-capture all those Fulham goals.

At this time, there were also no ready-made facilities to accommodate the television cameras. A match shown at the Cottage was only possible by the construction of an elaborate matrix of builders' scaffolding poles and boards around the tea bar and half-time scoreboard on the riverside terrace of the ground. The whole web of metal had to be dismantled again after the game!

When Fulham were away from home, the Saturday afternoon *Grandstand* agenda seemed long and uninteresting, as there was precious little 'real time' football information on ATV or BBC. Saturday afternoon sport comprised mainly ten-pin bowling, horse racing, motorcycle scrambling, rugby league and finally hours of Kent Walton's wrestling. The line, 'Hi there, grappling fans', introduced the viewer to the likes of Steve Logan, Mick McManus, Billy Two Rivers and (Mr TV) Jackie Pallo. He signed off each programme with his catchphrase 'Have a good week—till next week.' This was long before the advent of local independent radio stations like LBC that included up-to-the minute football coverage on a Saturday afternoon; association football came well down the pecking order. This was even before the age of the 'teleprinter', and often the final classified results were just quickly put up and read out. If you missed the slot, then it was a long wait for the Sunday papers.

As the Sixties wore on, some students would partially forsake their studies at college or night school late on a Wednesday evening to rush home through the smog on their bikes and bolt down a bowl of hot stew, in order to catch a half-hour highlight of a European Cup tie (usually Celtic, Manchester United or Liverpool). But that was it, and the absence of televised football kept you hungry for more. No slow motion replays, no cameras from every angle, no televised debates and little controversy.

This era was also before the start of the *News at Ten* programme, which would eventually, and very briefly, read out any of the midweek football results at the end of the televised news. Therefore, if Fulham were playing away from home somewhere remote, you would have to ensure that you put logistics in place that would enable you to be positioned in front of a television set (tuned to ATV) in good time for the three-minute 'window' between 10.25pm and 10.28pm to catch the result. If you failed in your quest, then it was a long night ahead 'not knowing'. There were no e–mails, mobiles, Internet, Ceefax or sky sports channels in those days. You daren't phone up a mate at eleven at night to ask him the score. Therefore, every possible combination of circumstance, incident and score would go racing through your mind, until the daily paper thudded onto the mat the next morning. You then rushed down and glanced gingerly at the results with one eye closed or with one hand covering the opponent's half of the score. Eventually this would be turned into a: 'Yes!', 'A draw's OK' or 'A damn 0–3'.

There were only a couple of periodicals covering football then. *Soccer Star* (confusingly similar to the ATV programme name) was a magazine more for the purists. It contained intelligent interviews, behind the scenes gossip, in-depth analyses of games, teams and statistics. This came out weekly with a different coloured front cover every week; it was priced at 9d at first, then 1/3d (4p and 6p). There was also *Charles Buchan's Football Monthly* that included more glossy pictures and magazine-style fonts and articles. This, however, was much more expensive at 2/6 (12.5p), and sometimes outside of our 'buying power' range.

The journalists used to love the name Fulham, and Fulham became the original 'F-word'. Somehow it was just *so* easy to come up with witty headlines for the Cottage fraternity. It wasn't so easy to generate similar witticisms for Chelsea. I rarely recall banner headlines like 'Chelsea's Chumps' or 'Chelsea's Charlies', but you could have a field day with Fulham. It was easy to put something derogatory both before and after the club name. Unfortunately, the headlines were rarely 'Fiery Fulham' or 'Fabulous Fulham', but there was a regular diet of Fulham...flop, flounder, fail or fumble. Putting the derogatory adjective *before* the club name gave rise to headlines like: frail, feeble, fickle, fussy or futile...Fulham.

Despite it all, the council house lads loved every minute. It's hard not to dwell on the sheer profundity of the *Fast Show's* pundit, Ron Manager, supposedly modelled on the late, great Alec Stock, and his summing up of the time: 'Marvellous wasn't it...hmmm?' *Yes it was.*

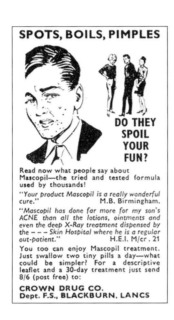

Balls, badges and boils—all important to the Sixties teenager!

Season 1965–66

The Build up

The start of the season

1965–66 saw the start of Vic Buckingham's first full season at the helm. Vic Buckingham had 'guested' for Fulham as a player during the war years. The long-standing board was still at the helm overseeing the club's fortunes: the Dean brothers, Jack Walsh and Noël (Chappie) D'Amato (vice chairman), with Tommy Trinder as chairman.

Playing and coaching staff

From a playing perspective, Mr Buckingham had already made a number of changes. The close season had seen the departure of two 'squad' players, forwards Reg Stratton to Colchester United and Bobby Howfield to Aldershot. The firm Fulham favourite, winger Trevor (Tosh) Chamberlain had retired. There were, however, two significant departures, thirty-three-year-old centre forward Maurice Cook to Reading, and the hugely popular thirty-six-year-old full back Jimmy Langley to Queens Park Rangers for £5,000. Despite his age, Langley had been a regular in the First Division the previous season. Langley was also a very popular player at the club, and had possessed a number of plus points: he was the club's penalty taker, he had an excellent free kick, he was a long throw expert and had scored over fifty goals in his career. More ominously, there appeared to be no ready replacement for him, although it was rumoured that Fulham were casting an eye over the Reading full back Colin Meldrum.

The backbone of the side were still at Fulham in the form of goalkeeper Tony Macedo, full back George Cohen, half back Bobby Robson, inside forward Johnny Haynes and 'play anywhere' forward Graham Leggat. In addition, the previous year's leading scorer with seventeen goals, Rodney Marsh, was beginning to blossom into a quality player. Johnny Haynes continued as Fulham's skipper for the forthcoming season.

The club had also made three acquisitions during the summer, but none of any real significance. Remaining true to their normal 'prudent' budgeting regime, none of these purchases had cost a significant amount of money. The club brought in former Spurs winger Terry Dyson (£5,000), former Busby Babe and Sheffield Wednesday inside forward Mark Pearson who came free from Sheffield Wednesday where he had suffered two broken legs, and finally John Ryan, a nineteen-year-old forward from Arsenal (free). Pearson was a rather controversial signing; he had worked with Buckingham before, but came with rather a bad boy/'Teddy boy' image and a reputed fiery temper. He had acquired the nickname 'Pancho' due to the long sideburns he used to sport.

Vic Buckingham had also appointed former Spurs player and teammate Ron Burgess as club coach, Burgess having previously been coaching amateur club Hendon. Long-serving former player Arthur Stevens provided the continuity as trainer. Retiring from the club was Frank Penn after almost *fifty* years of dedicated service to Fulham as player, physiotherapist and trainer. It was also a major surprise that trainer Joe Bacuzzi, the former Fulham player, had also left the back room staff after nearly thirty years' service. Buckingham had adopted the ideas he had learned from Spurs' Arthur Rowe, but had tailored the tactics to suit the long ball skills of Johnny Haynes. Although it seems amazing today, the start of the season saw Fulham appoint their first *full-time* physiotherapist in Eric Mardling.

Other changes

The club were talking of a 'new spirit' within Fulham, and, frankly, there had to be one. The brutal truth of the matter was that Fulham had survived in the First Division the previous season almost solely due to the fact that there had been two significantly *worse* teams than them in the shape of Wolves and Birmingham City. Certainly, in the main, they had not survived by the standard of their own performances; and even then it had been touch and go right up until Easter. A Fulham side struggling at the bottom of the table had become almost *de rigueur*.

Despite the fact that investment in the team had not been forthcoming from the board, there had been investment in the ground. The club could now boast the new Hammersmith end stand built at a cost of £25,000. The Stevenage Road stand had seen tip-up seats installed at a cost of £8,000. The dressing rooms, not considered First Division standard by Buckingham, had been completely refurbished. To top it off, the whole ground had been painted from 'top to toe'. In truth, the capital for these projects had not come from the board either, but had been raised solely by the efforts of the supporters and the club's 'Development Fund'. Some other internal projects had been delayed due to insufficient finance.

It had been rumoured that around this time Mr. Trinder had been offered the land behind the Hammersmith end at a very reasonable price, but had declined the offer. Incredibly, manager Buckingham himself was without a proper office, and had temporarily converted the boardroom into a makeshift bolthole. Buckingham also stated that the club's money was tied up for the next three years, committed to further ground improvements, and that there was little cash available for other expenditure such as...*players*!

The season saw a change to the club's playing strip, and the socks that had previously been all black with a white top were now white with a single black band halfway up. The club programme had retained its price at 6d (2.5p), but there was complete re-design, an enlarged format with a new green cover (designed by club photographer, Ken Coton).

In terms of football in general, the season saw the introduction of the use of substitutes. Any team would be allowed the use of *one* substitute, but would be allowed to use that substitute *only* if a player was injured. The whole issue of substitutes had been widely controversial, many managers intimating that the rule would be open to abuse, but eventually the new legislation was implemented. The season continued with the use of a brown or tan coloured football.

Pre-season

Fulham, without their own training ground, had completed their pre-season training at Hurlingham and Epsom Downs, and had also completed a three match tour of Belgium, winning two out of three matches, **AS Ostend 4–2** (Leggat, Marsh 2 and O'Connell) and **Crossing Molenbeek 5–3** (Dyson, Leggat, Brown, Robson, o.g), whilst losing the other to **La Gantoise 1–3** (Dyson). The loss of the third game was particularly disappointing, Brian O'Connell had been sent off for a tackle midway through the second half, and Fulham conceded three goals after leading.

The week before the start of the season, the first team and the reserves had played a 'double header' at **Peterborough United**. On this Saturday, the 'stiffs' won by **5–1**, and the first team drew **1–1**, the scorer being Rodney Marsh. On the following Monday, the first team drew **1–1** with Charlton Athletic, scorer Johnny Key. In this era, these games were known quaintly as 'Public Trials' rather than pre-season friendlies.

In an interview with Danny Blanchflower, Buckingham had stated that he expected to be given five years in all to perform a proper job, and stated, 'Success to me would mean that I would win either the League or the FA Cup in my term of office here.'

With the tight financial constraints facing the club, Blanchflower challenged him again, stating that maybe that this was a bit of a dream. Buckingham was unmoved, and he maintained his stance saying:

If I don't win the League or the FA Cup, then I will have failed. I don't mean that the club will have failed; they might finish second or have a good run, make a bit of money, get to a semi-final. But if we don't win something in five years, then I will think I will have personally failed.

Although many doubted Buckingham's optimism, no one doubted his sincerity. Those closest to the club agreed that he would improve the club all round both on and off the pitch. Buckingham's battle cry was 'We approach the season without fear'.

The Persona

The club still retained its family atmosphere, and there was a certain raffishness at the club, populated as it was by so many show business personalities. It was considered that these celebrities could put on a sparkling show by themselves at the Cottage, before the main footballing event! It was often remarked that the happy air of bohemianism did not always lend itself to sporting endeavours on the pitch. It was not unknown to see any combination of the following names at a Fulham home match: Edward Judd, Harry Fowler, Kenny Lynch, Honor Blackman and her husband Maurice Kaufmann, Ray Brooks, Peter Vaughan, Sean Connery, Johnny Speight and Eric Sykes.

The league's new arrivals

The First division welcomed back the famous **Newcastle United** after four years out of the top flight, and for the first time **Northampton Town**, one of the league's success stories who, in the space of just five years, had leapt up the divisions from the fourth to the First Division.

Club photograph prior to the start of the season. Back row: George Cohen, John Dempsey, Bobby Keetch, Tony Macedo, Jack McClelland, Barry Mealand, Fred Callaghan, Bobby Robson; centre row: Johnny Key, Stan Brown, Graham Leggat, Johnny Haynes, Rodney Marsh, Brian O'Connell; front: Mark Pearson, Terry Dyson.

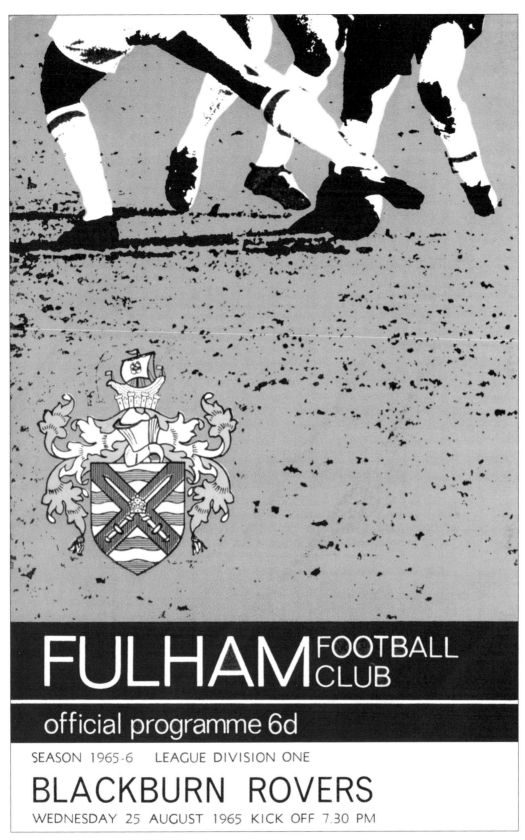

FULHAM FOOTBALL CLUB

official programme 6d

SEASON 1965-6   LEAGUE DIVISION ONE

BLACKBURN ROVERS
WEDNESDAY 25 AUGUST 1965 KICK OFF 7.30 PM

The programme for the opening home match of the season.

August 1965

In this month

* Edward Heath was elected Tory leader.
* Spy Kim Philby's OBE was cancelled.
* 55,000 attended a Beatles concert at Shea stadium in the USA.
* The architect Le Corbusier died.
* The first female high court judge was appointed.

'Help' by The Beatles and 'I Got You Babe' by Sonny and Cher topped the charts.

The matches

FULHAM'S OPENING fixture of the season took the team to Bloomfield Road and **Blackpool**. Chairman Tommy Trinder was appearing at the North Pier in Blackpool so was able to see the game, bedecked in the black and white scarf he wore to away games that came down to nearly his ankles! Barry Mealand came in as Jim Langley's replacement, and Terry Dyson made his league debut on the wing. Blackpool provided the enthusiasm and more of the fighting spirit, but Fulham were showing much more poise and calmness. The ponderous Fulham build-ups were being built mainly across the pitch, and were giving Blackpool ample time to cover.

Ready for the 'off'. The opening day line-up at Bloomfield Road. The team battled back to earn a 2–2 draw with a last-minute goal.

After a goalless first half, Johnny Key gave Fulham the lead six minutes into the second half with a shot from Johnny Haynes' defence splitting through pass. Blackpool, however, came back strongly, and equalised with twenty minutes to go through Ray Charnley from a pass by John Green. The game appeared to swing the Seasiders' way when Charnley netted again a few minutes later, but Fulham were reprieved and relieved when the referee disallowed the goal for a handling offence. Blackpool were also unfortunate not to be awarded a penalty when Tony Macedo clearly brought down their winger Leslie Lea in the area. However, the game sprang to life in the final ten minutes and Blackpool took the lead with just five minutes remaining with an effort from inside forward Green, centre forward Charnley returning the compliment this time with a fine pass. Vic Buckingham made his way back towards the dressing room in the last minute, and missed the Fulham equaliser scored in the dying seconds.

Man of the Match Key this time turned provider, beating the full back and providing a grass-cutting cross for Haynes to flick the ball into the corner of the net between Blackpool keeper Tony Waiters and the post. A number of Blackpool defenders had frozen, appealing unsuccessfully for offside. Most of the media credited Haynes with a clever flick, whilst others, less charitable, claimed that the ball had just hit Haynes and gone in. The game ended **2–2**, and the first point of the season was on the board.

The reviews of the match were strangely mixed, one reporter describing it as a 'drab encounter', whilst another described the final parts of the game as 'blood and thunder stuff, guaranteed to pack the terraces'. Fulham were pleased with their overall performance, but knew that they had to improve on their finishing. As an aside, the crowd at Blackpool was just over 15,000, whilst in west London, Jim Langley's debut for QPR came on the same opening day against London neighbours Brentford at Griffin Park. Brentford won 6–1, and this Third Division derby game attracted a similar 15,000 crowd!

In midweek, Fulham welcomed **Blackburn Rovers** to the Cottage. The game was almost postponed due to a polio epidemic. Blackburn's opening game of the season against Spurs had already been postponed. There had been thirty-five cases reported in Blackburn, and Fulham were liaising with the club and the Ministry of Health. There were no cases in Hammersmith and Fulham, and the medical officer gave the 'all clear' for the match to be played. Blackburn possessed the likes of former England captain Ronnie Clayton and England player Bryan Douglas. The Lancashire side also possessed young talent coming through such as Mick Ferguson, Keith Newton and a young Welsh centre half named Mike England. Graham Leggat dropped out due to a thigh strain, and Rodney Marsh, substitute on Saturday, took the centre forward's role.

On the night Fulham turned on the style. The team murdered Blackburn in the first half to lead 4–0, and ran out **5–2** winners. It was superb push and run stuff, which completely baffled the visitors. Every Fulham player played with a polish and determination, each slotting into their various roles, and delighting the crowd. Stan Brown netted the first in the tenth minute with a fine header after running forty yards to get onto the end of a swirling cross from Johnny Haynes. There was also a home debut goal for Terry Dyson in the twenty-sixth minute, when he flicked in Johnny Key's low centre. Five minutes later the score was three, when Marsh pushed a long forward pass through the middle for Key to arrow onto and score. Just seven minutes after that it was four; Johnny Haynes pushed through a superb forty-yard pass, Key latched onto it, continued a brave run, and again beat the Blackburn keeper Fred Else. This made it four Fulham goals in just twenty-eight breathtaking minutes.

Blackburn's George Sharples reduced the arrears ten minutes into the second half, with a swirling shot that only beat Tony Macedo due a sudden change in flight. The four-goal difference

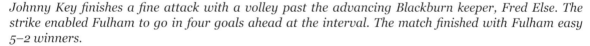

Johnny Key finishes a fine attack with a volley past the advancing Blackburn keeper, Fred Else. The strike enabled Fulham to go in four goals ahead at the interval. The match finished with Fulham easy 5–2 winners.

was restored, however, with twenty minutes to go, when Brown took his second with a low shot from sixteen yards. Fulham relaxed after that and conceded a careless last minute goal when Blackburn's Andy McEvoy headed in John Byrom's cross. Three points from two games was a very encouraging start. Although partially referring to the new stand and the change of kit, the media were prompted to headline, 'Five goal Fulham have new image'. Perhaps due to the polio scare, there are few details recorded on the game.

The good start had made Saturday's game with **Chelsea** even more mouth watering. Chelsea were already becoming an emerging force under the hard-nosed Tommy Docherty, with excellent youth players coming through into the team, coupled with some shrewd purchases. The previous season the Pensioners had won the League Cup, reached the semi-finals of the FA Cup, and were in with a shout for the league title until the very last minute. The youth products were Peter Bonetti, John Hollins, Ron Harris, Barry Bridges, Terry Venables and Bobby Tambling, augmented by the purchases of Eddie McCreadie, Marvin Hinton and George Graham. The crowd was well over 35,000, but the ground could have coped with a significantly larger attendance. There were major problems on the day as a number of supporters from both sides turned up late. The latecomers didn't feed into the ground properly and caused what initially looked like major blockages. Without modern communications, and in rather a panic measure, Fulham closed the gates, leaving thousands of angry supporters from both sides locked outside. Sean Connery was one of those watching the game.

An unchanged Fulham were this time up against a totally different team, and Chelsea took the lead early on when Tony Macedo tried to collect a mis-hit cross-cum-shot from Bobby Tambling; he dropped the ball and got into a total tangle. The ball fell invitingly to the Chelsea winger Bert Murray, who couldn't miss, and he flicked a low close-range shot into the net via the post. Fulham were quite strong during the entertaining first half hour, and Terry Dyson was unlucky when his deflected shot from George Cohen's cross hit the underside of the bar with Peter Bonetti beaten. Bobby Robson and Stan Brown were forced to add more defensive duties to their work to assist an out of form Bobby Keetch, and Barry Mealand was having a nightmare against Murray and George Graham on the wing. Barry Bridges then made it two for Chelsea with a bullet shot from a narrow angle that Macedo never saw, and George Graham scored the goal of the match. Tambling took an in-swinging corner kick, and Graham rose head and shoulders over the leaden-footed home defence to power home a header to make the score 0–3 at half time, and, effectively, game over.

Petulance and violence were already beginning to creep into the game. It started with a needless foul on Macedo by Eddie McCreadie after the whistle had gone; then Ron 'chopper' Harris scythed down Johnny Haynes from behind. This gave rise to an injury that left him hurt and limping. The match was being officiated by experienced Wolverhampton referee Jack Taylor. He tried not to use the notebook, relying instead on just finger wagging and stern glares, and must have taken some of the responsibility for the second half physical excesses.

In the second half heat, Chelsea began to tire a little, giving Fulham some opportunities to fight back. The match then made history inasmuch as Graham Leggat became Fulham's first ever substitute, replacing the injured Haynes in the first minute. With Haynes gone, what little chance Fulham had seemingly disappeared with him. Cohen made some forward surges and came closest to scoring, whilst Brown had a piledriver turned round the post by Bonetti. It was appropriate that the defensive players were those putting the efforts in on goal; Johnny Key, Brian O'Connell and Dyson were mere shadows of the players that had dismantled Blackburn so effectively just days earlier.

Fulham were being outclassed by a virile Chelsea outfit, and in the heat tempers began to rise; the last half hour was a rough, tetchy affair with Chelsea the main culprits. Keetch clashed with Graham, who went down clutching his back. This then gave rise to several other petty feuds, Dyson with McCreadie, and Keetch with Bridges. Even the normally placid Leggat who had only been on the field for a minute somehow became embroiled, he and Harris hacking lumps out of each other with the ball nowhere to be seen. Only in the last few minutes when Chelsea sensibly kept possession did the niggling finally begin to abate.

Chelsea's Shellito, Hinton and Hollins are all open-mouthed as Bonetti, for once, loses the ball. The Fulham forwards, outnumbered seven to two, fail to take advantage. Chelsea won this one convincingly 0–3.

Despite promptings by Robson and some fancy, mazy, but ultimately unfruitful runs by Rodney Marsh in the second half, Fulham were ineffective and devoid of ideas, a fact acknowledged by Buckingham, 'No excuses, we were beaten by the better team'. The game had been lost **0–3**, and it was down to earth with a bump. Both teams claimed several casualties from the match, and reported several others as 'walking wounded'.

September 1965

In this month

* ATV celebrated its tenth anniversary.
* Nobel Prize winner (Peace) Albert Schweitzer died.
* Aston Martin unveiled the four-seater DB6.

'I Can't Get No Satisfaction' by The Rolling Stones topped the charts.

The matches

FOLLOWING THEIR Chelsea defeat, Fulham travelled north to Lancashire and to Ewood Park midweek to attempt their first double of the season. **Blackburn Rovers** had made an inauspicious start and Fulham fancied their chances. A change was enforced with Graham Leggat deputising for the injured Johnny Haynes. Fulham played in their away kit. They received a rude awakening as early as the second minute when John Byrom scored to put the home side ahead. Fulham responded well to this early reverse with a mixture of sharp tackling and crisp passing that had Blackburn totally on the back foot, and it was no surprise when their slick attacking play brought an equaliser from Brian O'Connell ten minutes before the interval.

Fulham continued to play more of the football, but were completely undone as ten minutes after half time Blackburn's Andy McEvoy struck twice in a minute with individual flashes of brilliance to put the home side in the driving seat. The goals totally transformed a dour, rearguard action into a stroll for the Lancashire side. For the first, seven minutes after the interval, Mick Ferguson found Eire international McEvoy with a pass on the halfway line, and he burst through on a fifty-yard run, fending off a weak tackle from the pursuing Bobby Robson before drawing out and beating Tony Macedo. Scarcely had the crowd settled when McEvoy scored again and it was an even better goal. He exchanged passes with Byrom to burst through and beat Macedo with a tremendous rising thirty-yard drive. Fulham began to lose their composure, with Bobby Keetch finally being booked by referee Vic James for one punishing foul too many on his Blackburn tormentor-in-chief Byrom. Stan Brown's goal nine minutes from time, created by a neat move involving George Cohen and Leggat, was just a mere consolation; Fulham going down **2–3**. This had been a better performance overall than the Chelsea game, but then Rovers were certainly not an opposition of Chelsea's quality.

Consecutive defeats had dented confidence, and Fulham made changes, with Bobby Keetch taking Barry Mealand's place at left back and young John Dempsey coming in at centre half. Johnny Haynes was still out, but Buckingham continued with youth, replacing the England man with Fred Callaghan. Visitors **Tottenham Hotspur** had most of their big guns available, but also had some injuries. Fulham sensed that they could achieve something, as Spurs had not won away from north London in nine months; Spurs were, however, undefeated so far that season. The Spurs team included Bill Brown, Cyril Knowles, Alan Mullery, Dave Mackay, Jimmy Greaves and Alan Gilzean.

Fulham competed well in most areas of the pitch and showed plenty of spirit, but the team again looked terribly lightweight up front, Johnny Key, Brian O'Connell and Rodney Marsh all failing to put the Spurs defence under any kind of serious pressure, all three effectively marked out by Mackay, Brown (Laurie) and Knowles. Fulham also had none of the luck in and around the penalty area. Terry Dyson, facing his former colleagues for the first time and desperate to impress, tried hard, made some fine runs and tested Spurs keeper Brown with a header. Brown also saved well from one headed effort by Marsh whilst still on the ground. Fulham also had two shots cleared off the goal line by Knowles with the remainder of the Spurs defence completely beaten, but the final finishing was careless.

For a London derby there was little real passion in the game, and the encounter never rose to any great heights, gradually becoming a desultory and aimless skirmish. There was an element of

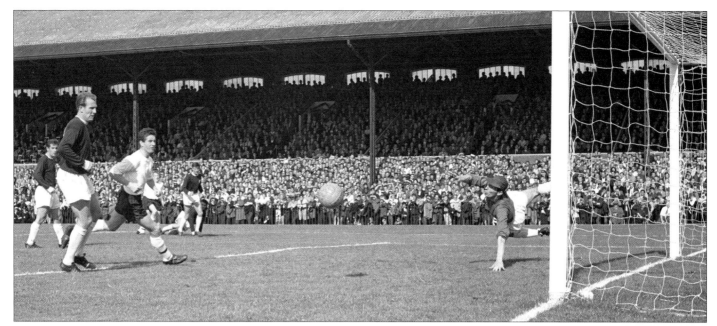

In a rare Fulham attack, Spurs keeper Bill Brown flies acrobatically across goal to beat out a goalbound shot. Brian O'Connell is unable to convert the rebound; Fulham losing 0–2.

controversy about the opening goal on thirty-five minutes when Spurs' Alan Gilzean received a Jimmy Greaves pass and put in a cross to forward Frank Saul. Goalkeeper Tony Macedo was injured as he rashly rushed out to intercept as the ball came over. He collided clumsily with the Spurs forward, but, despite an obvious injury to the Fulham goalkeeper, the referee allowed play to continue and Spurs reserve Eddie Clayton fired the loose ball into an empty net with Macedo still motionless on the ground. The goal appeared to knock the stuffing out of Fulham, and it was the second time in a week that Macedo had gifted the opening goal to the opposition in a London derby.

Spurs then pushed the ball around purposefully in the second half waiting for the next Fulham error, Macedo continuing to show poor judgement in the air. Greaves drifting in from the wing was given five reasonable chances, but all of the opportunities were ballooned into the crowd. Fulham finally paid for their lacklustre finishing when an unchallenged Mackay put Spurs firmly in control with a full-blooded drive from twenty-five yards that dipped. Macedo again completely misjudged the ball, diving over it and far too late to prevent the goal, and **0–2** proved to be the final result.

John Dempsey had taken his chance well with a stylish performance, often marking two Spurs forwards, and Bobby Robson had worked tirelessly, but at the end of the day there was no increase to the points tally, and after three consecutive losses, Buckingham was forced to admit, 'Our good start has dwindled away'.

Four days later, Fulham took on **Sheffield United** at the Cottage. The Blades had made an excellent start to the season, and were currently lying second in the league with seven points from five games, the Yorkshire side having already beaten Liverpool at Anfield. Their side on the night contained the likes of England Under-23 full back Len Badger, centre half Reg Matthewson, who would later become a Fulham player, and an excellent forward line that included Mick Jones, Alan Birchenall, Gil Reece and John Docherty, a familiar face to Brentford supporters. To boost the attack, Graham Leggat again replaced Fred Callaghan for Haynes' shirt. The match proved to be rather a stalemate, with Fulham determined not to concede after letting in eight in the previous three games. The match was played on a night of very high winds and torrential rain; there was even a crowd announcement warning supporters to stand clear of the edge of the terracing – probably reflecting the danger of being gusted into the Thames, and the football more than reflected the poor playing conditions.

This was a match where Rodney Marsh, 'whose play can resemble Pele's, or the biggest duffers in the local park', went through his whole repertoire. He was given two clear chances to score. Firstly, Matthewson's clumsy back pass gave Marsh a clear route to goal. Instead of shooting quickly, he elected instead to try and dribble around the goalkeeper. He was eventually tackled, and the United keeper Alan Hodgkinson easily saved his final weak effort. In the second half, he beat three United defenders with a superb run in the space of just a couple of yards, played himself into a perfect position, but delayed yet again. He was ultimately surrounded by a swarm of defenders and blazed his final effort well over the bar. The United defence gave little away playing an effective offside trap in the windy conditions, often catching several Fulham players offside at once.

Fulham got to grips with this tactic in the second half, but United pulled Keith Kettleborough and the rest of the midfield back into defence to smother the toothless Fulham attack. With so many players packing the United defence, the Fulham defence, for once, enjoyed a comparatively easy evening. John Dempsey marked Mick Jones out of the game, and the Fulham full backs dealt easily with the occasional threat from the United wingers. The draw was achieved, and the game ended **0−0**.

In light of the club's current form, it had to be seen as a point gained rather than one lost. A downside to the match was that just over 9,000 had turned up to watch, the lowest Cottage crowd for a league game since March 1963. The media called the match 'a shambles', adding that the general play was 'aimless, and lacking in the ordinary essentials of highly paid athleticism', finally summing up with, 'the lucky ones were those that stayed away!'

Despite the performance, however, Fulham took an unchanged side to meet **Liverpool** at Anfield on the ensuing Saturday. Fulham's record at Anfield was dismal, never having won there. Liverpool were also on good form having won four of the opening seven games, including a 5−1 away win at West Ham during the week. Johnny Haynes was still missing and again his absence showed.

The game ran true to form, and Fulham, rather unluckily, fell a goal behind early on when, in the fifth minute, the young Liverpool full back Chris Lawler rammed in an opportunist shot after Willie Stevenson's originally mis-hit shot had struck a divot and turned into the perfect pass. Fulham then put in a brave performance and managed to hold that scoreline until half time. The first half had seen little or no incident, and had lacked any real urgency or punch. Liverpool, although dominant in terms of possession, had been reluctant to shoot when they had created space in the Fulham area.

In the second half, Fulham improved, but again it seemed that the team were facing their usual problems: their sporadic attacks took just too long to reach the opposition penalty area, which gave the home defence plenty of time to re-group, the game at times often being played at almost a walking pace. Time after time, several promising Fulham attacks faded due to lack of forward movement. Fulham also began to become frustrated, being on the wrong end of several extremely dubious offside decisions, and their mood was not improved when Fulham's best forward Graham Leggat, who was giving centre half Ron Yeats a difficult time, was clearly brought down in the penalty area. Instead of the expected penalty, the referee awarded an indirect free kick, which came to nothing.

The Reds then compounded the injustice when they added a second goal on the hour through Roger Hunt. Ian St John pushed Peter Thompson's centre through the defence, and Hunt scored his fourth goal of the week with a right foot shot. Finally, in the last ten minutes, Fulham came to life. With just three minutes remaining, Terry Dyson lured Yeats out of position, leaving Johnny Key free to cut inside from the left and fire in a waspish right footer between Liverpool keeper Tommy Lawrence and the post. It was his fourth goal of the season. Indeed Fulham should have snatched a undeserved draw at the death, when Dyson, presented with a clear opportunity, attempted to dribble round Lawrence instead of shooting, and the chance was lost; Fulham lost the game **1−2**.

The following week, Fulham again were scheduled with a midweek fixture and travelled to Yorkshire and Bramall Lane to meet **Sheffield United** again. Brian O'Connell was out and Buckingham shuffled the pack, giving a debut to summer signing Mark Pearson; the team also welcomed back Johnny Haynes. Fulham again gave a good account of themselves, but their lack of striking power forced the team to defend for long periods. Sheffield United were not putting on the greatest of performances either, and the general aimless nature of the game allowed the Fulham goal to remain intact at half time.

Despite the match being goalless at the interval, Fulham began to put too much of the physical side of the game into their second half performance, and skipper Johnny Haynes, in his comeback game, and Rodney Marsh were both booked for skirmishes on the touchline. With sixty-five tedious minutes gone and Fulham looking likely to snatch a point, the deadlock was finally broken. John Docherty mis-kicked Gil Reece's corner, the ball fell fortunately to Barry Wagstaff and his shot from just two yards out flew into the net off Tony Macedo's shoulder. Several Fulham players complained to Preston referee Jack Kayley about the validity of the goal, but the effort was allowed to stand, causing tempers to become hot.

The goal forced Fulham to come out, and the Blades exploited the space, harassing the ragged Fulham defenders into several bad-tempered fouls. The game was effectively sealed five minutes from time, when United full back Len Badger made a determined solo run down the right, cut inside and fired in a fierce shot from an oblique angle, which Macedo appeared to obligingly punch into his own goal; it was Badger's first goal in senior football. Fulham went down **0–2**, their attack still not showing any real signs of gelling together.

It had been unfortunate for Fulham that five out of their first eight matches had been against teams bang in form and occupying places in the top eight of the table, but that was little consolation. The worrying statistic was that only three goals had been scored in the last six league games.

The game against **Aston Villa** at the Cottage was a chance to put the season back on track; Villa arrived three points better off than Fulham. The Midlands side possessed no real stars at the time, but centre forward Tony Hateley was one to watch, and experienced Wales international inside forward Phil Woosnam pulled the strings from the centre of the field. Fulham were given a boost with the return of Brian O'Connell, Mark Pearson reverting to substitute. Graham Leggat was recalled at centre forward in place of Rodney Marsh; Fulham were seemingly back to full strength.

The match, however, proved disastrous for Fulham, and the team were two goals down inside the first twenty minutes to the aforementioned Villa danger men Hateley and Woosnam. Both were excellently headed goals, after goalkeeper Tony Macedo had missed two centres. The first

Villa full back Aitken looks on anxiously as goalkeeper Colin Withers parries another piledriver from Graham Leggat. Leggat managed a hat-trick, but, aided by some eccentric goalkeeping by Tony Macedo, Fulham drooped, like the Thamesbank flags, to a 3–6 defeat.

arrived after just two minutes. Hateley was fouled, Macedo was badly positioned for the free kick, and Hateley outjumped John Dempsey to head in. Woosnam's goal was even worse, and there was hardly a Fulham defender in sight as the inside forward picked his spot from McLeod's cross, with Macedo again looking slow to go down. Finally, Leggat reduced the arrears six minutes before half time, deflecting in George Cohen's low cross in a packed goalmouth. Fulham, however, were not playing at all well, and were fortunate to go in just one goal behind.

What was proving to be an erratic encounter then turned to farce as a rain deluge temporarily turned the pitch into a lake and both teams had trouble standing, let alone playing. It was obvious that the conditions were going to be a nightmare for defenders, and so it proved. Villa appeared at first to be coping with the swamp slightly better, but the match turned round completely when slack Villa marking allowed Leggat to complete his hat trick early in the second half, with one left foot shot five minutes after half time, and one right foot shot in the fifty-seventh minute–giving Fulham a very unlikely 3–2 lead.

Fulham's fortunes looked to be changing at last, but two key incidents swung the match yet again. Terry Dyson, with an easy chance immediately after the third goal to make it four, scooped the ball yards wide of the far post with an open goal to aim at, and minutes later Macedo sustained a leg injury whilst making a do or die save on the goal line.

He was clearly hampered even after sustained treatment; this was of course long before the era of substitute goalkeepers. Skipper Johnny Haynes became involved in a lengthy discussion with Macedo, suggesting that he retired from the field, but bizarrely Macedo declined, gesturing that he wished to continue; it was a decision that backfired badly. With Macedo unable to jump, and clearly playing on just one leg and in slippery conditions, the away side went for the throat.

The Villains proceeded to score three further goals in a quick-fire six-minute spell through Mike Tindall, a beauty from thirty yards from Woosnam's pass, Hateley again and McLeod. Fulham's morale collapsed, and the defence looked even more wide open. Villa's Willie Hamilton completed the scoring fifteen minutes before the end for Villa to finish **3–6** winners. The second half had seen six goals in a twenty-five minute spell, and it had been only the second time since promotion in 1959 that Fulham had conceded six goals at home.

Although the scoreline had definitely flattered Villa, the Fulham performance had been very poor, and the crowd had responded with slow hand clapping, which couldn't have inspired confidence. The crowd had been especially annoyed with Fulham's naivety with regard to a substitution, especially as emergency goalkeeper Leggat had been playing; no one was sure why manager Buckingham had not intervened. Haynes had been frustrated by the whole episode, and his body language had clearly shown it. Bobby Robson had a nightmare in the half back role, and only Cohen and Leggat had emerged with any kind of pride, the media describing the rest of the team as 'looking and playing like wanderers in a football wilderness'. Buckingham responded that the club had no intention of changing the captain to try and relieve him of some of the responsibilities and burdens.

Buckingham did however hint that new blood was needed and said, 'Money is available, but so far we have not made any offers'. There were rumours that Fulham were about to bid £10,000 for six-foot Kilmarnock inside forward/wing half Jim McFadzean. The next Fulham programme made no mention whatsoever of the Villa debacle in the 'Voice of Fulham' section, preferring to sweep the match totally under the carpet!

Fulham had now lost six out of nine, and it was obvious, even at this early stage, that the team had significant problems. Last season's top scorer Marsh had already been virtually consigned to the reserves. Whether the fans were venting their displeasure regarding events on the pitch on the new Hammersmith end stand was uncertain, but the aluminium was already buckled and dented through deliberate kicking and over 100 bolts had been deliberately removed.

Fulham, low on confidence, then faced a tricky League Cup tie at Fourth Division **Wrexham.** The match drew a large, partisan crowd of 12,000, and there was a fiery cup-tie atmosphere inside the Racecourse Ground–Wrexham skipper Peter Jones had whipped his team up into a lather of aggression.

Fulham were clearly nervy early on, and Wrexham had missed a couple of good chances before Terry Dyson put Fulham ahead in the ninth minute. Wrexham's Martyn King then blazed over when it looked easier to equalise. Wrexham paid for those misses when Brian O'Connell put Fulham two ahead from Johnny Key's cross in the twenty-sixth minute. For all of Wrexham's frenetic efforts, Johnny Haynes had shown all the composure. Fulham had carved themselves just two scoring opportunities, and had taken both with an arrogant poise.

The second half, however, was a different story, and Wrexham dominated. The Fulham defence was reduced to last ditch clearances, and became panic stricken when King eventually reduced the lead midway through the half. An equaliser for the home side looked certain, but Wrexham lacked composure in the penalty box, despite the zest and pace shown in the other areas of the pitch. Fulham thankfully had just about enough in the tank, survived the last ten minutes of intense pressure, and scrambled through **2–1**.

Surprisingly, after the heavy Villa defeat, Buckingham made just one change to the side for the visit to Roker Park the next week to play **Sunderland,** Barry Mealand replacing Bobby Keetch at left back. The team responded with a significantly improved performance in front of a 40,000 crowd.

At first the game was all Sunderland, but their midfield drive soon petered out. It was Sunderland, however, who took an early lead in the seventh minute with a fine goal from twenty-five yards scored by Nick Sharkey following a shrewd pass from Scottish international Jim Baxter, who had dispossessed George Cohen. Sharkey beat three Fulham defenders in the run to goal, hesitating briefly before beating Tony Macedo with a shot into the roof of the net. Johnny Haynes then carved out three glorious scoring opportunities with calculated passes, two of which fell to Brian O'Connell, who missed both. O'Connell did make amends shortly afterwards however, when he equalised with a fine crashing header following a full-blooded right wing cross from Terry Dyson.

Fulham more than held their own in the second half, but were out of luck again when Sunderland winger George Mulhall raced into the area, and was upended by a combination of John Dempsey and Cohen. The referee awarded a penalty, and Baxter converted from the spot, sending Macedo the wrong way to regain the lead for Sunderland. It appeared that all Fulham's efforts would come to nothing, as a draw had been the very least that the team had deserved. With the crowd streaming for the exits and the referee looking at his watch, Fulham launched one final attack. Haynes intercepted Johnny Key's cross, pulled the ball down, sidestepped two Sunderland defenders and put over another perfect cross-field pass for Bobby Robson, returning to his native northeast, to slam home the equaliser with virtually the last kick of the game. The goal was his first of the season and earned Fulham a **2–2** draw.

It was the first league point that Sunderland had dropped at home that season. The two goals had been especially welcome, but it was still a concern that so many of the chances created by Haynes were still going begging. Haynes' performance again brought rave reviews, many commentators calling for his return to the England fold.

The match had been a 'first' for forty lucky supporters, who had been transported to the match in a brand new Continental luxury coach, loaned for demonstration purposes. The vehicle was longer than the maximum permitted on British roads at the time, and required a special permit from the Ministry of Transport. The coach possessed a German driver, and German and South African 'hostesses'. During the night trip, the supporters were able to sleep comfortably in bunks converted from the seats.

October 1965

In this month

* Edward Heath stated he would take Britain into the common market if the Tories were elected.
* Children's bodies were found on the Pennine moors.
* Thirty-six died as an aircraft crashed on landing at London Airport.
* Ian Brady and Myra Hindley were charged with the moors murders.
* The Abolition of the Death Penalty bill passed its final stages.
* The Prime Minister opened the Post Office Tower, the tallest building in Britain at 620 feet.
* The Beatles were awarded the MBE.

'Tears' by Ken Dodd topped the charts.

How the league was looking

Burnley, Leeds United and Sheffield United held joint top spot with fourteen points each, Chelsea and Manchester United were mid table, whilst Blackburn Rovers and Northampton held the relegation spots, Blackburn losing seven out of their opening eight league games.

The matches

BOOSTED BY the Sunderland result, Fulham faced **West Ham** at the Cottage, and it was long before the days of postponing First Division league matches for internationals, and both George Cohen and Bobby Moore were absent on international duty for England against Wales.

Buckingham gave a debut to Brian Nichols in Cohen's absence, Barry Mealand retained his position at full back, and Bobby Keetch returned to replace Stan Brown. West Ham's significant injury and form problems saw the team without Jack Burkett, stars Peter Brabrook and Ronnie Boyce, and goalkeeper Jim Standen, Eddie Bovington replacing Moore. West Ham's indifferent form had seen the club positioned just two places above Fulham, and just two points better off. In three consecutive matches West Ham had conceded a total of fifteen goals!

The game was played on a glorious October afternoon, but the match did not reflect the weather, and for the first half both teams struggled to find any kind of cohesion, the game being played at an extraordinarily slow pace. Even at this early stage, the Hammers seemed content with a goalless draw.

A West Ham clearance only succeeds in finding Johnny Haynes on the edge of the area. Haynes promptly volleys Fulham's second goal in a welcome 3–0 victory.

On the hour, however, Fulham's fortunes changed when Brian O'Connell's cross was sliced horribly over reserve goalkeeper Alan Dickie's head and into the roof of his own net by Hammers reserve full back John Charles for a classic own goal. The goal was a real gift, as Dickie had looked poised to collect the ball. Fulham were energised by this stroke of good luck, and Johnny Haynes added a second. Graham Leggat fired in a shot, and Hammers full back Dennis Burnett, making his West Ham debut, had plenty of time to clear the ball, but succeeded only in passing it to Haynes, who promptly despatched it back into the net with great precision. West Ham pushed forward to try and reduce the deficit, but Johnny Byrne was making no headway against the impressive John Dempsey. Byrne then dropped deeper, but Geoff Hurst had no luck at centre forward either.

Pushing forward led to a loss of concentration at the back, and Leggat put the result beyond doubt in the last minute, the goal proving to be another disaster for West Ham. Whilst the referee was attending to the injured Bobby Robson, Hammers centre half Ken Brown decided to take a quick goal kick. The kick was terribly mis-directed, and found only the surprised and unmarked Leggat, who intercepted easily, controlled the bounce and scored with a left-foot shot in off a post. A Fulham win by **3−0**, and a huge relief, even though every goal had been a gift and a comedy of West Ham errors.

Events on the pitch had become so bad at one point that the Hammers supporters decided to pelt Bobby Keetch with eggs. The majority of these did not break on the springy Craven Cottage turf, and Keetch, ably assisted by the Hammers centre forward Byrne, began to lob them back, giving the fans an unwanted egg shampoo, much to the amusement of Haynes. Fulham couldn't really bask in the glow of victory, the press labelling the game 'End of season stuff'. Others went further saying it was a 'disgrace to the First Division' and 'a poor excuse for a professional football match'. Brian Nichols' debut, however, had been very promising, with excellent tackling and timing. Apart from the gift goals, Fulham had struggled to make much positive headway up front. With most attacks being focussed on the right wing, Terry Dyson had again looked anonymous throughout.

Fulham's poor start had not been confined just to the first team. In the local London Challenge Cup, a competition that Fulham took seriously, a Fulham XI containing John Dempsey, Steve Earle, Mark Pearson and Rodney Marsh had drawn 2−2 with amateur side Kingstonian at the Cottage, with two late goals in the space of sixty seconds from Rodney Marsh sparing Fulham's blushes. The goals from Marsh earned him a first team recall. Predictably, Kingstonian won the replay 1−0 in front of 3,500 fans, even though the Fulham side that evening contained nine players with first team experience! The team were lucky to be beaten by just the one goal, and the nearest they came to equalising was a thirty-yard shot from Brian O'Connell that found the net, only to be disallowed because Rodney Marsh had strayed into an offside position.

The following sweltering Saturday saw a second consecutive London derby with Fulham facing **Arsenal**, currently lying second in the table, at Highbury. Highbury was another ground where Fulham had rarely found any luck, and the match proved to be no different. George Cohen was back from international duty, and Rodney Marsh was restored to the line-up in place of the previous week's goalscorer Graham Leggat, who was injured; John Dempsey and Bobby Keetch formed a double centre half pairing.

Fulham started poorly, and Jon Sammels almost put the Gunners ahead after just eight minutes with their first on-target shot. Cruel luck intervened shortly afterwards in the twenty-first minute, when full back Barry Mealand, having his first extended run in the team after Jim Langley's departure, went in for an injudicious tackle with George Armstrong and the loud crack which resulted left no-one in any doubt as to what had happened. He was stretchered off with a badly broken ankle, forcing Fulham to re-organise with Mark Pearson substituting, Keetch going to full back, and Brian O'Connell to half back. Just after the half hour, Arsenal scored. Frank McLintock heard the call from Sammels, and squared the ball to him to beat the diving Tony Macedo with a rasping cannonball drive from thirty yards. This roused Fulham, who were rewarded with a volleyed equaliser just seven minutes later through Terry Dyson. Johnny Key jinked his way

On a bogey ground, Arsenal goalkeeper Furnell backpedals as a Fulham effort lands on top of the net. Terry Dyson and Rodney Marsh look on hoping for better. On a hot afternoon Fulham unluckily went down 1–2.

skilfully across the penalty area with a deft, mazy run, beating four static Arsenal defenders in the process, before laying the ball across for the unmarked Dyson to score accurately with a simple chance from eight yards.

Whilst the team was still in the throes of re-organising, Joe Baker restored Arsenal's lead in the first thirty seconds of the second half. McLintock this time combined with George Armstrong, and from the resulting cross both John Radford and Baker lunged for the ball, and in it went, Baker being credited with the final touch. Fulham pressed forward again, and Dyson, Fulham's most persistent attacker, was unlucky not to equalise when his shot was palmed onto the angle of post and bar by the goalkeeper and finally scrambled away. The defence was playing well, and Dempsey had another outstanding game, subduing Arsenal's international Baker for most of the game. Keetch too was particularly robust, and despite being roundly booed by the Arsenal supporters, kept both George Eastham and Armstrong in check.

Arsenal did, however, continue to create the majority of the scoring chances, but were fairly profligate in front of goal. McLintock created a chance for Baker that he missed, and then Macedo saved a point blank header from Radford. Macedo again thwarted Baker when he shot against his body when clean through, and finally Armstrong hit the underside of the bar with a lob. Close to time it looked like Fulham would secure an unlikely draw, when keeper Jim Furnell only half blocked a drive from Rodney Marsh, but as the ball rolled towards the empty goal, Arsenal full back Billy McCullough raced back to clear the ball frantically off the goal line for a corner. In the end, despite a brave showing, Fulham went down **1–2**.

The press, however, were complimentary about Fulham's performance, with most agreeing that Fulham were unlucky not to get the draw, but in the game of points gathering it meant nothing. An unsatisfied Arsenal manager Billy Wright, however, disagreed, and said, 'We should have had six'. The match was officiated by John Osborne who would have an impact on next year's Fulham and Arsenal fixture. Despite the brave and hard-working performance it was obvious that goals were an issue, and just twelve goals in the last ten league games told its own story. The media said after the Arsenal game that the forward line had again carried 'little threat' and that due to this, Fulham never looked like saving the game. Buckingham admitted as much and confessed that he was, 'Spending every minute looking for someone with that crucial goal touch'. Barry Mealand attributed no blame to his sickening injury saying: 'It was no-one's fault, my studs caught in the turf as I stretched.'

In midweek, Fulham met First Division side **Northampton Town** at home in the next round of the League Cup. Fulham were extolling the virtues of the League Cup competition, but nine clubs had boycotted the competition, eight clubs from the First Division, and one (Wolves) from the Second Division. Even current holders Chelsea were not defending their title, because of European commitments. Fulham replaced the injured Mealand with Brian Nichols at left back, and Mark Pearson continued at right half. The Northampton side contained Theo Foley, who went on to become a respected radio commentator with LBC and other stations.

In a desperate gamble for goals, centre half John Dempsey was selected as an emergency centre forward, with Bobby Keetch returning to centre half. Vic Buckingham fell back on one of his favourite phrases, 'desperate situations require desperate solutions'. The idea of playing Dempsey at centre forward had originally come from former league referee Alf Bond, who had known Dempsey as a youth player when he had been an 'explosive' centre forward, scoring forty-four goals in one season. Fulham played well on the evening and were three goals up by half time against a wretched and disorganised Northampton side. Terry Dyson put Fulham on their way in the seventeenth minute when he hit home Haynes' pass from twenty yards. Dempsey got his first on the half hour with a firm header from Johnny Key's centre. Then, eight minutes before half time, Pearson put in a shot that was not cleared properly, and Dempsey promptly prodded the rebound in.

Immediately after the interval, Dempsey completed his hat trick when he shot Pearson's low cross into the net through a crowd of players; it was a hat trick in seventeen minutes for the 'experimental' centre forward. Terry Dyson completed the scoring a quarter of an hour from the end, when he converted a penalty after Rodney Marsh had been fouled in the box by Foley; Fulham strolled through the game to win by **5−0**.

The scoreline remains one of Fulham's largest margin League Cup victories. Remarkably, the three hat-trick goals were the first Dempsey had *ever* scored for Fulham at a senior level. Johnny Haynes had fashioned most of the goals with a superb display of inside forward play, ably supported by the enthusiastic Pearson. It was a shame that fewer than 8,000 spectators had watched the match.

The following weekend Fulham faced **Everton** on a very sunny afternoon at the Cottage, hoping that the Toffees would have a hangover from their tough European victory over Nuremburg on the previous Tuesday. Following his display at Arsenal, Mark Pearson kept his place. Despite being without goalkeeper Gordon West and centre half Brian Labone, Everton presented formidable opposition, their team that day including Ray Wilson, Jimmy Gabriel, Fred Pickering, Alex Scott and Alex Young alongside the young Colin Harvey. Everton were currently lying ninth in the league table.

With league confidence low, it was no surprise when ex-England centre forward Pickering put Everton ahead as early as the second minute; and it was a quite shambolic goal even by Fulham standards! Rodney Marsh slipped, and pushed Tony Macedo's long goal kick straight to Everton forward Johnny Morrissey instead of Johnny Haynes. Morrissey immediately lobbed the ball back onto the Fulham crossbar and whilst Fulham were in disarray with Macedo out of his goal, Pickering banged the rebound into an empty net. Fulham, however, rallied, and Bobby Robson was just wide with a shot after a three-man move.

After eighteen minutes Fulham were awarded their first league penalty of the season when the erratic Rodney Marsh was bundled over in the penalty box by a late tackle from Everton's Brian Harris. The award was a slightly dubious one, but new signing Terry Dyson took the responsibility himself to put Fulham level from the spot, sending the keeper the wrong way. Fuelled by this goal, Fulham raised their game, and Dempsey was just too high with a twenty-yard shot following a fine pass from Haynes.

Terry Dyson (half hidden) sends Everton goalkeeper Andy Rankin the wrong way from the penalty spot to equalise an early Everton goal. (The ball is partly hidden by Rankin's left leg.) Fulham won a thrilling encounter 3–2.

Fulham took the lead in the thirty-fourth minute when Pearson, running from midfield, took a pass from John Dempsey to blast a thirty-yard angled piledriver into the top corner of the Everton net, the shot appearing to pass through the hands of the Everton reserve keeper Andy Rankin; it was Pearson's first Fulham goal.

Everton showed that it was their turn to rally after the re-start, and Fulham had a lucky escape when Brian Nichols scythed Derek Temple down just outside the box, but fortunately the free kick was scrambled away. The Fulham defence, however, continued to give centre forward Pickering far too much space, and allowed him to snatch the equaliser. Macedo could not hold a hot shot from Jimmy Gabriel and from the rebound Pickering put away his second goal of the afternoon with a mis-kick that deceived the Fulham defenders and bounced into goal, despite George Cohen's despairing efforts on the line to keep it out.

Fulham would not be denied, however, and twice Dempsey, keeping his place at number nine after his midweek hat trick, came within a hair's breadth of scoring. He was positioning himself well, and giving the Everton defence a very uncomfortable afternoon. Pearson was also spraying around a number of constructive passes, which were accurately finding white shirts. Finally, from a Johnny Haynes corner, the mobile Dempsey took Marsh's juggling near-post flick-on and bundled in Fulham's third off a defender in a penalty box scramble.

The Everton players were furious with referee Lyden for allowing the goal to stand, claiming that Marsh had deliberately handled in the build up to the goal, but the goal stood. After this, the game became tetchy, with numerous late tackles going in from both sides. The rough stuff appeared to start when Pickering, looking for his hat trick, viciously felled keeper Macedo; he was booked, but lucky to stay on the field. In an act of apparent revenge, Bobby Keetch then took out Pickering, and was warned. As the bad feeling spread, Harris chopped down Pearson, who swung a fist, but fortunately it did not connect, and this particular flare-up ended amicably. Everton's Gabriel then had a goal ruled out for offside, which further inflamed the passions of the Merseysiders.

Everton appeared to lose their discipline, and ten minutes from time young nineteen-year-old star Harvey was eventually ordered off after one nasty incident too many. Dempsey innocuously pulled down Harvey from behind, and as the Fulham defender came over to apologise Harvey started throwing punches, right under the referee's nose. Pickering and Dempsey were also booked, and others were lucky to escape a booking. Trouble flared on the terraces as well, and a number of Everton supporters were ejected from the ground. However, despite some forceful play from Gabriel and some tenacious work from winger Alex Scott, Fulham managed to hold on to their **3–2** advantage.

It had been Fulham's best display and best result of the season, and the three goals were just what the doctor had ordered. Dyson had delivered his best game to date, always looking for the ball and causing the Everton defence problems. Certainly the Fulham team had shown a lot more zest and heart than in previous weeks.

Fulham took an unchanged side to face champions **Manchester United** at Old Trafford the following Saturday. Fulham believed they had a good goal ruled out in the seventeenth minute when United goalkeeper Pat Dunne, under pressure from Rodney Marsh, punched the forward's header against the underside of the bar. The goalkeeper caught the rebound on the goal line, and John Dempsey charged the goalkeeper, fairly in most people's view, who stepped back at least a foot over the line. The referee, however, ruled the effort out indicating a foul on the keeper despite Fulham's vehement protests. Shortly afterwards, Fulham went a goal behind in the twenty-third minute when David Herd, replacing the injured Denis Law at inside forward, rammed home a close-range sharp shot after a goalmouth scramble. Pat Crerand's initial shot had caused Macedo to fall with its power, and Herd tucked home the loose ball.

A glimmer of hope arose five minutes after half time when Rodney Marsh powered down the right and put in an accurate cross, which John Dempsey converted with a powerful header at the near post. United keeper Dunne almost stopped the ball with his foot, but the effort was too powerful. This equaliser was Dempsey's fifth goal in three games. Herd then hit the bar with another splendid shot and then restored United's lead in the fifty-eighth minute. Keeper Macedo could only parry and beat out Bobby Charlton's drive and Herd netted from the rebound. Both defences were in fine form with George Cohen keeping dangerous winger John Aston quiet. Mark Pearson, playing against his first club, Bobby Robson and Johnny Haynes were all instrumental in midfield providing dangerous ammunition for both Dempsey and Marsh up front, and Terry Dyson was again of great nuisance value in attack. Unfortunately, most of Fulham's efforts foundered against the United defence with Tony Dunne, Shay Brennan and Bill Foulkes also in fine form.

It looked on a number of occasions as if Fulham would fashion an equaliser, but the team again had *none* of the luck, especially when Dyson hit a fine shot that crashed against the post before

Experimental centre forward John Dempsey fires in another blaster which is too close for comfort, judging by the worried faces of United's Charlton, Crerand, Dunne and Foulkes. Despite another Dempsey effort, which did produce a goal, Fulham lost 1–4.

rebounding straight into the hands of the surprised goalkeeper Dunne. However, as time slipped away, the Red Devils broke to great advantage. Charlton brought down a cross and scored with a trademark shimmy and shuffle followed by a piledriver shot, and then, finally, Herd completed a fine hat trick, heading in a centre from Best in the closing minutes. In the end, Fulham wilted a little, and United ran out fairly comfortable **1–4** winners. Bobby Keetch had been furious with the one-sided refereeing saying: 'We expected a 50-50 share of the breaks.' The centre half added: 'I had a word with the referee as we walked off at the end. I was diplomatic, but I think I made our opinions plain enough.'

The media did agree that Fulham had played a lot better than the scoreline had suggested, and that the result had flattered Manchester United. One reporter said of the performance: 'My sympathy is completely with Fulham, when their only reward for much the more positive soccer was absolute disaster.' Apart from Dempsey, another positive was that Nichols seemed to be proving an able replacement for the injured Mealand, Buckingham commenting, 'Brian looked as good as anything on the park'.

The early success of converting Dempsey from a centre half to a centre forward brought a rather hasty comment from Buckingham: 'Dempsey is a centre forward, it is no longer an experiment, Fulham will make him a centre forward with his own particular style of play.' It would have been a tremendous boon for Fulham if the conversion had become permanent, as the club were, as usual, reluctant to open the cheque book and invest heavily in what they saw, even then, as a 'dicey market', but it was a typical Fulhamish comment as, after just three further league games, Dempsey was back in the centre half role!

On the final day of October, Fulham entertained newly promoted **Newcastle United** at the Cottage. The Magpies had made a mediocre start, and Fulham were optimistic. The Geordies had twelve points, three more than Fulham. Newcastle were managed by Joe Harvey, and the side included Dave Hollins, brother of Chelsea's John, in goal, and the experienced, balding Jim Iley. Graham Leggat returned in place of Rodney Marsh.

In truth, the game was a dismal affair from start to end on a very blustery day, with neither side playing much entertaining football. The play swung from end to end, and in the poor weather conditions there was a succession of missed chances, with Fulham being the worse culprits. Leggat had one opportunity, but was foiled by a point blank save from Hollins. The charismatic Trevor Hockey was the liveliest Newcastle forward on view, but he was up against George Cohen at his

Newcastle United's Craig desperately hooks the ball away from his own goal line as Leggat and Dempsey look to apply the finishing touch to the cross. Looking on, stranded, are the Newcastle goalkeeper Dave Hollins and the balding Jim Iley (still only 29).

Against the club he would later manage, Bobby Robson clears a rare Newcastle attack with consummate ease. Two very late goals secured the Cottagers two valuable points in a 2–0 victory in front of the television cameras.

commanding best. John Dempsey was less effective in this game at centre forward, but although he missed chances, he also had some atrocious luck with shots and headers that passed just the wrong side of the post. He finally did get the ball into the net and it looked a good goal, but for some reason the referee gave offside. Dempsey was upset by the decision, and raced half the length of the field to push the referee, and was lucky to escape without a caution. There were several needless petty fouls that punctuated play, but fortunately the referee was in a tolerant frame of mind.

Although Bobby Keetch and Brian Nichols kept things very tight at the back, the old goalscoring problem was still manifesting itself; all the forwards missed chances. Terry Dyson shot yards wide in the second half when it looked easier to score, and Johnny Key too flattered to deceive; too often all the Fulham forwards were being caught in an obvious offside trap. Trevor Hockey had one rare chance for the Geordies, but volleyed straight at Tony Macedo from six yards. Just as the game was about to peter out into a goalless draw, the persistence of Johnny Haynes prised open the Newcastle defence.

With just two minutes remaining, Newcastle's Ollie Burton needlessly brought down Haynes just inside Fulham's own half by pulling his shirt. Haynes rose and planted a sixty-yard free kick onto the head of Bobby Robson standing on the edge of the Newcastle area. Robson headed the ball goalwards, the ball bounced awkwardly in the box, and some slack Newcastle defending allowed Key to accept the knockdown and screw a shot across Hollins into the corner of the net. Newcastle, now pressing forward, were caught again on the break a minute later when, from a Newcastle attack, Macedo scooped up the ball and immediately supplied Haynes in the centre circle. Haynes ran forward with the ball as the Newcastle defence retreated. Haynes' pass found Dyson, who slipped the ball to Key, whose low hard centre found Leggat racing in, and he scored the second. Fulham ran out eventual **2–0** winners, and Alf Ramsey was amongst the 20,000 crowd to witness another superb Haynes display, worthy of an England recall.

The match secured a piece of history, as it was the second ever game to be shown on ATV's fledgling *Star Soccer* Sunday television series. The commentators struggled to make much of the game, but at least for the first time on a Sunday it was possible to re-live the goals from the day before. However, it was now a run of three successive home league victories for Fulham, which in terms of points was the critical issue.

November 1965

In this month

- * Seven died as hurricane winds battered Britain.
- * The Abolition of the Death Penalty and the Race Relations bills became law.
- * The provisional timetable for *Concorde* flights was issued.
- * Cassius Clay beat Floyd Patterson and retained the world heavyweight boxing title.
- * The Government introduced an experimental seventy mph speed limit on motorways.
- * Ian Smith declared UDI in Rhodesia.
- * Mary Whitehouse set up the 'Viewers and Listeners Association' to tackle bad taste and irresponsibility.

'Get Off My Cloud' by The Rolling Stones topped the charts.

How the league was looking

Burnley still held top spot, but Liverpool had shot up to second place, with Leeds third, and West Bromwich Albion fourth just a point behind. Arsenal had moved up to sixth. Manchester United and Chelsea were still hovering mid table. Blackburn were still anchored at the bottom, with West Ham occupying the other relegation spot, just ahead of Northampton Town on goal average.

The matches

FULHAM'S REWARD for overpowering Northampton Town in the previous round of the League Cup was the visit of another First Division side **Aston Villa** in midweek. The match was an opportunity for Fulham to erase the memories of the recent, heavy defeat in the corresponding league match, and to progress towards European football. Fulham had a significant opportunity to progress, as Villa were without three principal forwards in John McLeod, Willie Hamilton and Phil Woosnam. Graham Leggat was again preferred to Rodney Marsh, and so Fulham were unchanged. Fulham performed as well in the first half as they had all season and took the lead right on half time, when Johnny Haynes scored with a sweetly hit volley with the outside of his foot from Johnny Key's cross-field pass, the ball finding its way through a gap between Villa keeper

Leggat celebrates as Haynes' volley sneaks in to give Fulham the lead in the Fourth Round League Cup tie. Unfortunately Aston Villa poached a late equaliser to secure a 1–1 draw.

Colin Withers and the post. Johnny Key and Leggat were well supported by Haynes, who was again in England form, and Fulham looked likely to add further goals. Villa keeper Withers pushed Leggat's tremendous shot over his head, and was just able to run back and catch the ball on the goal line. Then Johnny Key crashed a shot against Withers' body and the rebound fell to John Dempsey, whose goalbound effort was cleared from the line by Villa's Alan Deakin.

Fulham played as well in the second half as they had in the first, and just a couple of goals were needed to round this match off as a classic win. Villa were restricted to just two chances: firstly, when Parke's header rebounded from a post straight into the arms of Tony Macedo, and secondly when Macedo had to make an incredible save to prevent Bobby Keetch's back header from becoming an own goal. Despite having much more of the possession and the chances, it proved a false dawn. Fulham took their foot off the accelerator and became casual with their finishing, allowing Villa reserve forward Barry Stobart to lob home a simple equaliser just twelve minutes from time. Alan Deakin, who had played so well in the league match, advanced unchecked and slipped a pass through the Fulham defence to Stobart. Macedo sensed the peril and wandered out of goal but too far, and Stobart was able to hook his shot high over him and into the net to earn Villa a replay at Villa Park, the game finishing **1–1**. Buckingham was unhappy with the performance and the result, saying: 'We should have won, we had 70% of the game.'

There was one positive piece of news to start the month, as Fulham announced that the club had signed eighteen-year-old Les Barrett on a professional contract, following two years as an amateur. He was originally signed as an inside forward, but could also play on the wing. Buckingham held a very high opinion of him as one for the future.

Whatever good work was being put down at Craven Cottage was consistently being undone away from home. In early November, Fulham travelled virtually unchanged to the Hawthorns with **West Bromwich Albion** in fine form and challenging the leaders; Stan Brown came in for Mark Pearson. It would be an interesting game, for if Fulham could overcome Aston Villa in the replay then the team would possibly face Albion again in the League Cup quarterfinal.

Again, the early part of the game saw Fulham put in plenty of effort. Tony Macedo made two fine saves to deny Tony Kaye, but Fulham created two glorious chances of their own in the first half hour to go ahead, one of which where Graham Leggat's header beat the keeper, but flashed a whisker over the open goal. Fulham fell one behind, however, on the half-hour when eighteen-year-old Albion forward Graham Lovett converted Kaye's centre with his head. Just before the

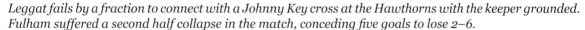

Leggat fails by a fraction to connect with a Johnny Key cross at the Hawthorns with the keeper grounded. Fulham suffered a second half collapse in the match, conceding five goals to lose 2–6.

interval, Macedo held Bobby Hope's snap shot just under the bar; the first half had finished pretty even.

Certainly Fulham were not prepared for the second half onslaught that followed. Leggat again came very close to the equaliser immediately after the interval, but one down very soon became three down. Three minutes after half time, Hope's through pass split the Fulham defence, and Tony Brown raced clear forty yards before crashing in a shot over Macedo via the underside of the bar. Five minutes later there was a carbon copy goal, this time Lovett sprinting clear thirty-five yards to hammer home. Fulham pulled one back on the hour when Terry Dyson beat the Albion keeper to a loose ball in the box, his lob leading to a headed effort from John Dempsey that goalkeeper Sheppard failed to block properly, it fell nicely for Leggat to walk the ball over the line from about a yard out; but this was about as good as it became.

Tony Brown added his second and Albion's fourth in the sixty-eighth minute, and just five minutes later Albion's Ray Wilson, playing in just his second game, expertly took Bobby Cram's pass and netted Albion's fifth. The game then became slightly tetchy with Dempsey being booked for a foul on Lovett, and Albion's Ray Fairfax receiving a similar reward following a foul on Leggat.

If the luck could not have become any worse, the accident-prone Macedo, who was, on this particular day, having a fine game, damaged his wrist and hand in making a save. On this occasion, he *did* leave the field twelve minutes from the end, and Leggat took over the gloves, with Brian O'Connell coming on as substitute. Albion's Clive Clark, who always did well against Fulham, shot another goal past the stand-in goalkeeper, and despite a long-range strike from Bobby Robson, against his former club, in the last minute, Fulham lost heavily, a seven goal second half leading to a final score of **2–6**.

The scoreline did in fact flatter Albion somewhat, and Fulham's performance had not been that disastrous in midfield and up front, but the game could not hide the fact that it was the second time that the defence had conceded six goals in the last *six weeks*. The scoreline, however, had done considerable damage to Fulham's morale, and only George Cohen and the recalled Stan Brown emerged from the defence with much credit. The worst aspect of the defeat was that it had seen Fulham pick up injuries to goalkeeper Macedo and goalscorer Robson. The reserve winger Terry Parmenter and Mark Pearson were also injured, and George Cohen soon be would be required again for England duty.

With these injuries, the last thing Fulham needed was a game two days later, but that was the date set aside for the fourth round League Cup **replay** against **Aston Villa** at Villa Park. Therefore for the second time in three days, a patched up Fulham squad set off up the motorway to the Midlands. Buckingham was forced to give a first team debut to goalkeeper Jack McClelland, Bobby Keetch deputised at right back for George Cohen, Fred Callaghan deputised for Bobby Robson, Stan Brown remained in for the injured Pearson, with John Dempsey moving back to centre half. Inside forward Brian O'Connell was forced to play an emergency centre forward role.

The game drew a disappointing 18,000 crowd to Villa Park. The first ten minutes were particularly worrying, as Keetch twice, and Brown were forced to clear from the goal line, but Fulham survived. Fulham hung on bravely until half time, with Haynes working tirelessly. On a greasy pitch, Fulham were technically superior to Villa in midfield with Dempsey dominating the back, but again the goalscoring hoodoo was in evidence. Johnny Haynes continued to push Fulham along, and the team created enough chances to have the Villa reserve goalkeeper John Gavan gasping. This was particularly so in the last few minutes of the first half when Terry Dyson's shot was blocked on the goal line by Alan Deakin, and Haynes' flick was turned away by full back Charlie Aitken.

After a dire first half, Villa could only play better, and unfortunately they did. Despite still looking a very brittle side, the Midlands side scored two second half goals. The first by Phil Woosnam was headed in seven minutes after half time, following an accurate cross by Villa winger Tony Scott. Fulham never seriously recovered from this reverse, although keeper Gavan did make one fine save from a stinging long-range shot from Fred Callaghan. Then just five minutes from time,

Woosnam scored again crashing in Charlie Aitken's centre to seal the tie for Villa, and Fulham, despite playing the more fluent, finer football, crashed out of the League Cup **0–2**.

Amazingly, the club programme the following week bemoaned the fact that Fulham were struggling to find a regular *goalscorer*, seemingly trying to gloss over the fact that the team had already conceded thirty-eight goals in the first sixteen matches, the second worst defensive record in the division. The charismatic Rodney Marsh had been in and out of the side all season, reflecting the on-off relationship he shared with manager Buckingham. Marsh had top scored in the previous season with seventeen goals in forty-one league matches, but had so far this season failed to find the net. Buckingham, frustrated by the other forwards, decided therefore to give him an extended run in the side.

The ensuing week saw **Nottingham Forest** visit the Cottage, two places above Fulham, but with the same number of points, and almost an identical record. Forest were not a team of stars at the time, but possessed young talent like Henry Newton and Ian Storey-Moore coming through to supplement a kernel of experience that included Colin Addison and John Barnwell (now the PFA representative). However, they were without their bustling centre forward Frank Wignall.

Fulham dropped Johnny Key and Bobby Keetch, who was made substitute, and were also still without Bobby Robson and Mark Pearson. Tony Macedo had recovered from his wrist injury, and George Cohen returned. Fred Callaghan continued at wing half, and Brian O'Connell also continued up front. John Dempsey dropped back to take Keetch's place at centre half, giving up the number nine shirt to Rodney Marsh.

Fulham were totally dominant early on, and the match was twenty minutes old before Forest were allowed to mount their first serious attack. Marsh duly obliged on the half hour with his first goal of the season, a fine headed goal as he soared above the Forest defenders to bullet home a header from Johnny Haynes' precision corner. The goal ensured that Fulham went in a goal up.

On the hour, Forest equalised with a gem through inside forward Chris Crowe, when he took advantage of a spread-eagled defence, opened up by Forest's Newton and Barnwell, and crashed a right footer past the advancing Macedo. Although Fulham tried, the team again lacked cohesion, and despite all the positional changes looked no nearer to finding a winning formula. Forest seemed obsessed with the draw that they had gained, and were penned inside their own half for long periods. They created little, and George Cohen and Brian Nichols easily snuffed out what they did create, but Fulham could not make the additional possession or territorial advantage count. They carved out numerous chances, but either delayed, or ballooned them all over the bar,

Brown and Dempsey look on anxiously, but Macedo deals with a routine shot easily. Forest's Barnwell is poised for any mistake. Despite an early Rodney Marsh goal, Fulham finally had to settle for a 1–1 draw with Nottingham Forest.

Terry Dyson being the most consistent culprit, with Marsh not far behind. One reporter calculated that no less than thirteen efforts, from between ten and fifteen yards out, had gone that way, and commented: 'If it had been a rugby match, Fulham would have won easily!' Despite their general play, Haynes hit the post twice, once in each half, and then seemed to have scored the winning goal late in the game, when he netted following a lobbed pass from Dyson. However, though there were few complaints from the Forest players, Norwich referee Tommy Dawes decided to disallow the goal for an infringement by Graham Leggat on the Forest keeper Peter Grummitt.

Photographs of the incident show no real contact between the two players; it was typical of Fulham's current fortunes. Even in injury time, Grummitt denied Haynes again when he fingertipped a backheader over the bar. However, the one positive side in the lacklustre **1–1** draw meant that it was now four home games unbeaten.

Rodney Marsh had a miserably poor game overall, easily held by veteran Forest centre half Bobby McKinlay, which did little to enhance his relationship with Buckingham. The one bright spot, however, was a brilliant display by George Cohen, who was seemingly playing right back, right half and right winger at the same time, all to equally good effect, creating chances and preventing goals. At least three of his 'goal inviting' crosses should have been put away, and he had deserved far better support and results. The media were now grooming George to be England captain, calling his display 'a masterly performance of guts, skill and sheer class'.

An unchanged Fulham travelled to Yorkshire and Hillsborough the following week for a contest against **Sheffield Wednesday**, and again the match proved to be very much of the same story as the previous week. In the first half, the Fulham attack was totally insipid, and it looked as if the team would score only by accident. Rodney Marsh showed individual flashes of brilliance, but Fulham lacked any kind of thrust, either through the middle or from the wings. Wednesday looked as if they might score at will in the first half, and from their first excursion into the Fulham penalty area in the second minute, John Fantham took debutant Jim McCalliog's pass, and smacked a shot against the Fulham right-hand post with Tony Macedo beaten.

Thanks to Macedo and a large slice of good fortune, Fulham kept the score down to one at the interval, David Ford's shot in the twenty-seventh minute proving decisive. The goal was the eighteen-year-old's first goal in league football, a simple finish as the ball arrived at his feet on the penalty spot. After the goal, Macedo then turned over another sizzling Fantham drive, and then Brian Nichols had to clear off the line after Macedo had dropped a cross from Wednesday's Colin Dobson.

In the second half, the attack pepped up a little, and the defence tightened considerably, giving Wednesday far fewer chances. However, with an impotent forward line, the match degenerated into a dull affair. George Cohen tried his best to pep up both defence and attack, but was the only bright spot in another depressingly poor display. Yet in the final few minutes, Fulham could have snatched an undeserved draw when Terry Dyson cut in from the wing, and his fine shot beat goalkeeper Peter Wicks, making his debut deputising for the injured Ron Springett, but the ball flashed inches wide of the upright. Otherwise Wicks had been more or less a spectator, touching the ball just nine times in the entire match! At the end, Fulham had been beaten **0–1**. Even the local media were not impressed, describing Fulham as 'without doubt the most mediocre side to play in Sheffield this season.' It certainly had been a mystery to the press why Wednesday had not scored 'a hatful'.

What was depressing about the current situation was that whilst tinkering with the forward positions of the experienced players, Vic Buckingham didn't appear to be looking at how the reserve side was performing. In the last eleven matches, the reserve team had won six, drawn four and lost only one, scoring *over thirty goals* in the process. John Ryan already had eight goals and young Steve Earle six, yet neither player had been given a sniff of first team action.

With Fulham in turmoil, the rumourmongers were carefully putting together a story that George Cohen (like Alan Mullery) was going to be purchased by Tottenham to replace broken leg victim Maurice Norman; thankfully, Fulham quickly quashed those rumours. On the downside, Bobby

Robson, who had hardly ever suffered serious injury in his entire career, had been forced to have an operation on a rare and serious condition to both feet that was causing the toes to turn downwards; strips of muscle had to be taken from the soles of both feet. The operation would put him on crutches initially, and keep him out of the team for some time.

The following Saturday saw the other newly promoted side **Northampton Town** visit the Cottage. In their first ever season in the top flight, the Cobblers were struggling for quality, currently lying bottom of the table. After having dispatched the club 5–0 from the League Cup earlier, this visit should have been a home banker. Johnny Key and Bobby Keetch returned, John Dempsey took the number nine shirt again and Brian O'Connell took the winger's shirt, with out of sorts Terry Dyson dropping to substitute.

It was a game where *nothing* went right, Fulham were not getting the run of the ball early on, and were soon one down. In the sixteenth minute, highly rated Northampton winger Tommy Robson evaded both George Cohen and Stan Brown to send over a pinpoint centre that was headed in by Bobby Brown. Lady luck then again took a hand in the proceedings. In the twenty-first minute, Tony Macedo, going for a cross, looked to be the victim of Bobby Hunt's flying elbow. Whether it was accidental or not was never discussed, but the sure outcome was that Macedo had broken his jaw. Normally the athletic PE trained substitute goalkeeper was Graham Leggat, but he was missing on this day through injury. However, Rodney Marsh, being quite tall, suddenly just *volunteered*, and ventured in between the sticks!

The crowd, already nervous, could hardly believe it. In one surreal incident, Marsh caught the ball, bounced it on the edge of the penalty area, and tried to kick clear. The mis-kick hit Northampton's Bobby Brown on the back of the head, and the rebound was bizarrely heading for goal until Brian Nichols rushed back and cleared! From this maelstrom, Fulham somehow managed to contrive an equaliser—substitute Dyson, Key and Dempsey combined, ending with Johnny Haynes shooting home through a ruck of players—but again this was as good as it became.

Northampton, sensing Marsh's unease in goal, went for the throat. Marsh then duly obliged the away side three minutes later, by making a hash of a simple chipped shot from Northampton's Bobby Hunt, allowing the ball to slip through his hands, and Northampton were in the ascendancy again at half time.

Other than the second goal, Marsh did reasonably well, and could not have been faulted for the other Northampton goals. It could also easily have been worse, as both Keetch and Brian Nichols were forced to turn goalbound shots off the goal line. Shortly after half time, Northampton scored the best goal of the match, Brown easily shaking off Keetch's ineffective challenge, before firing in a fierce ground shot into the corner, that even Macedo could not have stopped, let alone the diving Marsh. Fulham made a spirited attempt to try and reduce the arrears later in the game,

For once, a horizontal Coe in the Northampton goal is beaten but a defender clears from the line. Rodney Marsh hopes for a slip up. Later Marsh, now wearing the green goalkeeper's jersey, makes a brave but vain attempt to prevent Northampton's third goal. Northampton ran out 1–4 winners.

but there was very little zip up front. Fulham produced a ponderous and slow build up, with the ball going sideways and backwards rather than forwards, and the team demonstrated a lack of positioning and poise. The wingers seemed totally out of the game, and the remaining forwards crowded frantically in the middle, which led to confusion and communication problems.

Marsh was still busy at the other end, punching over a shot from Robson, and then smothering a shot from Joe Kiernan that thudded into his ribs. He received an ovation for his final save, turning over a header from Jim Hall that looked a goal all the way! Finally, Northampton sealed their win when Joe Broadfoot floated in a cross, and Brown headed in again. This one also seemed down to Keetch, who left the forward far too much room. In the end Northampton emerged easy **1–4** winners, a humiliating result for Fulham. The result handed Northampton their first *ever* away win in the First Division. It was also however, a happy return to the Cottage for Northampton's Broadfoot. The last time he had visited the Cottage, he had been a member of the Ipswich Town side that lost 10–1 to Fulham on Boxing Day 1963.

What was particularly galling was that Northampton's Bobby Brown, who had been an amateur with Fulham scoring four first team goals in eight outings in 1960, had cut the Fulham defence to ribbons, and had scored *three* of the four Northampton's goals. What was truly amazing was why Marsh had volunteered to be substitute keeper at all; he had *never played in goal before*! Marsh admitted the experience had been 'terrifying, with the ball flying at you from all angles'; he admitted he had not done very well. Some of the more cruel fans even suggested that being a striker, Marsh couldn't break the habit of trying to put the ball in the net. Certainly in his spell in goal, he seemed to rely on his feet a lot more than his hands.

Established star Macedo would be out for some time, and ATV had again chosen this Fulham game to be covered for *Star Soccer*. Although for the neutral observer the match probably made comical viewing, certainly not many Fulham supporters would have shared the sentiment. There had been fatalism in Fulham's play that looked particularly ominous.

Even the local media were now openly critical of the side and the management, offering the challenging question, 'Just how many of the present side are vital to the club's future, and how much longer can the club have any real hopes of staying in the First Division?' The local media reporter also stated that 'some hard thinking has to be done by Buckingham and the directors', and added, 'Although the clamour is for money to be spent on a centre forward, I am not sure that expenditure alone will be enough'.

December 1965

In this month

* Goldie the eagle escaped from London zoo for the second time in a year.
* The Government made plans for a Road Safety bill, including legal alcohol limits, and random breath tests.
* A Labour cabinet re-shuffle brought Barbara Castle to prominence as minister of transport.
* Richard Dimbleby died aged 52.
* Somerset Maugham died aged 91.
* Thirteen died after an oil rig collapsed in the North Sea.
* Two American *Gemini* spacecraft achieved the first rendezvous in space.

'Day Tripper' / 'We Can Work It Out' by The Beatles topped the charts.

How the league was looking

Liverpool had now taken over at the top, with Burnley three points behind; West Bromwich Albion, Sheffield United and Leeds United were keeping up the pressure two points behind Burnley. Manchester United were up to eighth, but Chelsea were still mid table. Blackburn were supporting the table, level on points with Fulham, but four clubs were just three points ahead of the bottom two including Blackpool and West Ham.

The matches

FULHAM TRAVELLED to the Victoria Ground the following week for the match against **Stoke City**, and despite the problems of the previous week gave a good account of themselves. The match gave a league debut to goalkeeper Jack McClelland, whom Fulham had signed on a surprise free transfer from Arsenal the year before. Jack McClelland had joined Arsenal in 1960, and had been given a tough role as understudy to the great Jack Kelsey and later Jim Furnell. Playing only eight games in the first two seasons, McClelland had played thirty-three games in goal for Arsenal in 1962–63 before being sidelined with a shoulder injury.

Buckingham gave youth a small chance by also giving a league debut to summer signing John Ryan and a first start of the season to young winger Terry Parmenter. Ryan had started his career at Maidstone before moving to Arsenal. Fulham were a goal down at half time through the Stoke veteran Roy Vernon after fifteen minutes. At this stage Stoke were moving the ball around sweetly, and it looked as if Fulham were on a hiding to nothing. McClelland was compelled to dive bravely at the feet of Stoke forwards on three separate occasions, to prevent certain goals.

In a second half played in extremely wet and windy conditions, Fulham gave a spirited display and were unluckily edged out. A blunder by experienced centre half Maurice Setters, allowing a ball to bounce over his head, freed Rodney Marsh to dance through and tap in the equaliser just five minutes after half time. Ten minutes later Setters, embarrassed by the error, headed just wide, and then charged upfield to restore Stoke's lead with a fierce shot that found the net via the crossbar. However, Fulham were still not done, and Marsh added a second equaliser with an excellent twenty-yard shot past the other Irish goalkeeper Bobby Irvine following a clever sortie down the left wing.

Although the Fulham defence was harassed and under pressure, McClelland was having an inspired game, making several excellent saves whilst, on occasions, being assisted by the woodwork. He was stopping efforts that he had no right to even see, let alone save. Then, just when it looked like their hard-working efforts would secure a deserved point, lady luck again hijacked the game, and Stoke's young star wing-half Alan Bloor blasted in an undeserved winner with just thirty *seconds* left on the clock, Fulham finally losing **2–3.**

Rodney Marsh, fresh from his goalkeeping duties, had looked the best forward on view. He had scored both Fulham goals, and had played much more like his old self, whilst youngsters Ryan and Parmenter had more than held their own. McClelland left the field to a standing ovation from the Stoke supporters. One reporter described his heroics as 'one of the most courageous displays of goalkeeping I have ever seen'. The brutal truth, however, was that no points had been added to the Fulham total again, and this was the kind of game and opponent where the team needed to pick up points. Psychologically, the defeat caused significant damage, however, as this result had seen Fulham finally drop to the bottom of the table.

Fulham with their current problems could have done without the visit of high-flying **Burnley** to the Cottage to mark the halfway point of the season. Burnley were a bogey team to Fulham and were riding on the crest of a wave, currently lying second in the table. Burnley were a side packed with experience, including goalkeeper Adam Blacklaw, midfielder Brian O'Neill, and a dazzling forward line that included Willie Morgan, Andy Lochhead, Northern Ireland international Willie Irvine and winger Ralph Coates. Mark Pearson came in for Stan Brown, and Graham Leggat for Johnny Key, and despite a promising debut the week before, Brian O'Connell was recalled to replace John Ryan.

All by myself! Graham Leggat dribbles into the penalty area to take on the Burnley defence. This effort, like most, came to nothing as the Clarets romped to a 2–5 win.

The match went painfully to form, and Fulham were 1–2 down at the interval. Both goals were preventable, and goalkeeper Jack McClelland was wholly or partially responsible for both. For the first in the eleventh minute, a through ball from Burnley's Gordon Harris was slipped into the Fulham defence. Both McClelland and John Dempsey hesitated fatally, allowing Irvine to nip in to score with a cross-shot that trickled into the empty net. Fulham's equaliser in the twenty-sixth minute was also fortunate, Burnley's Harris putting through his own goal whilst trying to prevent Terry Parmenter's left wing centre reaching Johnny Haynes.

Burnley then added a second goal five minutes before half time when McClelland seemed to have a sharp, ground level, cross-cum-shot from winger Morgan covered, but the ball bounced out of his hand, allowing Irvine to tap in an easy second from close range. O'Connell and Rodney Marsh had both come close, and Leggat had been just wide with a flying header, but generally Fulham were offering little as an attacking force. Fulham sensed some hope when the experienced Burnley full back Alex Elder was forced to leave the field injured, to be replaced by the young Sammy Todd.

In the second half, however, Burnley, as an attacking outfit, slipped into overdrive, and ran riot. The Clarets were a major force down the wings, and although George Cohen coped adequately,

Brian Nichols and Fred Callaghan were having a torrid time against Willie Morgan. In a four-minute spell shortly after half time, Burnley sealed the match with halfback Brian O'Neill and Irvine netting further excellent Burnley goals. O'Neill's in the fifty-first minute was a scorching twenty-five yard shot, and Irvine's converted chance, following a dazzling three man move in the fifty-fifth minute, allowed him to complete his personal hat trick. It looked at times as if the Fulham defence were giving the Burnley forwards shooting practice.

Pearson then managed to pull a goal back for Fulham fifteen minutes from time after Burnley keeper Blacklaw had failed to hold a sharp shot from Haynes. However, Fulham began to become frustrated by Burnley's superiority, and Pearson, renowned for his short fuse and booked previously for a nasty foul on Coates, was sent off with five minutes remaining after 'debating' a late penalty decision for Burnley with referee Wallace, given against John Dempsey for a foul on Willie Morgan. Brian Miller converted from the spot to complete the scoring. The numerical disadvantage did Fulham few favours, and Burnley ran out easy **2−5** winners.

There had been a new 'crackdown' by referees with regard to disputes and swearing, but most neutrals thought that 'Pancho' was a little unlucky to go off. The Saturday evening paper headlined 'Pearson off as Fulham crash'. There was little doubt that Burnley were a very good all-round side, but as one reporter cruelly put it, 'Fulham provided them with little more than a training match'.

With only half of the season completed, the Burnley game had sent the number of goals conceded rising to over fifty. The club still seemed very reluctant to buy, and it seemed their only choice was to persevere with young defenders Brian Nichols, John Dempsey and Fred Callaghan despite the maulings that they were receiving. The media were now noting that the team appeared to have little heart for a fightback when events were going badly on the pitch.

The next match against **Everton** on Merseyside saw Buckingham revert to experience. Stan Brown came back in for Fred Callaghan, and Terry Dyson for Terry Parmenter. There was also a much needed return by Bobby Robson following injury, and Mark Pearson moved up from wing half to inside forward to replace Brian O'Connell. Rumours had abounded that Johnny Haynes would be dropped for the match, but he took his customary place in the side, operating instead in an unfamiliar inside right/right wing position.

Goodison Park was another of Fulham's unlucky grounds, and the match was played in terrible muddy and rainy conditions on a gluepot of a pitch that seemed to impede both teams. It was certainly a match of physique rather than soccer artistry, and Fulham went in at half time two goals behind, after conceding both in the first quarter of an hour.

The first after eleven minutes came as both Everton wingers combined. Alex Scott pounced on a quick throw-in and sprinted clear of the Fulham defence in a thirty-yard run, and his deep centre was clouted first time on the volley by Derek Temple, and the ball flew in. Then, just five minutes later, the score was two. From a corner conceded by George Cohen, Temple put in an in-swinging effort to the near post, which was glanced home delightfully by Alex Young, the ball taking a deflection off Brian Nichols on its way in.

Both the goals originated from the wing, with Everton cleverly using the only dry areas of grass on the pitch. Once Cohen had mastered winger Derek Temple, Everton's chances began to wane. Rodney Marsh was only inches too high with a grand header, and Everton reserve goalkeeper Geoff Barnett had to fling himself to the left to make his only real save of the afternoon.

Fulham improved in the second half, with Graham Leggat much more of a physical threat but no goals were forthcoming. As an outside right, Haynes was up against England full back Ray Wilson, and he prised little change out of him. In the end, however, Fulham failed to seriously trouble the Everton defence in the second forty-five minutes, persisting with trying to charge through the centre of the slushy pitch.

Everton persisted in missing several chances, and Jack McClelland was again called upon to make a number of good saves. Perhaps Everton handed Fulham some measure of Christmas spirit by leaving it at **0−2**, but Vic Buckingham commented that he thought there had been an 'improved spirit' about the performance. Everton had avenged their defeat at the Cottage earlier in the season.

To be fair to Buckingham, the press had given a great deal of credit to both teams for being able to produce ninety minutes of entertaining football in swamp-like conditions.

Continuing bad weather led to the **postponement** of the Boxing Day fixture for the visit of **Leicester City** and gave Fulham some temporary respite; unfortunately the traditional corresponding fixture at Filbert Street the following day was not postponed. Vic Buckingham, without much cover decided, rather bizarrely, to play winger Brian O'Connell at left back for Brian Nichols.

On a bone-hard icy pitch, covered with a light dusting of snow, Fulham's current inadequacies were again painfully exposed. Although it was now beginning to sound like a broken record, Fulham were unlucky in the early exchanges when Mark Pearson's shot cannoned back off the post with Banks helpless on ten minutes. Spurred on by their good fortune, Leicester began to take control. Fulham, however, were not performing that badly, and their goal remained intact until just three minutes before half time.

Once the first goal went in, however, the floodgates opened, and some of the Fulham players lost heart. Leicester's Jackie Sinclair, signed from Dunfermline in the summer, remained fleet-footed, whilst the Fulham defenders skidded and slipped. He had a brilliant game, scoring twice and having a hand in the other three goals; he also scored the all-important first Leicester goal.

The second half was just three minutes old when Leicester's Davy Gibson made it two. Minutes later, Sinclair slipped around three defenders with ease before teeing the ball up for Bobby Roberts, who hit the target with a fierce drive. Fulham then began to come back, and George Cohen, in one of his several upfield sorties, put in a low shot that hit the foot of the post with Gordon Banks beaten. Banks was just able to prevent the rebound crossing the line. Ten minutes from time, Leicester's Mike Stringfellow made it four, and in the last seconds, Sinclair grabbed his second and Leicester's fifth from Gibson's centre to complete the rout; Fulham eventually lost **0–5**. Fulham were now without a league win in two months.

The media had noted that 'too many players seem to lose heart once they are trailing'. Few came out of the match with credit; George Cohen and Stan Brown were praised for their industry, and Johnny Haynes and Bobby Robson for some 'ideas', but all in all it was another hammering.

An outnumbered Rodney Marsh is crowded out by Leicester defenders at a frosty Filbert Street. The Christmas encounter was Marsh's last league game, ending in a 0–5 defeat.

The Leicester match saw Buckingham finally lose patience with Rodney Marsh, and after another barren match, Marsh would never again play a league match for Fulham.

Another issue for Buckingham arose when, after missing several days training, goalkeeper Tony Macedo, summoned to give an explanation, handed in a transfer request. Buckingham agreed that 'a move would be in the interests of both parties'. The formal statement put out, was that the request 'was purely personal, and unconnected with football'. Macedo had made similar requests in the past, so no one was really sure as to what would happen this time.

It appeared that Macedo had become disenchanted with football, and rumours implied that he wanted to quit the game altogether, and that he had asked the club for his cards (National Insurance Cards). Some reports further suggested that he had been suspended by the club. In the short term it was rumoured that only Plymouth Argyle had made any firm enquiry for him (£9,000). It appeared that Macedo had a number of off-field financial problems. He had lodged his own bankruptcy petition, and had appeared before the official receiver. These were dark times indeed for the Cottagers.

The ensuing club programme ran out the usual text—played well/unlucky/should have scored early on…etc—but the repetitive chant was now beginning to have a very hollow ring. With fifty-nine goals conceded so far, it was obvious that despite George Cohen's class and efforts, the defence was patently not good enough, and that with only six goals scored in the last seven games, a regular goal-scorer was a major priority. The harsh facts spoke for themselves that, in the months of November and December, Fulham had secured just *one* point from eight league games, which in anybody's book was nothing except relegation form; morale at the club could not have been lower.

January 1966

* Bakers put a penny (1d) on the price of a standard loaf which now cost 1s 4d (7p).
* 117 died as an Air India plane crashed into Mont Blanc.
* The Board of Trade banned nearly all trade between Britain and Rhodesia.
* Indira Ghandi was elected as the new Prime Minister of India.
* Beatle George Harrison married Patti Boyd.

'Keep On Running' by The Spencer Davis Group topped the charts.

How the league was looking

It was still Liverpool and Burnley leading the table separated by just two points, whilst Manchester United had found spectacular form, and shot up to third. Sheffield United and West Bromwich Albion had drifted badly to around mid table, where both Arsenal and Chelsea still remained. Fulham were still supporting the table, but just three points separated the bottom four clubs. West Ham were showing some improvement.

The matches

THE FIRST glimmer of a wind of change to sweep Craven Cottage was the appointment of Dave Sexton as Fulham's coach. Although young at just thirty-six, Sexton was already highly regarded. The tenure of Ron Burgess as Buckingham's number two at Fulham had been barely six months, and he departed Fulham to manage Bedford Town. Sexton had spent four years as Chelsea's coach, and whilst cutting his teeth at Stamford Bridge had earned a reputation as being responsible for the progress of many of Chelsea's current talented side. Sexton joined Fulham after surprisingly resigning from his position at Leyton Orient, and after rejecting offers from Birmingham City and Plymouth Argyle.

Fulham faced **Arsenal** on New Year's Day; it was a Saturday and this was before 1st January was a public holiday (it was not declared a public holiday until 1974). The Gunners were having only an average season and the north Londoners currently lay in mid-table. The Arsenal side was in transition with a mixture of young players like Peter Storey, Jon Sammels and John Radford coming through to complement the experience of Joe Baker, George Eastham and Don Howe. On the day, Arsenal were without first choice keeper Jim Furnell. His replacement was a certain Bob Wilson making a rare

The 'Wind of Change'. Buckingham welcomes a young Dave Sexton to the ground early in the New Year. Sexton's coaching was instrumental in turning around the side's fortunes in just three dramatic months!

start for Arsenal. Wilson, like Graham Leggat, was a former PE teacher, and had played for Arsenal previously as an amateur. This was his first year as a full-time professional.

Despite the Leicester debacle, Brian O'Connell retained his position at left back; Terry Parmenter was again included in place of Terry Dyson, whose bright start had faded badly; unfortunately, Bobby Robson was again unfit. Buckingham took a bold gamble by playing defender Bobby Keetch as a virtual ball winning inside forward in the number four shirt. In diplomatic terms Buckingham talked of Keetch's 'buccaneer approach' and 'his brand of enthusiasm', which was probably a euphemistic way of stating that he wanted him to put himself about a bit, keep a sharp eye on George Eastham and put some strong tackles in.

Early soccer coverage on ATV; Graham Leggat's winner against Arsenal retained all its glory on 'Star Soccer' the following day.

The matchday programme sent out a message of defiance, saying the club had 'no self pity', refuting that this was 'the same old Fulham going through its annual struggle against relegation', but rather 'a new Fulham having its teething troubles'. Vic Buckingham went public on a transfer target, naming St Mirren's Gerry Queen as a player he had identified to provide goals for Fulham. Ultimately the transfer didn't materialise as St Mirren turned down Fulham's 'substantial' offer. Queen, however, did come south three seasons later to play for Orient and Crystal Palace.

On this day Fulham played with a much greater sense of purpose, but in the initial stages it looked as if their luck was as far out as ever. Twice in a matter of seconds both Johnny Haynes and Graham Leggat had shots cleared off the line by Arsenal's Peter Storey and Ian Ure respectively, with the Arsenal defence in disarray.

Fulham finally won the game in the twenty-seventh minute with a goal from Leggat. Fulham won a free kick at a twenty-five-yard distance, awarded for a clumsy foul on Mark Pearson by Ian Ure. Haynes tapped the ball sideways to Leggat, whose first time effort thundered through a wall of defenders high into the net just inside the post, beating the partially unsighted Bob Wilson's despairing dive. Wilson managed to put a fingertip to the ball, but couldn't stop it.

The match never rose to any great artistic heights; Arsenal played the more constructive football, but seemed too easily put off by Fulham's hard tackling and defensive will. This was much more of a tenacious team effort with everyone pulling together. Due to the pitch, Fulham relied on 'down the middle' tactics, with the wingers coming inside, Leggat coming off better in his tussles with his Scottish counterpart Ian Ure.

Arsenal piled on the pressure as the blood and thunder game went on, but the Fulham defence, for once, would not be breached. George Cohen was again showing England class, rendering winger

No way through; Bob Wilson grabs this one, protected by McLintock, Ure and Neill. Bobby Keetch, in an unfamiliar forward's role, tries to bustle his way through. Fulham had the final say on New Year's Day, winning 1–0.

George Armstrong ineffective, and Alan Skirton's hesitancy on the other wing made makeshift full back O'Connell's job a great deal easier. John Dempsey continued where he had left off at Highbury, blotting out an irritable Joe Baker. It was a particularly satisfying match for goalkeeper Jack McClelland, as he had been shown the door by Arsenal the year before. He was on blinding international form, producing many fine saves, two especially, from a Frank McLintock header, and a spectacular palm over following a powerful goalbound header from Joe Baker, being described as world class.

Bobby Keetch too had done his part; his swashbuckling tackles and overall stamina had eventually worn down George Eastham. Keetch even managed a remarkable last minute overhead kick, well tipped over by the surprised Wilson. Arsenal, shocked by Fulham's tenacity, also had skipper Frank McLintock booked. Fulham eventually swamped Arsenal with their bottomless energy, and scraped home **1–0**; it was their first clean sheet for two months.

The match had attracted a crowd of over 26,000, and the result was made all the sweeter, for once, by watching the game again on *Star Soccer* the next day. The win was the ideal fillip that Fulham badly needed, but with tough fixtures to come, the team would have to sustain it. Following this encounter were a number of tough matches. Arsenal manager Billy Wright was furious with his team's performance, stating: 'We would not have scored if we had played all week.'

The following week saw the return to Lancashire and Turf Moor. **Burnley** were still second, and pressing strongly for the league title. Manager Buckingham made a strange decision and disturbed a winning side, by including 'transfer listed' Tony Macedo. Bobby Robson returned and the manager retained his faith in Terry Dyson despite the fact that the player had not scored since the middle of October. For the first time, Fulham, under improved tactics from Sexton, attempted to play a defensive 4–3–3 formation in order to grab a draw.

The improved spirit was again much in evidence, and the impressive John Dempsey broke up all early Burnley attacks. Macedo was busy punching out an Alex Elder centre, and saving another shot from full back John Angus. After twenty-three minutes Fulham missed the game's best chance to score; Haynes' shot was deflected off Burnley's Brian Miller to Mark Pearson, who broke through, but with the Burnley defence floundering, blazed over into the crowd from six yards when it looked a great deal easier to score. Bobby Keetch should also have scored, but headed over from virtually underneath the bar.

Macedo was still the busier of the two keepers, and he knew nothing of the Arthur Bellamy shot that flew just wide. The Fulham defence was breached just once when, seven minutes before half time, Burnley full back John Angus of all people, who scored just three league goals for Burnley in almost 450 matches, took a Ralph Coates pass, teed the ball up, and hit a dipping cross-shot from the corner of the penalty box that swerved and bounced past the bemused Macedo. That important goal touch still continued to frustrate and elude the Fulham team.

In the second half, Fulham were marginally the better footballing side. In the new formation they defended deeply and relied on counter-attacks. The team did look a little disorganised, and the forward players were not too sure of their individual roles. The forwards frustrated Johnny Haynes to a degree, as his continual promptings were wasted by the players being repeatedly caught offside. Burnley brought on centre forward Andy Lochhead, but he could not beat Macedo, who again dealt capably with a drive from Todd, whilst Gordon Harris blazed wildly over.

Fulham sensed that the Burnley forwards were having an off day, and abandoned some of their defensive outlook to search for a late equaliser. Late in the game, Dyson was unlucky twice, once with a brilliantly taken volley that flew just wide of a post with Blacklaw beaten, and then with a thirty-five yard drive that Blacklaw saved with difficulty. In the end, despite a late Fulham rally, the one Burnley goal proved enough; the game finished **0–1** and gave Burnley the double.

The match also proved the end of the road for winger Terry Dyson, as, apart from a single cameo substitute appearance the following season, he never again made another first team league appearance. It was the first real sign of Vic Buckingham making comprehensive changes. At least the Burnley match had been a dogged 'backs to the wall' display that was much improved on the efforts of four weeks previously.

In front of a substantial crowd, Law and Charlton watch as Bobby Robson tries to slip the ball through to makeshift forward Bobby Keetch. Despite their endeavours, Fulham were edged out 0–1. It was Keetch's final league game.

A visit from in-form fourth-placed **Manchester United** the following week was again the last thing Fulham really needed. The game drew a large crowd, and the sellers of fake merchandise and unofficial posters were all positioned around the entrance to Bishops Park, giving the impression of a sea of red and white. The Busby Babes had Harry Gregg in goal in place of Pat Dunne, whilst his Irish namesake Tony Dunne replaced Shay Brennan. United were also without England winger John Connelly. Nevertheless, the Red Devils still fielded a formidable team including Pat Crerand, Nobby Stiles, George Best, Denis Law, Bobby Charlton and David Herd. Fulham persisted with Brian O'Connell at left back, but Mark Pearson was missing against his former club. The biggest surprise was the inclusion of Bobby Keetch in an unfamiliar number eight shirt. Keetch had obviously been told to shake up the forwards as well, and put himself about.

The crowd of 33,000 watched a match that was a lot closer than most imagined it would be. It was a bitterly cold and icy afternoon, and Tony Macedo played in tracksuit bottoms. Herd put in a cross-shot just wide early on, and Law miscued when in a good position. United took the lead with a trademark Bobby Charlton missile from twenty yards on the half hour, after Law and Best had neatly created the opening. Charlton let the ball run for a couple of yards, before firing a blistering shot into the top of the net that gave Macedo no chance at all.

Graham Leggat had a header just wide, and Gregg was forced to react smartly to push a long-range shot from Bobby Robson around the post. As the half wore on, however, United looked more and more comfortable. When they were able to win possession, Fulham again had none of the luck. Just before half time, Haynes was brought down in the box, when his shirt was clearly grabbed; the incident appeared to be a glaring penalty, but referee Brandwood waved play on.

Midway through the second half, a twenty-five yarder from Robson rebounded forcefully from the bar before Gregg had moved, and the same player then forced the goalkeeper into another scrambling save at the foot of a post. But all in all, Keetch looked totally out of place paired up front with Leggat, Terry Parmenter looked a little lost against international full back Tony Dunne, and Johnny Key was still woefully wayward up front.

As Fulham pressed forward for the elusive equaliser using the long ball, United countered with swift passing. Dunne shot into the side netting, Macedo saved another Charlton bullet by advancing to beyond his six-yard line, and Dempsey kicked wildly out of the goalmouth after Best had created the opening in the Fulham defence. The game finished **0–1**, and gave United the double.

The entertaining Denis Law had gone through his usual bag of tricks, the repertoire including bicycle kicks, overhead kicks, blowing kisses to his teammates, holding his shirt cuffs, and chatting humorously with the home crowd. Law actually played the final five minutes with just one boot on, carrying the other, explaining: 'It was hurting a bit, so I took it off – but I only needed the one anyway!'

To be fair, Fulham had shown plenty of honest endeavour and spirit, but in the end the team had capitulated to class football. The defence, especially Macedo, Cohen and Dempsey, had all played well, but the lightweight forwards had again failed to make any impact against Pat Crerand, Bill Foulkes and Nobby Stiles.

The match signalled the end of the Fulham careers of both Johnny Key and Bobby Keetch, neither of whom would start a first team league match again. Buckingham was honest in his post-match summary when he said: 'We were outplayed in ability, but fought to the last.' Again the match was covered for television, in *Match of the Day*.

Taking a break from league football and the pressures of relegation, Fulham took a second trip of the season to Bramall Lane the following week to face **Sheffield United** in the FA Cup. Jack McClelland played in goal, as the transfer-listed Tony Macedo would have been cup-tied if subsequently transferred to another club. Buckingham treated the game as an experiment, clearly seeing Fulham's league future to be of paramount importance, and the FA Cup as just a distraction— he made seven changes in all. He predicted that the fans would see 'a different Fulham'. In reality, it was mostly the same team, but playing in different positions in the forward line. Rodney Marsh came in for Johnny Key, and Mark Pearson replaced Bobby Robson. It was another damp and foggy afternoon, and Fulham gave another foggy performance on a wet, slippery pitch covered in sand and puddles; the team were never really in it. Two goals from Alan Birchenall (permanently mis-named in the Fulham programmes as either 'Ken' or 'Keith' Birchenall) secured the win alongside a third from Woodward.

The Blades dominated from the start and their wingers were soon weaving magic, with the twin strikers looking dangerous every time a ball came over. Soon after the start, Mick Jones put in a powerful header that beat Jack McClelland, but was kicked off the line by Brian O'Connell. However, it took Sheffield just eight minutes to take the lead through Birchenall. Stan Brown mis-directed a header back to McClelland, and whilst the defence hesitated, Birchenall seized on the chance and lobbed McClelland cleverly.

With a little fortune, four minutes later, Fulham could have been level. United goalkeeper Alan Hodgkinson made the save of the half, diving full length to hold and keep out a full-blooded effort from Terry Dyson. It could have been more but for the brilliance of McClelland. He dived full length to push a shot from Jones round the post, and then repeated the feat when United's Gil Reece put in a similar effort. Despite the home side's pressure, Fulham kept the score down to just one before half time.

The second half was much the same. Johnny Haynes did have one piledriver early on well saved by Hodgkinson, but when this failed to go in, a great deal of Fulham's resolve melted away. McClelland saved well twice from Alan Woodward, and was helpless when a third effort from the winger passed just the wrong side of the post. The Fulham defence was reduced to kicking the ball anywhere, but it brought only another wave of United pressure. Birchenall took his second in the sixty-fourth minute, heading in cleanly from Woodward's centre. Then, just minutes later, Woodward put the tie beyond doubt, touching home from a few yards in a simple finish after a strong run by centre half Reg Matthewson had created the chance.

Seeking damage limitation, Fulham pushed John Dempsey up front. Dempsey replied by sneaking in to head a consolation goal, deflected in off United's Joe Shaw. McClelland had another good game, but the rotation of the forwards had changed nothing at all. Fulham lost **1−3**, and were out of the competition at the first hurdle. To make matters worse, Rodney Marsh broke a bone in his foot. Buckingham's prediction of a new Fulham had proven to be just mere hope, and he said: 'No excuses, they were, by far, the more direct side.'

The writing had been on the wall for both Bobby Keetch and Rodney Marsh, neither of whom had really seen eye to eye with Buckingham. Both were flamboyant individualists, not really in the manager's style. Marsh recalled Buckingham talking to himself, Keetch and others on the training pitch regarding the fineries of the game. Marsh recalled that Buckingham did a little tap dance, and sang a song about 'having rhythm' or similar. Then he said: 'If you understand that, you'll understand football'. Keetch replied: 'You prat' and sashayed away leaving Marsh smiling. The FA Cup match was Rodney Marsh's swansong as a Fulham player. In the space of one turbulent month, Buckingham had brought the curtain down on the Fulham careers of Dyson, Marsh, Key and Keetch, and Brian O'Connell would follow a month later.

With only one league goal in the last five games, Fulham's record was pitiful and there appeared to be no ready answers. With the 'old guard' rejected and Terry Parmenter not really ready, Buckingham gambled with one last throw of the dice, which he 'rolled' in the next home match against **Blackpool**.

Returning to the league endeavours, Buckingham finally made wholesale changes: Tony Macedo was withdrawn again, with Jack McClelland resuming in goal, established defender Brian Nichols replaced Brian O'Connell, and Fred Callaghan came in for Bobby Keetch. However, there were two other significant inclusions. Firstly Steve Earle, himself transfer-listed due to lack of first team opportunities, took Johnny Key's place at number seven. Earle had scored eight goals in just twenty appearances for the reserves, and so was worthy of his chance; the match was his first league game for fifteen months. Steve Earle recalls:

> *I had had a bust-up with Vic Buckingham at the Roehampton training ground that resulted in me not even speaking to him for twelve months. I was put on the [transfer] list, but Buckingham had no intention of selling me. Frustrated, I went to see him and he gave me a 30% pay rise and put me back in the team!*

The most surprising second inclusion, however, was that of Leslie Barrett at number eight. The eighteen-year-old had been a professional for just three months, and had made just eight reserve

Steve Earle, on his return to the team, just fails to connect during the match against Blackpool. Makeshift centre forward Stan Brown watches intently, as does debutant Leslie Barrett. Also in the picture are Alan Ball (far left) and England full back, and now radio commentator, Jimmy Armfield (between Brown and Earle). Despite Fulham dominating for most of the match, the game ended as a 0–0 stalemate.

appearances. Battersea born Barrett had supported Chelsea as a youngster. He had undergone three trials with Chelsea, and at the end of the third trial, Chelsea had rejected him! Fulham had not made the same mistake and had signed him straightaway. An all round sportsman, Les had also excelled in both cricket and athletics.

For the match, Mr 'play anywhere' Stan Brown wore the very unfamiliar number nine shirt, and Terry Parmenter was returned to the wing. Johnny Haynes was, for once, apparently dropped from the side, George Cohen taking over the captaincy.

Blackpool were themselves struggling, and were just three points ahead of Fulham in eighteenth place. The Seasiders included in their squad ex England goalkeeper Tony Waiters, injured on the day, and ex England defender Jimmy Armfield, now a successful radio commentator, alongside veteran striker Ray Charnley. On the whole it was an ageing side, but did contain one very bright spark in the form of flame-haired eighteen-year-old 'dynamo' Alan Ball, and also the young Hugh Fisher. Fulham must have viewed this match as an opportunity and a must for two points. Buckingham said: 'I believe these changes are warranted by our position. I mean no disrespect or discredit to those who are replaced today. But I sincerely believe that these younger players are worthy of a chance of proving what they can do.'

With so many changes, the match itself was very disappointing, with precious little of note to recall, both sides creating very little. The youthful Fulham side put in plenty of effort, but were unable to break down a dogged Blackpool defence in which Armfield excelled. George Cohen's performance shone out like a beacon amongst the mediocrity around him. Mark Pearson, however, failed in his attempt to imitate Haynes and his role; his passing often went astray, and he was often dispossessed. Stan Brown looked uncomfortable at centre forward, despite having played there in earlier years. Blackpool should have taken the lead in the second minute when John Dempsey misjudged a long kick and Graham Oates rushed clear with just Jack McClelland to beat. Fortunately, he shot a yard wide. Stan Brown, however, did have one clear chance when put through by Pearson, but his first time shot was just inches wide.

When Fulham most needed experience, Bobby Robson went off injured with a pulled calf muscle, and young John Ryan was given a little first team action as his substitute at centre forward with Brown dropping back; he strove manfully, but to little effect. Blackpool may well have won the game late on with steadier finishing: Leslie Lea hit a post, McClelland pushed out Armfield's shot from the rebound, and then saved the final third shot from Graham Oates. Overall, in the course of the match, the Blackpool forwards proved to be as profligate as the Fulham front line. Despite Fulham dominating the second half, the game finished **0−0**, but at least it was another valuable point gained.

The match proved promising for Earle, and Barrett, who, despite missing two gilt-edged chances, and having one saved by Blackpool stand-in goalkeeper Alan Taylor, had what was described as a 'sparkling debut'. The media were pleased with the effort Fulham put in, and most remarked that, with a little cooler finishing, Fulham would have won comfortably. The press added that 'the youngsters played with enthusiasm, determination and guts'.

February 1966

In this month

- * The Companies Bill was passed which forced firms to reveal their donations to political parties.
- * 133 were killed when an airliner crashed into Tokyo bay.
- * The Government produced a prototype for a fast breeder reactor at Dounreay in Scotland.
- * Watneys put a penny on the price of a pint of bitter which now cost 1/8d (8.5p)
- * Buster Keaton died.
- * Freddie Laker purchased three BAC 111 planes, and set up an 'all jet airline' for the holiday market.

'19th Nervous Breakdown' by The Rolling Stones topped the charts.

How the league was looking

Liverpool were now well ahead of Burnley at the top, and looking very strong, whilst both Leeds United and Manchester United were just a point behind Burnley. Chelsea had at last found some form, rising to seventh, Arsenal were still mid table. West Ham now seemed clear of trouble. Fulham were still supporting the table, and losing touch with all the other teams except Blackburn. Sheffield Wednesday and Sunderland had both slipped nearer to the relegation zone.

The matches

BUCKINGHAM MUST have seen some glimmer of hope in the Blackpool performance, as he named a virtually unchanged side for the trip to face **Chelsea** at Stamford Bridge, Graham Leggat replacing Steve Earle temporarily, with Johnny Haynes still omitted from the line-up. Chelsea had already won nine away matches, but had yet to discover that sort of form at the Bridge. The Pensioners, however, had won their last six games on the trot, and so were on very good form.

The match, again attended by over 35,000, began in standard form and Fulham, on yet another of their unluckier grounds found themselves two goals down inside the first half an hour. In the tenth minute, Chelsea's George Graham made an interception, and found winger Bobby Tambling poorly marked, and he left footed the ball under the diving Jack McClelland and into the net. Fulham were very unhappy with the goal, as both Tambling and another Chelsea forward Barry Bridges appeared to be at least two yards offside, and both partially obscuring McClelland's vision. Then, in the twenty-seventh minute, Chelsea starlet Peter Osgood, dubbed the 'Wizard of Oz',

A ray of hope as Graham Leggat, despite the close attention of Chelsea defenders McCreadie and Harris, volleys home via the crossbar past a startled Bonetti. The goal gave the Cottagers some hope, but a goal line clearance by Peter Osgood late in the game saw a point disappear, Fulham losing 1–2.

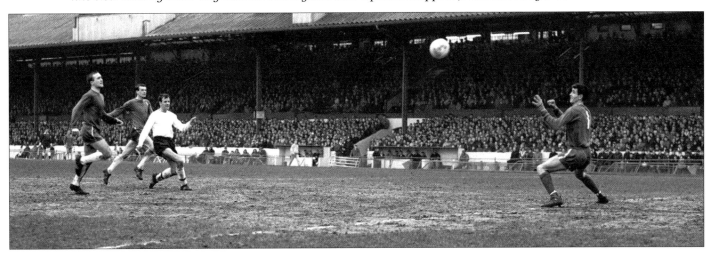

made it two. He robbed a rather hesitant Stan Brown, back defending on the edge of his own area, and ran on a few yards before scoring with an accurate tight angled shot, wide of McClelland and just inside a post.

Three minutes after the re-start, Fulham obtained a foothold and Leggat, Fulham's best forward, immediately pulled a goal back. Les Barrett found Brown, who made a forceful run down the centre, and fed Leggat, who cracked home a fierce volley off the underside of the bar that left Peter Bonetti standing. Fulham then dominated the second half against a very ordinary and casual Chelsea, and saw a point go drown the drain in the last minutes.

Fred Callaghan, pushing forward, spectacularly back-heeled a cross past Bonetti, but of all places for a centre forward to be, the ubiquitous Osgood was standing right on the goal-line and headed the ball out of the open goal. The chance was gone, and the game was lost **1–2**. The near neighbours had also succeeded in doing the double over Fulham. Even though Fulham were a little short on finesse, the team were at least now starting to show that they were willing to make a fight of things.

Already out of the FA Cup and facing a blank weekend the following Saturday, Vic Buckingham arranged a **friendly** with **Portsmouth** at Fratton Park for the following Friday evening. Buckingham then experimented in a bid to try and find that elusive winning combination. On the evening, the teams played out an entertaining 2–2 draw. Stan Brown, continuing with the number nine shirt, put Fulham ahead, and although Portsmouth equalised through McCann, a goal by Steve Earle nine minutes from time had looked to be enough to give Fulham victory, but a very unfortunate last minute own goal by George Cohen gave Portsmouth a share of the spoils. Dave Sexton was already seeing signs of a recovery, and stated, 'After the last two weeks, my hopes of avoiding relegation have risen considerably. I am happy with the club's crop of young players'.

A second consecutive away trip beckoned and on the following Saturday, Fulham took part in a second consecutive London derby against **Tottenham Hotspur** at a sunny White Hart Lane in front of over 31,000. The Tottenham ground had never been lucky for Fulham, who, as usual, were forced to play in their blue away colours. Vic Buckingham restored Johnny Haynes to the line-up, wearing a rather confusing number nine shirt. Buckingham, still looking for that elusive forward, missed the game, away on another scouting mission. The game saw a first half few would have ever believed.

Any hopes of a continuing improvement looked to have gone completely out the window as Fulham found themselves 0–3 down after just thirteen minutes, Spurs managing to score three goals in the space of just eight minutes. Diminutive Cliff Jones netted the first in only the fifth minute, when he soared above the Fulham defence to head home Jimmy Robertson's accurate centre. Then just six minutes later, Jones added a second. Spurs aces Jimmy Greaves and Alan Mullery opened up Fulham's left flank, and Jones again leapt highest to head Robertson's cross past Jack McClelland. George Cohen appeared to be at fault for the goal, allowing Jones too much room. Things became even worse just two minutes later, a super solo run by Greaves giving Spurs forward Frank Saul the chance of an easy finish. Fulham were reeling, and the Fulham faithful began to wonder whether Spurs would score double figures that afternoon. One of Jones' headed goals was particularly brave; the effort saw him collide with a post when scoring, only to emerge spitting out blood and teeth. At this time, Fulham put another marker on livewire winger Robertson, who was giving Brian Nichols a torrid time.

Fulham's response to this adversity was just as remarkable, as the team then promptly scored three goals themselves in the space of just *seven* minutes. Firstly, Graham Leggat scored with an acrobatic angled header from Les Barrett's cross on twenty-three minutes, and then four minutes later Spurs defender Phil Beal attempted a clumsy overhead kick clearance which only succeeded in presenting Steve Earle with the ball, and despite a slight suspicion of handball Earle thumped home the second from twelve yards. Bobby Robson was then unbelievably unlucky when his fierce shot rebounded off a post and ran virtually the whole length of the goal line before being cleared. Then, remarkably, Barrett took a Haynes pass, from an opening created by Mark Pearson, and

From Haynes' pass (back of picture), and Pearson's assist, Les Barrett leaves former Fulham player Alan Mullery gasping as he crashes home the first goal of his career. This was Fulham's third goal against Tottenham in the space of just seven minutes, and levelled the scores. Thanks to a controversial goal, a fortunate Spurs side won the match 3–4.

thundered in the equaliser for his first senior goal on the half hour; it was Spurs' turn to be stunned.

However, just as it looked as if the luck was turning, controversy stepped in again. The Fulham rearguard slipped up once again four minutes before half time when George Cohen apparently played Jones onside from Greaves' pass, and he waltzed through to complete his hat trick. The linesman raised his flag immediately for offside, and with the Fulham team expecting a free kick, the referee over-ruled the official, gave the advantage to Spurs, and awarded the goal. Fulham were disgusted with the very dubious decision, and complained at length about the award. Predictably the protests didn't alter the referee's mind, and was a real kick in the teeth. Seven goals had been scored before half time.

Fulham kept up the quality in the second half, but both teams had obviously been given orders to 'tighten up'. In the second half, a fast and clever Fulham took the game to Tottenham, and the Spurs goalmouth led a charmed life. Supplied with ammunition from Johnny Haynes, Cohen and Robson were just wide with shots; Barrett missed an open goal, and was then thwarted when his point blank header drew a magnificent save from Spurs keeper Pat Jennings.

The Spurs forwards were forced to help out in the overworked defence, and little was seen of their attacking players in the second half. Despite Fulham's undoubted superiority, the second half produced no further goals, and Tottenham nervously hung on for an undeserved victory, Fulham losing **3–4**.

The club programme summed it up as: 'Plenty of goals, but still no luck.' The media commented: 'Fulham were cruelly deprived of their first away win of the season which has gone all against them.' Fulham had looked much more of a team, showing plenty of fight and spirit, and Earle and Barrett were firing much needed goals. With this victory, Tottenham became the fourth club to achieve the double over Fulham in the previous five weeks.

Fulham, however, had to accept realistically that maybe that was it. Anchored at the bottom, the team had given it their best shot, but those efforts had not been quite good enough. The club had picked up just four points from their last *fourteen* games, losing eleven, and the club's away form had looked embarrassing. Fulham had picked up just two draws out of fifteen away league matches, (two points out of thirty), losing the last eleven on the spin, and had been despatched easily from both the League Cup and FA Cup away from home. If the team were to stand any chance at all, this would have to radically improve. Realistically, Fulham had just fifteen points and there were just thirteen (unlucky?) matches left to play. *In reality, the last rites had been read, and relegation now seemed a formality.*

If there was any team you would not want to face when you were at rock bottom, that team was **Liverpool.** The Reds were already steaming towards the league title, being nine points clear at the top, whilst Fulham were now five points adrift from safety at the bottom. Liverpool seemed to have the perfect blend; they possessed established experience in Tommy Lawrence, Gerry Byrne, Gordon Milne, Ron Yeats and Willie Stevenson in defence, with Roger Hunt, Ian Callaghan, Ian St John and Peter Thompson in attack. This powerful Liverpool squad was supported by youth players like Chris Lawler, Geoff Strong and a young Tommy Smith.

As with the visit from Manchester United earlier, Putney seemed to be a mass of red and white. So loud were the travelling supporters, their singing from the ground could be heard as far away as Putney Bridge. The atmosphere was electric, and the main question was, were Liverpool going to deliver the *coup de grace*? Vic Buckingham was again absent from the match; he was away watching forward George Kerr of Barnsley. The only thing Fulham had going for them was that Craven Cottage was not Liverpool's happiest hunting ground.

In front of another 31,000 crowd on a windy afternoon, Fulham set about Liverpool like tigers. Fulham received a quick wake up call when Jack McClelland made a diving save from Milne before any Fulham player had touched the ball, and then a Lawler centre was flicked on by Thompson to Hunt who shot over. Finally, Ian Callaghan fired just over the Fulham bar; it had been all Liverpool in the first few minutes. Then, against the odds, Steve Earle gave Fulham the lead with a beautiful near post header from a right wing cross after just ten minutes and Liverpool were rocked.

Johnny Haynes won the ball in midfield and supplied Graham Leggat, who re-found Haynes on the wing continuing the move. Haynes moved forward to almost the corner flag, glanced up and sent over a head-high teasing cross, and Earle moved in between Smith and Byrne to score with a glancing downward header, squeezing his effort between Lawrence and his near post. At

Sheer defiance; Watched anxiously by Pearson, Brown and Cohen, goalkeeper Jack McClelland leaps spectacularly to palm a curling goal-bound effort from Liverpool's Thompson over the crossbar to safety. Liverpool stars Hunt and St John watch yet another Merseyside effort repelled by the brave Fulham defence.

Above: the goal that started the fightback. Steve Earle has just slammed in the vital second goal past the fallen Tommy Lawrence in the 2–0 victory over Liverpool. Leggat congratulates Earle, and Brown does a dance for joy! Liverpool defenders Lawler and Yeats appeal in vain for the handball decision that never came. Below: at two down, a frustrated St John launches himself at 'Pancho' Pearson. The tackle and ensuing fracas earned the Liverpool forward an 'early bath'.

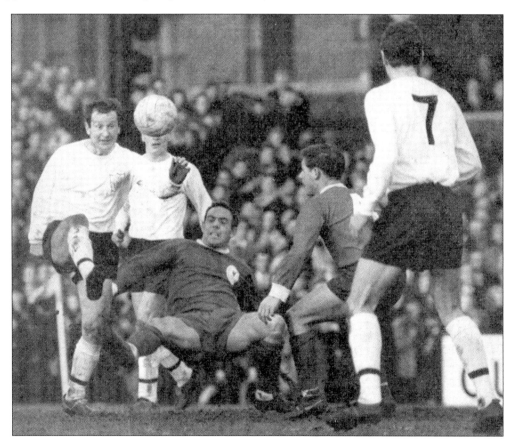

last Fulham were looking capable of mixing it physically with stronger opponents and were winning the majority of the fifty-fifty balls, while the Liverpool players were beginning to react to some of the tackling.

A cross from Callaghan passed across the entire Fulham defence, and it seemed certain that Liverpool would equalise when Hunt carved out a clear opening for St John, but McClelland came out bravely, diving at the Scottish international's feet, and saving a certain goal. Then Stan Brown, keeping a tight rein on England forward Hunt, deflected his shot for a corner.

It was not all one-way traffic, however, and a fine Les Barrett run brought a full length save from Lawrence, and Leggat shot just over after great approach work by George Cohen and Haynes. Finally Brian Nichols tripped Callaghan, but Yeats headed the resulting free kick over the bar. Fulham's defence was on the rack at this time, but holding firm.

Although struggling with the wind, Liverpool fought back amazingly after half time, with John Dempsey and Cohen repelling wave after wave of Liverpool attacks. McClelland foiled Hunt and then palmed away Thompson's curling shot bound for the top corner. Fulham's only response was a typical long-range effort from Bobby Robson that grazed the bar. Just as it seemed a matter of time before Liverpool equalised, Fulham broke away and scored again, and again the scorer was Steve Earle.

Leggat again started the move, and found Barrett on the left wing. Barrett cut inside, beat two players then stumbled, but managed to get the ball back to Leggat. Leggat immediately passed the ball through to Earle in the box and although Earle was hemmed in and controlled the ball with his hand to some degree as it bounced up, the Liverpool defenders did not put in an effective challenge, and Earle kept his head before smashing a cross-shot past Lawrence to send the fans into raptures. Lawler and Yeats complained bitterly about the goal being awarded, but it stood. It was the first piece of luck that had gone Fulham's way for some time. The goal award provoked significant crowd trouble at the Hammersmith end of the ground, and police were called in.

Fulham, now sensing a shock, launched into biting and determined tackles, never letting Liverpool settle on the ball. As Fulham played out the last ten minutes, Mark Pearson slowed the game down and was the victim of a crude tackle from behind from St John that floored him. Pearson, on rising, reacted angrily to the foul trying to grab St John's shirt and then his hair. St John, losing his temper, threw punches at Pearson that barely made contact. Pearson, however, fell pole-axed and lay in a 'crucified' position on the Cottage pitch. Referee Aldous had no option other than to send off St John. Ron Yeats was also booked for a tackle and subsequent comments to a linesman. A second Liverpool player was lucky not to go off moments later for another deliberate kick at Cohen. The match drifted from that point, but at the final whistle, hardly anyone in the ground could believe the **2–0** scoreline.

Arriving home, many fans thought that they must have been dreaming until the *Evening Standard* came out with: 'Fulham shock the leaders – St John sent off near the end.' The result was made even more glorious by its showing on *Match of the Day*. The performance had been no fluke, and certainly Liverpool had made the grave mistake of underestimating Fulham. Some of the press reactions, however, were mixed; some hailed Fulham's performance, and said that Liverpool had been 'well beaten', whilst others claimed that Liverpool's defeat had been 'daylight robbery'! For Ian St John, the dismissal would mean a hefty suspension, as it was the fourth time he had been sent off in five years since joining Liverpool from Motherwell.

Fulham seemed to have played almost a 3–4–3 formation, with Cohen, Dempsey and Nichols at the back, Brown and Pearson as defending wing halves, Robson and Haynes as attacking inside forwards, with Earle, Leggat and Barrett up front. Could Buckingham have found some kind of winning formula at last? Only time would tell.

March 1966

In this month

* The Labour party were re-elected in the general election.
* James Callaghan stated that Britain would switch to decimal currency in 1971.
* The BBC announced plans to broadcast in colour.
* 130 died as a Boeing 707 crashed into Mount Fuji.
* The Government announced plans to abolish National Assistance, and replace it with a Ministry of Social Security.
* The World Cup went missing.
* *Arkle* won his third successive Cheltenham gold cup.

'The Sun Ain't Gonna Shine Any More' by The Walker Brothers topped the charts.

How the league was looking

Liverpool were pulling further ahead at the top, whilst Leeds United, Burnley and Manchester United were all separated by just one point for second place. Chelsea were now sixth with Everton rising to eighth. West Ham had joined Arsenal mid table. Fulham were still propping up the table, Blackburn were just one point ahead and Blackpool were now slipping into trouble in twentieth place. Northampton were just two points better off, and Sheffield Wednesday were now also in trouble.

The matches

THE FA Cup fifth round brought a blank week for Fulham at the start of the month, leaving the team unable to immediately build on their success over Liverpool, but they were now eager for the fight. The team *had* to break their away 'blanks', as they had not won away in the league since beating Nottingham Forest (3–2) in September 1964, *an amazing run of thirty-one matches covering eighteen months!*

The unchanged team travelled to Villa Park on the following Saturday for the second time that season. Fulham also had the impetus of **Aston Villa** being without the influential Phil Woosnam and Willie Hamilton. The team immediately started where they had left off against

Under construction: Villa's stand and Fulham's recovery. An unmarked Leggat rises to head Fulham's opening goal inside two minutes at Villa Park. In a stunning performance, a rejuvenated Fulham ran out 5–2 winners, securing victory away from home for the first time in eighteen months.

Liverpool. Within two minutes Graham Leggat had given Fulham the lead with a trademark downward header from a Johnny Haynes floated free kick from near the corner flag. Villa were really asleep, and goalkeeper Colin Withers made no attempt for the ball as it hit the six-yard box, and Leggat headed in easily. Villa pulled themselves level against the run of play in the eighteenth minute. Tony Scott beat Stan Brown on the wing, and centred for Tony Hateley to head an excellent trademark bullet goal. Scott was injured in the build up, and Fulham were pleased to see him substituted. Fulham continued to force the pace, and it was no surprise when Steve Earle restored the lead ten minutes before half time. Haynes floated in another accurate corner, Withers was again at fault as he inexplicably dropped the ball, and Earle scored with a shot on the turn through a ruck of Villa players; this enabled Fulham to go in at the interval 2–1 up.

In the second half Fulham's performance became even better, and with their first real attack of the second half the team scored again. Haynes beat two Villa midfield players with a beautiful body swerve, Brian Nichols picked up the pass and as the ball came across, Leggat helped the ball on, and Earle again, with ample time, converted easily. There were a few flutters when Villa pulled a goal back with a quarter of an hour to go, Alan Deakin heading in a McLeod cross, but Fulham kept their concentration and near the end Steve Earle laid on a simple chance for Les Barrett, who devoured the chance eagerly. To perfectly round off the afternoon, Leggat netted the fifth goal just seconds before the end. Taking Earle's pass, he scythed through the entire Villa defence before slotting the ball over the advancing goalkeeper. A Haynes-inspired Fulham had won **5–2**, reducing Villa to a shambles. The team had also equalled their best ever away performance in the top flight.

The game finally broke their away hoodoo, and was ample revenge for the earlier League Cup exit on the same ground. The two league games between the clubs that season had produced no fewer than sixteen goals! The Villa fans, though, were less than impressed and police were called to protect George Cohen and Jack McClelland from cans and bottles that were landing in the goalmouth. Steve Earle was delighted; he was on the transfer list but admitted, 'Things look a lot rosier now'. Vic Buckingham added a note of caution: 'Make no mistake there's still a long way to go before this little struggle is over.' Significantly, the result had lifted Fulham off the bottom of the table, but the team were still three points behind Blackpool, who had a game in hand. Blackpool had beaten Leeds twice, and strugglers Newcastle United and Sunderland had also won, so Fulham, at this stage, couldn't rely on other teams losing.

The following week Fulham entertained **Sunderland** at the Cottage. The Mackems were seven points in front of Fulham but were not good travellers, having only secured one away win all season. Fulham, as expected, were unchanged. The Sunderland team contained a number of Scottish and Irish players, including centre half Charlie Hurley, Jim Baxter and Neil Martin.

The Eire centre half Hurley had been doubtful from the off, and ran out with his left knee heavily bandaged, his lack of mobility obvious. It didn't take Fulham long to spot this or exploit it. In the ninth minute, Bobby Robson found Steve Earle with a pass on the left, Earle chased the loose ball, beat the static defender Bobby Parke and put in a hard low centre. Hurley, under pressure from Graham Leggat but with ample time to clear, somehow turned the ball clumsily into his own net as his left leg 'gave way'. Again an early goal was just the tonic Fulham needed, and the team played with a newfound zest and confidence.

Leggat then added a second in the eighteenth minute. Robson won the ball tenaciously and put in an excellent lobbed centre; Leggat was forced to move slightly backwards to reach it, but still had enough power to beat Hurley in the air and to send an arcing header over the despairing keeper Jimmy Montgomery and into the net. Leggat, in rampaging form, also netted the third ten minutes before half time. He won the ball from Sunderland's Martin Harvey outside the box, ran a few paces unchallenged before cracking in a shot so hard that the ball hit the stanchion behind the goal before rebounding out into play. In a rampant first half that saw Sunderland rarely out of their own half, Jim Baxter was a colossus at the back, abandoning his midfield role and desperately trying to keep the marauding Fulham forwards at bay. Mark Pearson shot over from yet another

Left: a jubilant Leggat wheels away after Sunderland's Hurley, prostrate in the goal, turns Earle's cross into his own net to give Fulham their first goal in a 3–0 win. It was Fulham's third successive victory in their bid for survival.

Right: Graham Leggat jack-knifes to win the ball against Hurley. His header arcs into the net for Fulham's second goal against Sunderland. Far right: Leggat celebrates, with Steve Earle about to join in.

Johnny Haynes pass, and Earle then thumped the Sunderland bar; Fulham led 3–0 at the interval.

With Baxter helping at the back, there was no real Sunderland presence up front and the Fulham defence coped easily. Earle, Leggat and Les Barrett, although not tall, were terrifying the Sunderland defence feeding off terrific ground passes supplied from Haynes playing very deep and still wearing the unlikely number nine shirt. The second half continued in the same vein; Leggat was unlucky not to claim his hat trick early in the second half, when Pearson and Earle combined to put him through, his first time effort being scrambled off the line by Hurley.

Baxter was dragging Sunderland back into the game now, but George Cohen and John Dempsey were coping well with any pressure, with Stan Brown having plenty of time as sweeper. Fulham came again and hit the bar once more, a thirty-yard screamer from Robson from yet another Haynes pass; Montgomery never saw it. Fulham could and should have netted six, the Sunderland defence had been torn to shreds, but Fulham, sensing that the game was now won, played out time to record their third successive win with an all-round team performance. Final result **3–0**.

Haynes, unsurprisingly, was voted Man of the Match. 'What precision passing!' quoted the *Evening Standard*, under the banner headline 'Lively Fulham win in Style'. Blackpool had also won against West Ham 2–1, but significantly Blackburn and Northampton had both lost. The gap on Northampton and Blackpool was now just three points. A neutral would have struggled to guess which of the two sides that day was threatened with relegation. Ian McColl the Sunderland manager conceded: 'The way Fulham are going they could win the championship! They must be playing better than anyone at this stage.' And the Liverpool manager Bill Shankly, not one given to sentiment, also added: 'Few could understand how Fulham managed to beat us, now they should be beginning to see.'

Fulham travelled unchanged again to Upton Park the following week, seeking their fourth successive win and their own first double. **West Ham** were without centre half Ken Brown and centre forward

Johnny Byrne. The Hammers were lying around mid table, and Fulham must have hoped that the east London side would have one eye on their European commitments.

The first twenty minutes were very difficult, and this time there was no early goal to fire Fulham. The team received an early scare when Hammers winger John Sissons just failed to connect with Geoff Hurst's cross. Sissons then fired over himself, and full back Denis Burnett had a shot blocked, and finally Hurst ballooned over from close range. In the twenty-first minute Fulham should have scored; Graham Leggat won possession in the centre circle from Jack Burkett, and hared off towards the West Ham goal, with the entire Hammers team in pursuit. Fortunately for the Hammers, keeper Jim Standen raced out and as Leggat shot from the edge of the box, Standen somehow blocked the shot. Two minutes later the scene was re-enacted the other way round, Jack McClelland bravely saving from Hurst when sent clear.

Fulham's tough tackling was winning few friends, but the method was proving very effective. It was now great end-to-end and full-blooded stuff. McClelland was forced to make the save of the match, magnificently tipping over Jimmy Bloomfield's header, but two minutes later it was Fulham's turn to storm back, and John Dempsey nodded Bobby Robson's corner kick against the bar. Hammers ace Peter Brabrook beat two men and shot over, and a cunning lob from Johnny Haynes was just about scrambled over the bar by Standen.

Someone had to score soon, but the Hammers were making more of the running. Then, just three minutes before half time, Fulham broke away for a surprise goal. Steve Earle collected George Cohen's pass, cut inside and hit a right footer, the shot was partially stopped by Hammers goalkeeper Standen, but he couldn't hold the ball, and it spun and rolled slowly over the line. Not a classic goal by any means, but no Fulham player or supporter was complaining.

Tails up, Fulham doubled their lead immediately, just thirty seconds after the interval. This time it *was* a goal to really set the crowd talking. Les Barrett took a superb pass from Haynes, controlled the ball immaculately and beat three West Ham defenders for speed, including Bobby Moore, before moving into the box and crashing a shot high into the roof of the West Ham net wide of Standen. McClelland still had to make two fine saves from Eddie Bovingdon and Hurst, but Fulham were now in full flow, and Barrett headed just wide.

In the sixty-fifth minute, things became even better, and, following a mistake from a West Ham defender, Fulham sealed the game. Martin Peters, of all people, standing in the centre circle

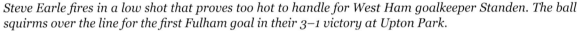

Steve Earle fires in a low shot that proves too hot to handle for West Ham goalkeeper Standen. The ball squirms over the line for the first Fulham goal in their 3–1 victory at Upton Park.

attempting to clear, back-headed the ball instead straight to Leggat, who was standing in an offside position, by at least ten yards. The Scot coolly ran on before nonchalantly lobbing Standen from the edge of the penalty box and it was 3–0. Fulham had now notched three goals in twenty-three minutes. Fulham were given a slight wake-up call ten minutes later when the ever-dangerous Hurst headed in a cross with a quarter of an hour remaining, but Fulham held on. McClelland had looked very firm, Haynes had controlled the centre of the field and Barrett always looked a real handful up front. The **3–1** win gave Fulham their first double of the season by an aggregate of 6–1.

It had been an amazing turnaround; the team that had recently realised just one goal from six league matches had now rattled in seventeen in their last six: (Earle 7, Leggat 6 and Barrett 3, plus one own goal). On the day, Northampton had drawn, Blackpool had won again and now seemed clear; Sheffield Wednesday also won.

The only dark point in this glorious month was the departure of forward Rodney Marsh. It was no secret that Buckingham had not been a fan of Marsh, having tried, and failed, to make him train harder, take the game more seriously and become a team player rather than just a solo act. Marsh would argue that he had tried his hardest to please Buckingham, but that Vic had tried to change his game so much, from being a dribbler to a frontrunner who used his weight, that the enjoyment had completely gone out of his game.

Buckingham had sometimes publicly called Rodney 'a clown', a comment Marsh resented. He was currently out of favour, but it was a major surprise when it emerged that Buckingham had sold him to wily Alec Stock managing and fashioning an emerging QPR team just down the road in Shepherd's Bush. The sum was reported to be a paltry £15,000.

Although Rod's style of play could be infuriating at times, he possessed amazing dribbling and ball skills, and the previous season had been the leading goalscorer for a First Division club. Yet, here he was being sold to a club that were *two divisions below Fulham*—he was also just twenty-one years old. The transfer would rank as one of Fulham's biggest ever mistakes, as Marsh would hit over one hundred goals for QPR and later become an England international. He would again return to the First Division with both QPR and Manchester City, and rejoin Fulham a decade later. He had joined Fulham straight from school, and his departure was a big shock. Amazingly, Marsh's departure was not even covered by the club programme. Marsh made an immediate impact, inevitably scoring the QPR equaliser on his debut. As Fulham had always shown a reluctance to spend, one had to assume that the fee received for Marsh went a long way in purchasing the forward who would ultimately replace him.

Steve Earle remembers:

Rodney would do things in training just to annoy Vic Buckingham, and Vic would some days send him off—or cancel training altogether! Rodney was a great personality. I remember going to his house for a party and his mum was in the kitchen. He asked her to throw him a meat pie, which she did—through the serving-hatch! Rodney trapped it on his foot, flicked it up, caught it and then started eating it as if it was normal! When we were apprentices, Rodney was always getting called into the office for breaking windows in the Cottage—in the end, we weren't allowed any footballs in the courtyard, so we played with tennis balls instead!

April 1966

In this month

* The World Cup was found.
* The British Airports Authority (BAA) was formed.
* The Sussex downs were designated an area of outstanding natural beauty.
* Hindley and Brady went on trial for the moors murders.
* The state opening of Parliament was televised for the first time.
* The first regular cross-channel services by Hovercraft commenced between Ramsgate and Calais.
* Giant panda Chi-Chi flew in to attempt to breed with An-An.
* Authors C.S. Forester and Evelyn Waugh died.
* Brezhnev became the Soviet leader.

'You Don't Have To Say You Love Me' by Dusty Springfield topped the charts.

How the league was looking

It was 'as you were' in the top four places, with Liverpool now eight points ahead of the chasing pack of Burnley, Leeds United and Manchester United; Chelsea were now fifth. Arsenal and West Ham were still both mid table. Fulham were now *off* the bottom, with Blackburn on the base rung. Northampton and Sheffield Wednesday were just two and three points away. Blackpool's form had improved, and they now looked safe.

The matches

FULHAM TOOK on **West Bromwich Albion** at the Cottage at the beginning of April with confidence now sky-high. Albion were eighth and a very good side. The Baggies were also already League Cup winners, having defeated West Ham in the final 5–3 on aggregate. At this time, the League Cup final was always contested over two legs, home and away.

Albion were without defender Stan Jones and skipper Graham Williams. Fulham also had an enforced change with George Cohen again on England duty. Vic Buckingham's decision was again a strange one. Having experienced a torrid time at left back, forward Brian O'Connell was this time given the right back shirt. Fulham would be seeking revenge for the 2–6 drubbing at the Hawthorns earlier in the season.

Again, as in three out of the previous four games, Fulham scored within the first ten minutes. In the fifth minute, Johnny Haynes took a pass from Les Barrett after a brilliant overlapping run by Brian Nichols that took out three Albion defenders. He ran the ball into the area past static defending, and smashed a beautiful sidefoot cross-shot into the side of the net, ending up smiling flat on his face alongside the photographers beside the goal. Albion fought back strongly, with quicksilver winger Clive Clark giving O'Connell a tough time. Clark ultimately received a free kick from Graham Lovett in the twenty-second minute, beat O'Connell for pace, and produced a fine low centre across the Fulham goalmouth that found Jeff Astle, and he was able to tap the ball easily past Jack McClelland.

Albion then committed the cardinal sin of dropping their concentration for a couple of minutes just after they had scored, which proved fatal. Albion's defence immediately allowed Haynes time on the ball, and again he was able to put in an unchallenged shot from outside the area. The ball clipped Albion's centre half Danny Campbell on the heel, spun and rocketed past the wrong-footed and stranded Albion keeper Graham Potter.

The second half was a very tense affair, with Fulham holding on a fair bit against a more fluent side, and looking slightly shaky in defence when under pressure. Mark Pearson was providing a lot of the graft, and Haynes most of the class. As the Albion threat increased, Fulham withdrew into deep defence. Large gaps appeared in the Fulham midfield, which were exploited by the eager

Johnny Haynes goes flat on his face alongside the press, after slotting an early goal in Fulham's fifth successive win, 2–1 against West Bromwich Albion. A delighted Bobby Robson salutes the strike.

Albion front line. Their numerous dangerous attacks foundered as they found Jack McClelland in superb form, his handling and quick reactions foiling the Albion forwards, especially the dangerous John Kaye, time and again. John Dempsey was again totally commanding in the air, and Stan Brown again excelled as sweeper.

The Albion blitz continued right up until the final whistle. Fulham tired visibly and could hardly put one foot in front of the other, but although the strain was beginning to show, the team did just enough through sheer endeavour and spirit, to hold on to record their fifth successive win, by a **2–1** margin. The media accepted that although they had been slightly outclassed, Fulham's tenacity and sheer guts had earned them the two points.

Even Vic Buckingham was forced to admit with a smile, 'Fortune smiled on us'. It was strange that Haynes, who had not scored for three and a half months, came up with the two goals when they were *really* required. Some of the press gave the winner as an own goal, but most credited it to Haynes. It was befitting that the goals came on that day, as Haynes had just been named as *Evening Standard* footballer of the month for March. A Fulham team that had won just five league games all season, prior to the start of the great run, had now won five league games on the spin. There were a number of postponed matches on the day, but significantly Northampton, away from home, beat Aston Villa who were now themselves slipping badly. Fulham were still only two points behind Northampton but with two games in hand. The Albion match proved to be the last game in a Fulham shirt for Brian O'Connell.

The one other piece of news breaking that week was that Fulham had broken their record for a transfer by signing nineteen-year-old Allan Clarke from Walsall. The record fee was £35,000. Clarke had been watched several times by Buckingham and was no doubt his number one transfer target. The club had made an original offer that had been turned down, but finally proposed a fee that Walsall could not refuse. Clarke, from the Midlands, had twice turned down the chance to go to London, but took little time to weigh up the offer this time, as it seemed apparent that no Midlands club were prepared to offer the transfer fee that Fulham were putting forward.

Clarke admitted to being excited about the prospect of playing in the same side as Johnny Haynes. Despite his tender age, Clarke had been playing in the Walsall league side for two seasons, having made his debut in October 1963 at seventeen. He had already scored forty-one league goals in just seventy-two league matches for the Saddlers.

Lean, mean and keen. A young nineteen-year-old Allan Clarke shortly after his arrival at the Cottage, ready to make his mark on the First Division.

He was quite a versatile player, and had appeared for Walsall at inside right, centre forward and inside left. He had also been Walsall's top scorer the previous season (1964–65) with twenty-three goals.

Clarke arrived at Fulham with a very high reputation. His transfer fee was brokered by the fee received for Rodney Marsh supplemented by supporters' club money, with the remainder coming from the board. Although the transfer figure seems miniscule today, it is worth remembering that Clarke's transfer cost the same amount as the entire new Hammersmith end stand development, and the refurbishment of the Stevenage Road stand put together!

Six days later, on Good Friday, came the second consecutive home match and the Bank Holiday morning saw 39,000 cram into the Cottage to see if Fulham could continue their miraculous form. Like the Liverpool game it would be a huge test, as **Leeds United** were also an emerging force. The Peacocks had been: runners up in the League the previous year, Cup finalists the previous year, were third in the league currently and also in the semi-final of the Inter Cities Fairs Cup. Leeds also appeared to have the right mix of youth and experience; experience in the form of Jack Charlton, Willie Bell, Billy Bremner, Jim Storrie and Alan Peacock, augmented by significant youth talent in Paul Reaney, Norman Hunter, Peter Lorimer, Johnny Giles and Eddie Gray.

Fulham, to their credit, kept up their form, launching a barrage of scintillating attacks on the Leeds defence in the early stages. The team put in a flurry of early shots, but significantly this time there was no early goal. Steve Earle should have scored, but drove wide with the goalkeeper helpless on the ground; Johnny Haynes also shot wide. Within this opening quarter of an hour, the Leeds goalkeeper Gary Sprake also had to pull off two magnificent stops from Bobby Robson and Graham Leggat to prevent Fulham taking a very deserved lead.

Unfortunately, it was Leeds that grew the stronger after this siege. After absorbing the best that Fulham could throw at them, Leeds began to launch swift counter-attacks from deep within a superbly organised defence. Leeds eventually took a first half lead when Jim Storrie swept in a drive from twelve yards. To make matters worse, Johnny Haynes badly bruised a leg muscle in the first half, disrupting Fulham's rhythm. He did not re-appear for the second half, and the match gave Allan Clarke his first Fulham appearance as a substitute—ironically, he would join Leeds three years later.

Fulham re-launched themselves after the interval, with an all out attack. The team were almost caught out at the back as first Willie Bell and then Peter Lorimer hammered shots against the Fulham woodwork. Fulham survived, however, and were rewarded when Leggat broke into the

Bobby Robson neatly sends the Leeds goalkeeper Gary Sprake the wrong way from the penalty spot to equalise Leeds' first-half goal. The Peacocks recovered to finally win 1-3 at the Cottage, putting an abrupt stop to Fulham's winning run.

Leeds penalty area only to be pulled down from behind by Leeds full back Bell; a cast iron penalty. Robson had been given the role of penalty taker, as Terry Dyson was not in the side. Robson took the penalty, the experienced international being reminded by the nineteen-year-old debutant Clarke to 'take your time son!', and sent Sprake the wrong way from the spot.

The question now was could they build on it? Frustratingly they couldn't, and the Leeds know-how began to tell. Fulham sadly did not look the same side without Haynes, and were behind again just five minutes later. Following a foul, Johnny Giles floated a perfect forty-yard free kick onto the head of winger Albert Johanneson, and he nodded the ball high into the corner of the net. Fulham tried to rally, but were finally floored, a quarter of an hour from time, by the goal of the match. A defence-splitting forty-yard pass from Lorimer found Storrie. He immediately flicked the ball forward to Johanneson. The winger produced a clever back-flick that allowed Billy Bremner space to pick up the ball and drive in low and hard from fifteen yards.

It had been difficult to cope with the Leeds front line, Peter Lorimer had given Brian Nichols a very difficult time, and speedy winger Johanneson had troubled George Cohen throughout; centre forward Storrie had also been constantly menacing. Fulham had played their part in a storming game, but the Leeds performance had been even better, acknowledged by the press as 'a powerful and polished show'. At least it was said that the visitors had won the encounter, rather than Fulham having lost it. Nevertheless, Fulham's winning run had hit the buffers. To make the **1−3** result worse, news filtered through that Northampton had taken a point from Liverpool.

Fulham were able to have a little respite after that match, as the following day's game at **Nottingham Forest** was **postponed** very late on, due to a waterlogged pitch after heavy rain that day.

After losing to the Yorkshire giants, it was with some trepidation that Fulham set off northwards for the reciprocal evening encounter with **Leeds United** just four days later. The injury to Johnny Haynes was a big blow, but Allan Clarke started the match as Haynes' replacement with Graham Leggat dropping deeper. Fulham were in their changed blue strip, and Leeds were without their Wales international keeper Gary Sprake, reserve David Harvey making his league debut.

In a way, despite the Liverpool result, it proved to be *the* result of the season. Fulham were forced to fight an almost ninety-minute rearguard action. John Dempsey was absolutely outstanding in the Elland Road mud and rain, but there were eleven heroes. In the first half Jack McClelland saved well from Albert Johannsen, and later pushed a Jim Storrie effort onto the crossbar, but that was as difficult as the game became.

Fulham began to grow in confidence, and Leeds, looking sadly out of touch, were being made to look cumbersome by a skilled and spirited Fulham. Fulham were quick in the tackle and were defending stoutly, whilst at the same time launching clever counter-attacks. Even when Billy Bremner joined in supporting the midfield, Leeds never seemed to move the ball quickly enough to break the Fulham defence down. Fulham also received some 'divine' assistance when Leeds suffered injuries to key players Mike O'Grady and Paul Reaney, Jimmy Greenhoff substituting for O'Grady.

Fulham naturally had the opportunity for a couple of breakaways and from one, just fifteen minutes from time, Mark Pearson took a half chance to give Fulham the lead. Leggat tenaciously won possession in his own half and ran diagonally across the field in a corkscrew motion and down the right wing. He ran almost seventy yards unchallenged, while at least four Leeds defenders remained virtually motionless. Leggat flicked the ball accurately across to Pearson, who placed the ball beautifully past the stranded goalkeeper into the corner of the net; the goal was his first goal in four months. The goal was the death blow to Leeds; they tried hard to pull the game out of the fire, but it was Fulham who carried the greater danger in the thrill-packed closing stages. The Fulham wingers tested a Leeds defence that never looked happy in the mud. The experienced guiding hands of George Cohen and Bobby Robson then took over and ensured that the Fulham defence was not breached, and the single goal proved to be enough to give Fulham the points; Fulham held on to win **1−0**.

The press summed the match up with the message: 'Their recent efforts emphasised what we already knew; there are many worse sides above them in the table.' Another wrote: 'Whilst looking second best for most of the time, their [Fulham's] determination in defence and ability to make the most of snap openings, entitled them to the points.' What was now frustrating was that Northampton had also won again on the night beating Stoke 1–0, and were now matching Fulham match by match, result by result. The league table was now becoming very tight, and six points now covered the bottom ten clubs. The match finished Leeds United's hopes of becoming League champions.

Sheffield Wednesday visited the Cottage five days later and were now also down amongst the dead men, sitting just four points in front of Fulham but holding fifteenth position. The Owls also possessed no outstanding stars, but quality and experience in Ron Springett, Don Megson, Johnny Fantham and Gerry Young, coupled with youth in Vic Mobley and the young Jim McCalliog recently signed from Chelsea.

The omens looked good as again three early goals went in, the trouble was that two of the three were Wednesday's. Fulham were asleep from the kick off, and conceded a first minute corner. Graham Pugh's right wing corner was completely missed by John Dempsey, Vic Mobley headed the ball back into the goalmouth, and the Fulham defence stood almost paralysed as the unmarked David Ford's powered backheader put Sheffield Wednesday ahead.

Fulham rushed straight to the other goal, Allan Clarke neatly pulled down a cross, allowing Les Barrett to put in a tremendous shot that Ron Springett saved well. Normal service was seemingly resumed when Barrett equalised just two minutes later. Fulham forced a corner, a short kick was played out to Mark Pearson, and he fed Barrett, who poked in a head high shot from eighteen yards. It looked as if Springett had stopped the effort, but the greasy ball slipped out of his hands and into the net just inside a post, the shot having just enough power to creep across the goal line.

Fulham had not learned their earlier lesson, however, and further slack defending allowed Jim McCalliog to restore Wednesday's lead after just nine minutes. McCalliog started the move with Wilf Smith, and he found John Quinn on the wing. Quinn produced an accurate head high cross that was headed in neatly by the alert, but totally unmarked, McCalliog. Without Johnny Haynes, the centre of the field was in trouble and Fulham were looking less than solid in a virtual 4–2–4 formation.

The team were currently being given the runaround by a confident and slick Wednesday. Pugh skimmed a header a fraction wide of a Fulham post, but Dempsey could have levelled but just failed to connect with Steve Earle's clever free kick. Happily Fulham just about survived until half time, but faced worse news in the dressing room that Northampton were leading at Tottenham. It was now do or die.

Fulham looked a different side after the break, and emerged with far greater determination, forcing Wednesday onto the back foot. The team received a quick reward for their efforts when Graham Leggat squared the match again ten minutes after half time. George Cohen made a superb run down the right wing, and from his accurate cross, delivered from almost the corner flag, Leggat bravely launched himself, and his flying header from almost a prone position, rocketed in spectacularly.

Even better was to follow, when fifteen minutes later Earle put Fulham ahead for the first time in the match. Full back Brian Nichols sent a long free kick from the halfway line into the Wednesday box, which appeared straightforward to clear. Unfortunately Mobley and fellow defenders got in each other's way and, as panic ensued, Earle emerged from a ruck of defenders in the penalty box to keep his head and slide the dropping ball past the unsighted goalkeeper.

Four minutes later, Fulham cemented the victory with another penalty converted by Bobby Robson. The spot kick was awarded by referee Harry New, after Wednesday's centre half Mobley had brought down Earle in the box when he was clean through. Robson's straight penalty thundered into the roof of the net. Certainly Fulham's forward pressure had paid off in the second half, Leggat leading the line, ably supported by the tenacious wing play of Les Barrett, who was already looking a real 'find'. Fulham's style caused Wednesday to lose their rhythm, their composure and finally their tempers.

Quite why Wednesday capitulated so badly in the second half was not easy to fathom, though a number of experts considered that their minds had possibly been on the following week's FA Cup semi-final with Chelsea. This **4–2** result had made it now seven wins for Fulham in eight games.

Allan Clarke's second home game was certainly steady, but he already spoke like a confident veteran: 'Being substitute is enough for me in the first few weeks, it gave me an invaluable chance to watch my new colleagues in action, and to judge the pace of the First Division'. Blackburn Rovers now looked *gone* from the division, and the gap between Fulham and Northampton stood at just two points. As usual at this time of year, the shock results were beginning to flow in. Aston Villa had beaten second place Burnley, Sunderland had beaten Chelsea, and Northampton had picked up a valuable draw at Tottenham. Only Blackpool had experienced a bad day, losing 0–3 at home to Nottingham Forest.

Just two days later, a tired Fulham used up the first of their games in hand, taking on sixth placed **Leicester City** at the Cottage, following December's Boxing Day postponement. The match provided a real opportunity to catch Northampton Town, and the Northampton team had turned up to watch the encounter. Johnny Haynes was still missing, and it was a squally unpleasant evening with persistent rain and very muddy conditions. With regard to the pitch, the media remarked that 'half the Thames could have overflowed on it, without making a great deal of difference'. Despite the weather, a healthy 18,000 turned up to push Fulham on.

What followed was a nightmare; nothing for Fulham went right on the night. The defence in the poor conditions looked all at sea, despite John Dempsey and Stan Brown's efforts. The team played very much like they had done during the first half on the previous Saturday, but this time, however, Fulham *were* punished. Twice in the first five minutes, Fulham were in terrible trouble; keeper Jack McClelland had to go into a virtual sliding tackle to expedite a goal line clearance from Jackie Sinclair. A couple of minutes later, Brian Nichols was forced to perform an overhead kick on the goal line to prevent Derek Dougan's header from dropping into an empty goal; and it wasn't long before Leicester were ahead.

In the fourteenth minute, Sinclair cruised over the mud, and sent in a centre that Dougan touched home with his head without having to jump from the ground. Fulham were given a further let-off two minutes later, when Leicester's Tom Sweenie had a goal mysteriously disallowed. It soon began to look as if this was going to be 'one of those nights', when five minutes later Leicester scored again. Leicester's Paul Matthews on his 'wrong' left wing, made a fine run, Sweenie combined with Sinclair and the Leicester winger's shot was crashed into his own goal by the sliding Brian Nichols. Fulham were unlucky a few minutes later when they had a clear penalty shout against John Sjoberg turned down. Just before half time Fulham carved out a rare chance, but Gordon Banks denied Graham Leggat with an amazing reaction save from just two yards, many spectators swearing the ball had crossed the line.

In the second half, Fulham were given a chance on the hour to reduce the arrears when Leicester full back Peter Rodrigues brought down Les Barrett in the box and Fulham were awarded another penalty, their third in consecutive home matches. On this night, however, it wasn't to be. Bobby Robson hit his penalty hard and high, but straight, allowing the elastic Banks to twist, turn and send the ball high over the bar.

A few Fulham heads dropped, and two minutes later Leicester broke away with quick, long passes to clinch the game, Sinclair's cross being nonchalantly touched home by Dougan. Just to add insult to injury, six minutes from time McClelland failed to hold a hard centre from Leicester full back Ritchie Norman in the rain, and Sinclair tucked in his deserved goal from close range.

Both sides had shown equal courage, effort and spirit, but Leicester had just had that extra class in attack, especially in the shape of Sinclair and Dougan who had virtually won the match on their own. Fulham had often been outpaced and out-thought by the clever midfield of Leicester. The two points had been lost, giving a significant confidence booster to Northampton; the match ended **0–4**. The result gave yet another club the double over Fulham, this time with an embarrassing 0–9 aggregate. The survival odds were once again heavily stacked against Fulham.

The Monday result made the crunch away match against **Northampton Town** on the Saturday certainly a 'four pointer', *and one of the most important games ever in Fulham's history.* A very large record crowd of 24,500 had poured into the County Ground to witness the encounter. The stakes were very high, and although it wasn't shouted aloud, both teams knew that the losing side would probably be the one relegated. The good news for Fulham was that Johnny Haynes was back. Allan Clarke, however, kept his place up front, with Graham Leggat moving to the wing leaving Les Barrett as substitute.

As expected, the game was a full-blooded encounter, and Fulham's nerves were frayed after Monday's debacle. Northampton set the pace with fast-thinking, quick-tackling football and it was no surprise when George Hudson put the home side ahead on thirteen minutes. Northampton captain Joe Kiernan advanced on goal unhindered, and put in a hard shot that Jack McClelland could only beat out. Hudson, following up, slammed home the rebound.

Fortunately Fulham responded quickly, Brian Nichols and Mark Pearson putting together a move just six minutes later that led to Bobby Robson equalising with a twenty-five yard rocket shot that beat Northampton keeper Norman Coe all ends up before dipping into the top corner. Fulham were still struggling to hang on, and at a bad time against a more purposeful home side, Robson turned villain.

The half back slipped and made a hash of a headed clearance from Walden's centre, the ball dropped nicely to captain Kiernan well outside the penalty area, and he put Northampton ahead again with a fiery shot, just ten minutes before half time. Leggat then had three chances in three amazing minutes. He shot wide, and then over and finally drew a great save from Coe following Pearson's adroit pass. It was tense, tough and exciting stuff, but Fulham just could not find the spark that had ignited previous performances.

Fulham emerged a far more determined side, but were given a stroke of luck that probably changed their whole future. In a spell of home pressure, Northampton pushed forward again, and another great effort from Hudson beat keeper McClelland, hit the underside of the bar and bounced down on the line and up, McClelland finally pawing the ball away. To most of the crowd it looked as if the ball had crossed the line, but the linesman, trying to keep up with play, slipped in the mud, had little view of the incident and no goal was awarded. This increased Fulham's desire to win, and the last twenty-five minutes turned out to be Steve Earle's match.

In the sixty-fourth minute Earle put Fulham level, clipping the ball home just inside the right-hand post from George Cohen's cross after the full back had made another of his characteristic and inspiring forays down the right flank. Both sides, now sensing that a point each would not be enough, attacked and counter-attacked. Johnny Haynes was now pulling the strings from both wings, and was beginning to bewilder Northampton with his slide-rule passes.

Both teams began to look so tired in the last twenty minutes, like two punch drunk boxers slugging it out, that a draw seemed inevitable. Seven minutes from the end, Fulham's hearts were in their mouths again, however, when Northampton's Graham Moore was played onside from a Fulham deflection. In a one-on-one situation he missed a match-winning opportunity from just five yards.

Then with just one minute to go, Leggat's floating right wing cross pulled back from the dead ball line found Earle ten yards out, Earle picked his spot and headed in beautifully, putting Fulham ahead for the first time in the match. This goal sparked an all out assault and stampede on the Fulham penalty area, and Northampton forced a desperate corner in injury time, bringing everyone up.

From the ensuing goalmouth scramble, the ball was cleared by Brian Nichols to Earle standing alone with Leggat, both unmarked just inside their own half. Earle took the ball on his own, set off like a greyhound and ran sixty yards, pursued by the Northampton rearguard. Leggat acted as a decoy for a pass, but Earle instead rounded the advancing goalkeeper Coe and pushed the ball into an empty net. It was all over, a **4–2** win, and the result meant that it was now eight wins in

A muddy and exhausted Johnny Haynes is embraced and acknowledged by ecstatic Fulham supporters as he leaves the field following the crucial 4–2 win at Northampton.

ten matches. Certainly it was sweet revenge for the 1–4 defeat at the Cottage a few dark months before.

Such was the emotion that the final whistle prompted a Fulham pitch invasion, and the players were forced to run the gauntlet of backslaps and handshakes, to chants of 'Easy, Easy'; it was a momentous day indeed. The crowd that day would stand as the largest crowd ever to witness a match at the County Ground. John Dempsey remembers: 'As the crowds came on the field after the game, a woman [home supporter] tried to hit me with her umbrella, very upset that her team had lost 2-4.'

Still the gallant Northampton side would not lie down, and just two days later, the Cobblers produced another great result beating Sunderland. This particular duel was destined to keep going to the wire, and the result forced tired Fulham to match that pace.

Fulham visited **Nottingham Forest**'s City Ground the next night to play their remaining game in hand; this time there was no slip up. By way of importance the match was Johnny Haynes' 500th appearance for Fulham.

The unchanged side played well, and Forest were totally out of sorts. Forest put Fulham under some pressure early on when two wayward Bobby Robson passes gave away possession and Jack McClelland tipped a Colin Addison header over the bar. Gradually Fulham's superior football told, and they took the lead in the

The Fulham team take the field at Nottingham almost safe from relegation. For Johnny Haynes (centre) the match represented his 500th Fulham game. He received the ideal present, a 2–1 win.

twenty-first minute. Johnny Haynes pushed the ball into the penalty area, Allan Clarke's shot rebounded to Steve Earle, whose shot was also blocked, but the ball ran nicely to Graham Leggat who comprehensively beat Forest keeper Peter Grummitt from close range. Haynes then had a shot held on the line.

In the thirty-third minute, Haynes was injured in a tackle, and limped off to be replaced by Les Barrett. During the transition period Forest equalised through Sammy Chapman. Fulham were undeterred, however, and regained the lead just four minutes later. Clarke moved the ball forward to Mark Pearson, who fed Leggat. Grummitt was only able to parry Leggat's stinging shot, and Pearson ran the rebound over the line before the keeper could recover.

In the second half Fulham came close to extending their lead, when Barrett drove against Grummitt from close range. Forest applied some late pressure, with McClelland saving from Joe Baker, as he had done in January when Baker was with Arsenal, and twice John Dempsey had to be quick to clear his lines, but in truth Fulham held on comfortably, and were seldom troubled, recording a **2–1** win. Ironically, with this defeat, Nottingham Forest also plunged into the relegation mire.

Forest had clearly been undone by the scheming play and experience of Robson, Haynes and Pearson, and Johnny Haynes felt compelled to say: 'I can't ever remember Fulham playing as well as they are now.' Incredibly, it was now nine wins in eleven games, and the paper headline next day agreed: 'Fulham Almost Safe'.

The word *almost* was the key word. On the hot sunny Saturday, as the team took on **Stoke City**, unchanged Fulham played their eighth game in April in the space of just twenty-eight days. One last successful push was all that was needed; one point would probably be enough. Stoke were without Peter Dobing, and an eighteen-year-old local novice John Farmer was in goal. Stoke's position was just below mid table, so the Potteries side had little to play for. The club programme summed up the nerve-wracking position:

This is our last home match of the season, a time when we should be taking a quiet and reflective look back over the last eight months. But how the blazes can we look back, or forward, when our whole attention is riveted firmly to the next ninety nervous minutes ahead?

A look at the league table showed an incredible three points separating the twenty-first placed team from the thirteenth placed team. In theory any one of those nine clubs could accompany Blackburn Rovers to the Second Division.

After just ten minutes disaster struck, when George Cohen was stretchered off with a serious leg injury. Cohen had hared across the penalty area and partially blocked a shot from Stoke winger Harry Burrows, taking the full impact of the follow through on his left knee. He immediately dropped to the ground requesting assistance from the stretcher-bearers. He left the pitch, travelling immediately to St Stephen's hospital to have a number of stitches inserted in the wound. Apart from Fulham's need, Cohen was also out of the next England pre-World Cup warm-up match. The injury, a complete accident, forced an immediate re-shuffle, with Les Barrett coming on as substitute, and Stan Brown switching to full back.

This was already a 'patched up' Fulham side, with Johnny Haynes nursing a calf injury, and playing only thanks to an injection, and both Mark Pearson and Steve Earle nowhere near fully fit. Despite

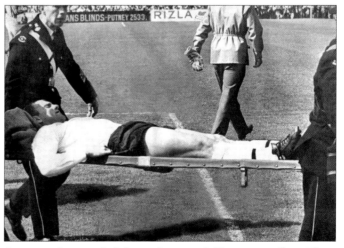

Just a point needed for safety, and disaster strikes. The agony shows on George Cohen's face as he is stretchered off with a badly gashed knee just ten minutes into the vital last home game with Stoke City.

In a forty-five minute onslaught, Steve Earle and Allan Clarke search desperately for the elusive second half equaliser, but find little space amongst the packed Stoke City defence.

their much-improved chance of survival, the tension was now beginning to show, and on a dry bumpy pitch, passes were going astray. Fulham were producing little as an attacking force, although Farmer saved from Earle, and Pearson had a header tipped over.

Stoke mounted a few counter-attacks of their own, and from one of these, after thirty-five minutes, another Stoke reserve, Gerry Bridgwood, took John Ritchie's pass and attacked down the right. Pearson missed his tackle and Bridgwood beat another defender before slamming in a low cross-shot that surprised and deceived the advancing Jack McClelland, and Fulham were a goal down. Up to this point John Dempsey again alongside McClelland had proved to be equal to everything Stoke had put to them, but now the team *had* to find an equaliser. Fulham stormed back, and Farmer blocked two Graham Leggat efforts with his body, and Eric Skeels kicked Earle's shot off the line.

The second half was one long agonising forty-five minutes. Fulham were much improved, but found the young Stoke keeper Farmer in inspired form, saving everything thrown at him with a mixture of luck, bravery and good keeping skills. The longer the game went on, the more the tension increased. Firstly, Farmer parried Barrett's searing volley, then bravely dived at Earle's feet to block a certain goal. Pearson was now increasingly handicapped by his injury, but couldn't be substituted, therefore striker Leggat dropped deeper, leaving Pearson a limping 'passenger' up front.

Fulham then appealed for a penalty when Maurice Setters clearly handled Bobby Robson's shot, but the referee shook his head. Then came the miss of the match; Pearson won the ball, drew the goalkeeper and put over an inviting cross, but Barrett, under pressure, headed wide of an open goal. Stoke, well organised, hung on, superbly marshalled by the rugged Setters, hacking away attack after attack, and in a rare dangerous Stoke breakaway, Brian Nichols desperately cleared John Ritchie's goal bound header off the line. Would Fulham fall at the final hurdle?

With just eight minutes to go, Fulham forced a corner, and from it Farmer was clearly fouled and impeded by a combination of Leggat and Allan Clarke as he jumped for the ball. Farmer dropped it and, in the ensuing melee, Barrett put in a shot that was headed off the line by Tony Allen; following this, Mark Pearson then bundled the Stoke skipper Allen unceremoniously into the goal. As the ball bounced crazily around the Stoke goalmouth, Dempsey, who had come up, headed the ball back into the goalmouth, the rushed Stoke clearance came out to him yet again. This time Dempsey returned the ball in to Clarke. Clarke demonstrated all of his predatory instincts by shooting first and asking questions afterwards, slamming the ball into the open net from just feet out; the referee awarded the goal. Stoke were not happy with the goal, but to their credit didn't protest too much; the goal however would never have been allowed to stand today. Players and supporters celebrated with joy, the roar could have been heard in Putney High Street. It was Clarke's first goal for Fulham, and he would *never* score a more important one.

The goal that meant everything! Stoke keeper Farmer has dropped the ball, and Leggat's grounded. A Stoke defender appeals for a foul. Allan Clarke doesn't wait, and slams the ball into an empty goal; it was his first for the club. The goal gave Fulham a 1–1 draw, and ensured First Division survival, sending gallant Northampton down.

The final whistle blew on a **1–1** draw—had the result been enough? Aston Villa had slipped to twenty-first position, but on this day the Midlanders had beaten Arsenal 3–0. The critical result was that Blackpool had beaten Northampton 3–0. The result ensured that Blackpool survived in the First Division for another year, but it also meant that Northampton Town were relegated, their gallant fight for First Division survival finally over. *Fulham were finally safe.* The result and season was particularly tough on Northampton, and the Cobblers never really recovered from relegation. Within four seasons, they were back in the Fourth Division. George Cohen, listening intently to the match commentaries on the radio, celebrated jubilantly from his hospital bed.

May 1966

In this month

* The seventy mph speed limit was continued until 1967.
* Brady and Hindley were sentenced to life imprisonment for the moors murders.
* Everton beat Sheffield Wednesday 3–2 in the Cup Final after being two goals down.

'Pretty Flamingo' by Manfred Mann topped the charts.

How the league was looking

Liverpool were going to be champions, with either Leeds United or Burnley as runners up. Chelsea's rise in form had pushed the team to fourth. Manchester United had dropped to sixth. Tottenham had slumped badly to mid table. West Ham and Arsenal were also still mid table. Fulham's amazing run had seen them safe from relegation, Blackburn marooned, accompanied finally by Northampton. Aston Villa, Nottingham Forest, Blackpool and Sheffield Wednesday had all been lucky to survive in a final relegation scramble.

The matches

THE FINAL match of the season, away at **Newcastle United**, was of course an anti-climax; Fulham, now safe and relaxed, could at last play without any fear. Bobby Drake came in for just his second game in two years, replacing the injured George Cohen, and Buckingham rested the half fit Mark Pearson, replacing him with Fred Callaghan. The match was another significant milestone for Johnny Haynes who surpassed Eddie Lowe's record total relating to the number of games played for Fulham; Haynes now had 512 to his credit.

The two teams played out a casual but very entertaining **1–1** draw, with Bobby Robson scoring his fourth goal in eight games. Fulham took the lead inside ten minutes with a classic goal. Stan Brown took a quick throw and found Graham Leggat, who made a fine right wing run. His cross found Clarke who, with some clever footwork, back-heeled the ball, setting up Robson who scored with a blistering long-range twenty-five yard drive; Clarke was having his best game in a Fulham shirt to date. It was Robson's second goal in his native northeast that season, but would prove to be his last for the club.

Fulham should have won, and were denied a certain penalty when a Newcastle defender clearly handled the ball on its way to the net. Defences were generally on top, but Fulham loosened their grip on the game, and allowed Newcastle to steal an undeserved equaliser. Alan Suddick, after a fine run, forced a corner off Bobby Drake, and took the corner kick himself. The ball swung high over the Fulham defence allowing giant centre half John McGrath to soar high and head home powerfully from ten yards, giving Jack McClelland no chance.

In the second half, Newcastle were generally on top in terms of possession, and the game became a swinging end-to-end battle, and it took two brilliant point blank saves from McClelland to finally earn Fulham yet another point. Steve Earle, Graham Leggat and the ever-youthful Johnny Haynes were all on top form. In truth, however, Fulham were just pleased to see the game and the season out.

1965–66 Season Summary

IT WAS hardly surprising that the season would be remembered as *The Great Escape* after Fulham's usual mild flirtations with relegation. It was, however, the third time in the last five seasons that Fulham had finished just two places from the bottom of the First Division. In February the team had been dead and buried with just fifteen points from twenty-nine games, when from that point, their displays of derring-do produced championship winning form with twenty points from just thirteen games (a possible twenty-six points). If that form had been present all season, Fulham would have netted around sixty-five points, and would have been League champions!

Some of the early season's games, especially those at the Cottage against Aston Villa, Northampton and Burnley, had been embarrassingly poor, but later performances against Liverpool, Sunderland, Leeds (away) and Northampton had been out of the top drawer. A team that had won just five games out of the first twenty-nine had then won nine of the next eleven. A team that had picked up only two draws away from home all season after fifteen away games, were undefeated away from home for the remainder of the season, picking up eleven points out of twelve.

A team that had scored just thirty-five times in twenty-eight league matches (average 1.25 goals per game) had then scored thirty-two goals in just fourteen games (average 2.30 goals per game). A team that had conceded sixty-seven goals in twenty-nine games (average 2.30 goals per game) then tightened up and conceded just eighteen in the last thirteen games (average 1.30 goals per game). Effectively, the Fulham team had almost doubled their scoring rate and halved their conceding rate.

It was clear that Fulham's revival had coincided with the arrival of Dave Sexton at the turn of the year. Immediately the team possessed more shape and determination. Steve Earle recalls:

> *To my mind, Sexton was the first real coach I'd had since signing for Fulham. Before that, training consisted of a two-lap warm-up and a five-a-side. Dave was the first to introduce game-related training, and he showed a lot of interest in the younger players.*

John Dempsey agreed, recalling that:

> *Sexton made all the difference when he came in. He changed how we trained, and improved all the players. He was a very good coach, and really worked out how we should play. It was a very sad day for Fulham when he left.*

To his credit, Buckingham had also taken the bull by the horns and dispensed with some of the under performing players, and his gamble with youth had ultimately paid off. A number of the regular players had been replaced and Fulham seemed to have finally found their own decent mix of youth and experience. The core of the four excellent international players in George Cohen, Bobby Robson, Johnny Haynes and Graham Leggat had been complemented by an experienced journeyman in Mark Pearson and the consistency of Stan Brown, and consolidated by some exciting new young talent in Jack McClelland, Brian Nichols, John Dempsey (outstanding in defence and attack all season), Steve Earle and Les Barrett. Add to this a centre forward with a future in Allan Clarke, and for once the prospects for the future looked a lot rosier. No-one had been ever present in the league, and only six players had played thirty or more league games, and twenty-three players in all had been tried.

As the team prepared immediately for a long holiday/tour of Asia, the main talking point was whether Fulham's inspirational full back George Cohen would be fit for England and the 1966 World Cup that was due to start very soon. The gashed knee Cohen had sustained was a bad one; to his horror he could see clear through to the bone. Cohen was in hospital for ten days, he could barely walk, and considered himself out of the England squad. Vic Buckingham, to his credit, had other ideas. He picked Cohen up from hospital, and said to him, 'George, you have to walk', and made Cohen get up and walk out of the hospital unaided.

He then helped and supervised Cohen in a hard, strict training regime that ultimately enabled him to be fit for international duty. Cohen admitted later that Buckingham had been right, saying, 'The more I walked, the easier it became'. Cohen trained on his own at Hurlingham, desperately trying to beat the deadline he had set himself. After several weeks of worry, he made it and when the World Cup squad assembled, he was ready. As an added fillip, and after a remarkably consistent campaign, George Cohen was voted runner-up to Manchester United's Bobby Charlton in the poll for the Footballer of the Year, an honour that gave him tremendous pride.

League Division One - Season 1965-66 - Final Table

		P	W	D	L	F	A	W	D	L	F	A	Pts
1	Liverpool	42	17	2	2	52	15	9	7	5	27	19	61
2	Leeds United	42	14	4	3	49	15	9	5	7	30	23	55
3	Burnley	42	15	3	3	45	20	9	4	8	34	27	55
4	Manchester United	42	12	8	1	50	20	6	7	8	34	39	51
5	Chelsea	42	11	4	6	30	21	11	3	7	35	32	51
6	West Bromwich Albion	42	11	6	4	58	34	8	6	7	33	35	50
7	Leicester City	42	12	4	5	40	28	9	3	9	40	37	49
8	Tottenham Hotspur	42	11	6	4	55	37	5	6	10	20	29	44
9	Sheffield United	42	11	6	4	37	25	5	5	11	19	34	43
10	Stoke City	42	12	6	3	42	22	3	6	12	23	42	42
11	Everton	42	12	6	3	39	19	3	5	13	17	43	41
12	West Ham United	42	12	5	4	46	33	3	4	14	24	50	39
13	Blackpool	42	9	5	7	36	29	5	4	12	19	36	37
14	Arsenal	42	8	8	5	36	31	4	5	12	26	44	37
15	Newcastle United	42	10	5	6	26	20	4	4	13	24	43	37
16	Aston Villa	42	10	3	8	39	34	5	3	13	30	46	36
17	Sheffield Wednesday	42	11	6	4	35	18	3	2	16	21	48	36
18	Nottingham Forest	42	11	3	7	31	26	3	5	13	25	46	36
19	Sunderland	42	13	2	6	36	28	1	6	14	15	44	36
20	**Fulham**	**42**	**9**	**4**	**8**	**34**	**37**	**5**	**3**	**13**	**33**	**48**	**35**
21	Northampton	42	8	6	7	31	32	2	7	12	24	60	33
22	Blackburn Rovers	42	6	1	14	30	36	2	3	16	27	52	20

Steve Earle celebrates his hat trick at Northampton.

1965–66 Season's Results

	Sat, August 21	A	Blackpool	D	2–2	Key, Haynes		15,280
	Wed, August 25	H	Blackburn Rovers	W	5–2	Brown 2, Key 2, Dyson		14,880
	Sat, August 28	H	Chelsea	L	0–3			34,097
	Wed, September 1	A	Blackburn Rovers	L	2–3	Brown, O'Connell		10,497
	Sat, September 4	H	Tottenham Hotspur	L	0–2			28,178
	Wed, September 8	H	Sheffield United	D	0–0			9,785
	Sat, September 11	A	Liverpool	L	1–2	Key		46,382
	Wed, September 15	A	Sheffield United	L	0–2			17,967
	Sat, September 18	H	Aston Villa	L	3–6	Leggat 3		12,634
FL Cup 2	*Wed, September 22*	*A*	*Wrexham*	*W*	*2–1*	*O'Connell, Dyson*		*12,001*
	Sat, September 25	A	Sunderland	D	2–2	O'Connell, Robson		39,292
	Sat, October 2	H	West Ham United	W	3–0	Haynes, Leggat, og		22,310
	Sat, October 9	A	Arsenal	L	1–2	Dyson		32,318
FL Cup 3	*Wed, October 13*	*H*	*Northampton Town*	*W*	*5–0*	*Dempsey 3, Dyson 2 (1 pen)*		*7,834*
	Sat, October 16	H	Everton	W	3–2	Dempsey, Dyson (pen), Pearson		18,110
	Sat, October 23	A	Manchester United	L	1–4	Dempsey		32,716
	Sat, October 30	H	Newcastle United	W	2–0	Key, Leggat		19,226
FL Cup 4	*Wed, November 3*	*H*	*Aston Villa*	*D*	*1–1*	*Haynes*		*10,083*
	Sat, November 6	A	West Bromwich Albion	L	2–6	Leggat, Robson		20,170
FL Cup 4R	*Mon, November 8*	*A*	*Aston Villa*	*L*	*0–2*			*18,536*
	Sat, November 13	H	Nottingham Forest	D	1–1	Marsh		13,863
	Sat, November 20	A	Sheffield Wednesday	L	0–1			16,030
	Sat, November 27	H	Northampton Town	L	1–4	Haynes		11,339
	Sat, December 4	A	Stoke City	L	2–3	Marsh 2		14,871
	Sat, December 11	H	Burnley	L	2–5	Haynes, Pearson		12,092
	Sat, December 18	A	Everton	L	0–2			20,670
	Tues, December 28	A	Leicester City	L	0–5			20,164
	Sat, January 1	H	Arsenal	W	1–0	Leggat		25,801
	Sat, January 8	A	Burnley	L	0–1			17,200
	Sat, January 15	H	Manchester United	L	0–1			33,018
FA Cup 3	*Sat, January 22*	*A*	*Sheffield United*	*L*	*1–3*	*Dempsey*		*18,009*
	Sat, January 29	H	Blackpool	D	0–0			12,093
	Sat, February 5	A	Chelsea	L	1–2	Leggat		35,438
	Sat, February 19	A	Tottenham Hotspur	L	3–4	Earle, Leggat, Barrett		31,719
	Sat, February 26	H	Liverpool	W	2–0	Earle 2		31,616
	Sat, March 12	A	Aston Villa	W	5–2	Earle 2, Leggat 2, Barrett		13,829
	Sat, March 19	H	Sunderland	W	3–0	Leggat 2, og		20,918
	Sat, March 26	A	West Ham United	W	3–1	Earle, Leggat, Barrett		18,997
	Sat, April 2	H	West Bromwich Albion	W	2–1	Haynes 2		20,426
	Fri, April 8	H	Leeds United	L	1–3	Robson (pen)		38,960
	Tues, April 12	A	Leeds United	W	1–0	Pearson		33,968
	Sat, April 16	H	Sheffield Wednesday	W	4–2	Barrett, Earle, Leggat, Robson (pen)		20,980
	Mon, April 18	H	Leicester City	L	0–4			18,014
	Sat, April 23	A	Northampton Town	W	4–2	Earle 3, Robson		24,532
	Tues, April 26	A	Nottingham Forest	W	2–1	Leggat, Pearson		19,618
	Sat, April 30	H	Stoke City	D	1–1	Clarke		25,491
	Sat, May 7	A	Newcastle United	D	1–1	Robson		18,810

1965–66 Season

APPEARANCES (maximum 47):

Football League Division 1: Cohen 39, Dempsey 38, Brown 36, Robson 36, Haynes 33, Leggat 32 (+1), Nichols 27, Pearson 24 (+1), Dyson 21 (+1), Macedo 21, McClelland 21, Key 20, O'Connell 20, Keetch 19, Marsh 17, Earle 15, Barrett 12 (+2), Callaghan 9, Clarke 7 (+1), Mealand 7, Parmenter 6, Drake 1, Ryan 1 (+1).

FA Cup, all one appearance: Brown, Cohen, Dempsey, Dyson, Haynes, Keetch, Leggat, McClelland, Marsh, O'Connell, Pearson.

FL Cup: Dempsey 4, Dyson 4, Haynes 4, Key 4, Cohen 3, Keetch 3, Leggat 3, Macedo 3, Nichols 3, Robson 3, Brown 2, O'Connell 2, Pearson 2, Callaghan 1, Marsh 1, McClelland 1, Mealand 1.

TOTAL: Cohen 43, Dempsey 43, Robson 39, Brown 39, Haynes 38, Leggat 36 (+1), Nichols 30, Pearson 27 (+1), Dyson 26 (+1), Macedo 24, Key 24, O'Connell 23, Keetch 23, McClelland 23, Marsh 19, Earle 15, Barrett 12 (+2), Callaghan 10, Mealand 8, Clarke 7 (+1), Parmenter 6, Drake 1, Ryan 1 (+1).

GOALSCORERS (all competitions):

Leggat 16, Earle 10, Haynes 7, Robson 6, Dyson 6, Dempsey 6, Key 5, Barrett 4, Pearson 4, Marsh 3, O'Connell 3, Brown 3, Clarke 1, og 2.

George Cohen—most league appearances.   *Graham Leggat—most goals.*

June 1966

In this month

* Phillips petroleum made the richest North Sea oil strike yet.
* The AA announced its first rise in subscriptions since 1905, from two to three guineas (£2.10 to £3.15).
* The first *Till Death Us Do Part* episode was broadcast.
* Mary Quant and Peter Sellers were each awarded the OBE.
* Walter McGowan became the world flyweight boxing champion.
* James White was sentenced to eighteen years for his part in the great train robbery.
* Barclays bank introduced the first credit card, Barclaycard.
* France left NATO.
* An un-manned spacecraft soft-landed on the moon.
* The Irish Prime Minister banned the UVF (Ulster Volunteer Force).

'Strangers In The Night' by Frank Sinatra topped the charts.

How the league was won

Liverpool won the league by a clear six points, Leeds United pipping Burnley to the runner's up spot on goal average. Manchester United were fourth and Chelsea fifth. Tottenham finished eighth, West Ham mid table and Arsenal fourteenth. Blackburn Rovers and Northampton Town were both relegated. Fulham drew clear in twentieth place, and above Fulham only *two* points separated Sunderland in nineteenth place from Blackpool in thirteenth place.

The Far Eastern Tour

AFTER THE rigours of the season, Fulham took eighteen players in June on a close season tour-cum-holiday in **Asia**, where they would meet and play local representative sides in exhibition matches. First Division Sheffield Wednesday, following their Cup Final defeat, would also be making the trip. In what was one of the earliest 'sponsorship deals', the tour was supported and underwritten by, of all companies, British American Tobacco Co. Ltd. (BAT)!

The outbound journey included five stopping points, and took a weary Fulham party some nineteen hours. The team would have a number of social engagements, and during the time there would visit and coach local schoolboys and visit training colleges and RAF units serving in the

Relaxed at last, the players enjoy their Far East tour. Pictured dining are (left to right around the table) Ryan, Sexton, Brown, Callaghan, Macedo, Earle, Moss, McClelland, Haynes and Pearson. Pictured enjoying a boat trip are (left to right) Barrett, Earle, Robson, Conway and Clarke.

area. The club were well looked after on the tour, and stayed at some point at the famous Raffles Hotel.

The matches would be a constant battle against dehydration and humidity, but Fulham would become more accustomed to the conditions as the time went on. There were a number of instances of, what was termed diplomatically, 'upset stomachs' to deal with!

Steve Earle recalls that Allan Clarke was badly affected by sunburn on a boat trip, and said: 'They had to cover him in bandages like a mummy, he was in bits.' Clarke played in this state in one of the tour matches, but still managed to score twice! Earle also shared a room on the tour with Bobby Robson who was less than comfortable with the insects and other creepy-crawlies that abounded. Earle placed a toy insect in Robson's bed, and when Robson's feet touched the 'bug' he leapt in the air, and proceeded to beat the bed for a number of minutes until he spotted the culprit. He then proceeded to chase Earle round the Raffles hotel for ten minutes!

The matches on the tour normally took place at 8pm. The pitches were often hard, but were made easier by the occasional welcome intervention of heavy rainfall.

A summary of the tour results is as follows:

29 May - Hong Kong. Attendance: not known
Fulham 2 Combined Chinese XI 2 (Leggat and Earle) (HT 1–0)

1 June - Hong Kong. Attendance: not known
Sheffield Wednesday 5 Fulham 2 (Leggat 2) (HT 1–1)

4 June - Singapore, Jalan Besar Stadium. Attendance: 12,000
Fulham 6 Singapore 0 (Leggat 2, Clarke 2, Robson and Ryan) (HT 4–0)

7 June - Penang City, Penang City Stadium. Attendance: 19,000–20,000
Fulham 1 Asian All Stars 0 (Leggat) (HT 0–0)

11 June - Kuala Lumpur, Merdeka Stadium. Attendance: 10,000
Fulham 5 Sheffield Wednesday 3 (Leggat 3, Pearson and Haynes) (HT 2–1)

14 June - Singapore, Jalan Besar Stadium. Attendance: 13,000
Fulham 4 Sheffield Wednesday 2 (Leggat 2, Pearson and Earle) (HT 3–1)

Supplementary notes to the matches:

29 May match – Combined Chinese XI:
☐ Match played in the Hong Kong Government Stadium. Fulham robbed of a 2–1 win by a last minute equaliser.

1 June match – Sheffield Wednesday:
☐ The match marked Jimmy Conway's first appearance in a Fulham shirt.
☐ Four goals in ten minutes early in the second half saw Fulham lose out to the humidity.

4 June match – Singapore:
☐ Described by Buckingham as 'a bit of a frolic', Fulham scored four early goals and then eased off.
☐ Fred Callaghan broke his nose in the game, it was re-set in Penang, and he took no further part in the tour.

7 June match – Asian All Stars:
☐ Fulham had a little leisure time in the idyllic environment of Penang.
☐ The All Star XI was a brainchild of the Malaysian Prime Minister Tunku Abdul Rahman. The side consisted of players drawn from Hong Kong, Korea, India, Burma, Vietnam and China. The game marked the first time that they had ever played together.
☐ The game against the Asian All Stars XI drew a record crowd of between 19,000 and 20,000.

Graham Leggat's headed goal came three minutes from time.

☐ Allan Clarke returned quickly to England in order to keep an important meeting in Nottingham on 11 June—his marriage.

11 June match – Sheffield Wednesday:

☐ Fulham's 5–3 win over Sheffield Wednesday was achieved with two goals in the last two minutes.

☐ Fulham played their best football of the tour, and Graham Leggat excelled with a hat trick. (Some reports credit Leggat with four goals.)

14 June match – Sheffield Wednesday:

☐ The game saw a record attendance at the Jalan Besar Stadium.

☐ Fulham conceded an early goal, but scored three before half time. Steve Earle wrapped up the victory shortly after half time.

Tour Summary

P	W	D	L	F	A
6	4	1	1	20	12

Scorers

Leggat 11, Earle 2, Clarke 2, Pearson 2, Haynes 1, Robson 1, Ryan 1.

Graham Leggat scored in every game, including the three matches against Sheffield Wednesday. He became quite a hero to the locals who marvelled at his powerful shooting and eye for goal. Modest as ever, Leggat said: 'The team score the goals, I just put my name on 'em.'

The return

The exhausted team flew back on the 15 June, and it was an even longer trip of some twenty-two hours. The team arrived back in the UK on the 16 June, to be met by Fulham Director Chappie D'Amato.

In summing up the tour, Buckingham said:

Whilst open to accusations of self-adulation, I would sincerely say that the Fulham flag flew high on the tour both on and off the field. The players brought only credit to their club, and deserve the utmost praise for their efforts.

The Close Season 1966

At this time:

July

* The Government produced a Prices and Incomes bill.
* Brigitte Bardot married Gunter Sachs, and Frank Sinatra married Mia Farrow.
* Jim Ryan knocked 2.3 seconds off the mile record.
* Richard Speck killed nine student nurses in America.
* Prime Minister Harold Wilson imposed a 'prices and incomes freeze' to beat the crisis.
* ***England won the World Cup***.

'Sunny Afternoon' by The Kinks topped the charts.

Early August

* The comedian Lenny Bruce died of a drug overdose.
* The Kray twins were arrested.
* Chairman Mao proclaimed the 'cultural revolution' in China.

'With A Girl Like You' by The Troggs topped the charts.

The events

AFTER THE traumatic season, the Fulham board, management, team and supporters took a deserved holiday. The current affairs are included here to retain the 'feel' of the 1966 period!

Season 1966–67

The Build up

The start of the season

1966–67 saw no changes to the Fulham board of directors. The long-standing board still comprised the Dean brothers, Jack Walsh and Noël (Chappie) D'Amato (vice chairman), with Tommy Trinder as chairman. Fulham's league crowds had risen significantly over the previous season from an average of 17,691 to 21,160, a rise of over 18.5%. Fulham were proud to announce that the club had *not* raised season ticket prices for the coming season, and were offering, for adults, season tickets from seven guineas £7–7s–0d (£7.35p) up to a maximum price of ten guineas £10–10s–0d (£10.50p). From a stadium point of view, it was now possible for the first time ever to purchase alcoholic drinks at Craven Cottage; there were facilities under all the stands except the Putney Terrace.

Fulham pride

Probably the proudest moment ever for the club was that now, within its ranks, Fulham had a World Cup winner, George Cohen being one of the glorious eleven that had lifted the Jules Rimet trophy at Wembley on that special day in July. It was a fitting pinnacle for a player who had been a consummate professional with both Fulham and England. Cohen would remain as club captain for the ensuing season.

Playing and coaching staff

At the end of the season, Buckingham continued with his root and branch clearout at the club; the departures were not particularly surprising. The least known of all the names was Tony Goodgame who had not made the first team. He had been given a free transfer and had joined Leyton Orient. Johnny Key was also given a free transfer after nine seasons, 181 appearances and thirty-seven goals, and had joined Second Division Coventry City. Key would assist Coventry ably in their successful bid for promotion to the First Division. Brian ('Pat') O'Connell was given a free transfer after eight seasons, 170 appearances and twenty-eight goals, and elected to join Second Division Crystal Palace; he played for Palace for just one season.

Probably the most renowned name on the list was that of Bobby Keetch, also given a free transfer. Keetch was Fulham through and through, and was devastated at being released by the club. Although never the greatest footballer, Keetch had always brought considerable commitment and honesty to the club. Many considered that, for his character alone, the club were a great deal poorer for his departure. He left after five seasons, 120 appearances and two goals. The *bon viveur* and drinking partner of Greaves and Moore almost retired from the game altogether, and was without a club for almost six months. He ultimately joined Queens Park Rangers to be re-united with former Fulham colleagues Jim Langley and Rodney Marsh. Keetch did not stay long, however, making only fifty-one league appearances, and after a short playing spell in South Africa left the game altogether to concentrate on art and antiques. The three players departing had made over 400 appearances for Fulham between them.

The departures had a further significance as Key, O'Connell and Keetch, along with Marsh who had left in March, were all from London and the Home Counties, and Fulham had been their only serious professional club from school. It seemed as if some of Fulham's 'family' core had been removed. The squad had though been increased inasmuch as Vic Buckingham had signed two significant players from Irish club Stella Maris Bohemians for very reasonable fees. They were twenty-year-old midfield player Jimmy Conway and twenty-year-old centre forward Turlough O'Connor. Jimmy Conway arrived with a glowing reputation, and was considered as 'another Johnny Haynes'. Both were signed before the Asian close season tour. There were also three lesser signings, which were eighteen-year-old full back Mike Pentecost signed from non-league Sutton United, nineteen-year-old defender Hugh Cunningham signed on a free transfer from Glasgow Celtic, and young eighteen-year-old goalkeeper Ian Seymour signed for a nominal £1,250 fee from non-league club Tonbridge.

The major blow that had occurred during the close season was the departure of coach Dave Sexton after just eight months. Sexton had been instrumental in Fulham's successful survival struggle the previous season. Fulham had offered Sexton a position as assistant manager, and had also offered him the same financial 'package', but Sexton had accepted an offer to become coach at Arsenal. As his replacement, Buckingham had appointed the former Charlton centre half Gordon Jago on a two-year contract. The new thirty-three-year-old coach had been manager of Eastbourne United for the previous four years. Jago had turned down offers from Plymouth Argyle and Coventry City to join Fulham. He was now Fulham's third coach in a year.

Buckingham was quick to quash the 'doom merchant theorists' who suggested that Fulham without Sexton were already as good as relegated. Buckingham was quick to point out that 'success was down to the players, not just coaching' and that it was not 'the end of the world'.

Privately, however, Buckingham was seething at the timing of Sexton's departure during the pre-season build up, and talked of his 'annoyance' and that 'he didn't think much of that', but was magnanimous enough to say that 'a wind of change' had blown through the Cottage on Sexton's arrival, and that he 'must record his value'. Buckingham added that Sexton was 'a damn good coach who did a good job for us.' Buckingham admitted that with the quality of players that Fulham had, he had never envisaged the problems they would initially find themselves in, and would ultimately extricate themselves from. He said that he did not want to experience it again, and neither would the players or the supporters.

Other changes

Fulham had made a further change to their playing strip for the following season, whereby a single white stripe had been added to the sides of the shorts. The programme was still 6d, but it was again a new-style programme with a new cover. Fulham would be a club that embraced Alf Ramsey's 'wingless wonders' approach, and would play as lined up in the programme in a 4–3–3 formation. The First Division clubs were now playing some matches with a white football rather than the traditional brown/tan colour, to aid clarity on television.

Pre-season

Aside from football, one of the great Fulham family traditions was the annual cricket encounter against Putney Cricket Club at Putney Lower Common. On this occasion Putney batted first and declared at 181 for six. In reply, Fulham, in white naturally, never looked like reaching that total, but held on doggedly with one wicket left to force a creditable draw when stumps were drawn at 146 for nine. Graham Leggat hit a six and top scored with thirty-one. Fulham's eleven was: Mardling (physiotherapist), Robson, Clarke, Ryan, Drake, Haynes, Leggat, Stevens (coach), Earle, Dempsey and Hill. One wonders whether the cry of 'Earle's caught' ever arose! With footballers being such precious commodities nowadays, one also wonders whether a similar kind of encounter would be allowed to take place today.

Two weeks before the start of the season, Fulham played a friendly match with **Millwall** at the Den. Millwall were a good side and had just been promoted to the Second Division. At one stage Fulham were 2–0 down, former Fulham player Mike Brown scoring in the first minute, with veteran Len Julians adding a second on just thirteen minutes. Millwall were pressing strongly at this stage for further goals, but then Bobby Robson pulled a goal back with a penalty, following a handball offence.

In the second half, Allan Clarke put Fulham level, beating one player for speed, and then holding off two other defenders before scoring with a cracking cross-shot that Millwall keeper Lawrie Leslie hardly saw. Johnny Haynes then put Fulham ahead with a similar super long range shot from over thirty yards past the unsighted keeper, before Graham Leggat slid in a fourth near the end from an accurate cross from Steve Earle. Fulham had been impressive in a very hard workout to win **4–2**.

After his World Cup winning exploits, George Cohen returned to re-join the squad. Vic Buckingham suggested he should take a few days off. Cohen agreed but continued to train intensely. In the end his wife Daphne pleaded with Buckingham to take him back! Buckingham agreed to take Cohen back into the squad for a small pre-season tour of Belgium, as long as Cohen came 'just for the holiday'. In true Cohen fashion, George turned down the request, and refused to go unless he could be considered as part of the playing squad. In the end Buckingham had no option but to agree!

Fulham completed the short pre-season tour of Belgium, winning one match and losing one. The initial game against **Olympic Charleroi** resulted in a **4–2** victory, the Fulham scorers (Clarke 2 (1 pen), Callaghan and Haynes), and the second against **RFC Liegeois**, a much tougher match, resulted in a **2–3** defeat, Dempsey and Earle the scorers. Vic Buckingham's war cry for the coming season was: 'We start the season in good spirit, aiming for the top.'

The league's new arrivals

The division welcomed **Southampton** and **Manchester City** in place of the relegated Blackburn Rovers and Northampton Town. True to their frugal nature, Fulham had ordered just the one new flag to put alongside the others on the riverside terrace—that of Southampton. Manchester City had lost their First Division status just three seasons previously, but Fulham had an inkling that City would be back sooner rather than later, and had therefore kept their original flag!

Official photograph at the beginning of the season. Back row: Robson, Brown, Cohen, McClelland, Dempsey, Nichols, Barrett; front row: Clarke, Earle, Pearson, Haynes, Leggat.

FULHAM
FOOTBALL CLUB

OFFICIAL
PROGRAMME **6**ᴰ

SEASON 1966-7 LEAGUE DIVISION ONE
EVERTON
SATURDAY 20 AUGUST KICK OFF 3 PM

The programme for the opening home match of the season.

August 1966

In this month

* Plans were announced for a 385ft skyscraper in the West End, called Centre Point.
* Francis Chichester set off on his lone round the world voyage.
* The Hawker Harrier, the world's first vertical take off jet aircraft, was unveiled.
* Three policemen were murdered on a west London street.
* In Vietnam, twenty U.S. soldiers died when U.S. planes napalmed Americans by mistake.

'Yellow Submarine' / 'Eleanor Rigby' by The Beatles topped the charts.

The matches

FULHAM STARTED their campaign against FA Cup winners **Everton** at Craven Cottage. The game saw the presence of three World Cup winners at the Cottage: both England full backs George Cohen and Ray Wilson, alongside dynamo Alan Ball whom Everton had signed from Blackpool just five days earlier. The fee had been £110,000, a new record transfer fee for a player involving British clubs. Ball had also claimed a hat trick on a previous visit to the Cottage.

Buckingham decided to start the season in controversial fashion by omitting England international Johnny Haynes from the team, and went as far as to say privately that 'Fulham were a better team without him'! He was convinced, probably wrongly, that Haynes was not pulling his weight. It was a boiling almost tropically hot day and the attendance, even allowing for holidays, was a very disappointing 21,000. The first half was very even; certainly honours were even defensively and in the middle of the field, but all in all, the fare on offer was pretty dreary stuff.

Ball was prominent from the start, and in the main move of the first half, ten minutes before half time, he put Alex Scott away down the right hand side. From his perfect cross, Fred Pickering beat Jack McClelland with a thumping header that vibrated the bar, and Alex Young blazed the rebound over. Towards the end of the first half, George Cohen was beginning to move upfield and from attacking moves both Graham Leggat and Allan Clarke went close with powerful drives. Seemingly influenced by the World Cup, both teams seemed to have adopted a defensive approach, playing very deep, often putting eight or more men behind the ball and relying on breakaways. Without Haynes' spark, Fulham found it even harder to break down the Everton defensive wall, and created few scoring opportunities.

The tempo increased in the second half, and in the fifty-second minute, McClelland made the save of the match. Pickering, again supplied by Ball, hit a first time shot that brought a full length one-handed save from the Fulham keeper. The Toffees, however definitely possessed the edge up front, and from a breakaway on the hour, Alan Ball, who had given a Man of the Match performance on his debut, put Everton ahead. Stan Brown brought down Ball on the edge of the penalty area, and, from the resulting free kick delivered by Scott, Ball turned swiftly in the penalty area, and from fifteen yards swept the ball first time high into the roof of the net with the Fulham defence mesmerised.

Fulham huffed and puffed for the remainder of the game, and although Leggat and Clarke again went close, Fulham never really looked like scoring. Everton goalkeeper Gordon West had a particularly easy afternoon, the ball too often travelling sideways or backwards in Fulham attacks. All the forwards, except the clever deep-lying Clarke, were looking distinctly off colour. Mark Pearson spent more time helping out the defence, and his role as a replacement for Haynes was a memorable failure. Ball's 'robust' approach to tackling had the Fulham fans booing and one jumping tackle on Pearson was particularly ugly. Pearson himself raised ironic cheers for an avenging, charging tackle on Ball soon afterwards. The home crowd quickly forgot Ball's World Cup exploits, but he had given Everton leadership and bite, just the kind that Fulham were clearly lacking.

Clarke had done well, but had missed Haynes' passes. The Fulham crowd were aware of the absence of craft, and began chanting, '*We want Haynes*', as the game began to ebb away. Haynes could be seen reading a newspaper at the players' entrance on the corner of the pitch, looking far removed from the whole episode. The lethargic match finished **0−1**, and it was certainly not the start Vic Buckingham had been looking for.

Haynes demanded to see chairman Tommy Trinder to discuss the position. He was invited to the boardroom where a silverware award was to be presented to George Cohen for his World Cup exploits. Haynes himself was also going to be given an award for his fiftieth England cap, even though, bizarrely, this had been over four years ago! Haynes did not show up, but the presentation to George Cohen went ahead. It was this decision by Buckingham that probably began to isolate him from some of the players.

The team for the first away fixture, at Turf Moor. Back row: Brown, Cohen, McClelland, Dempsey, Robson, Nichols; front row: Earle, Clarke, Haynes, Pearson, Leggat.

A visit to **Burnley** in midweek was also not the best first away match of the season, given Fulham's dismal record at Turf Moor. Buckingham, seeing the error of his ways, or under pressure from Trinder, immediately restored Johnny Haynes to the line-up; Burnley were without dangerous winger Ralph Coates. Haynes' inclusion didn't make a great deal of difference, and another indifferent Fulham performance ensued, the first half hour being devoid of almost any kind of entertainment. Fulham persevered with the defensive 4−3−3, giving the defence a numerical advantage if nothing else. Burnley striker Andy Lochhead missed a number of clear chances before heading Burnley in front, but even a goal failed to stir the crowd or the teams into any sort of life. The main talking point of the half was a badly timed tackle by John Dempsey that floored Lochhead, giving rise to some heated exchanges.

In the second half, Mark Pearson moved upfield and the forward presence at last started to have some meaning. However, just as Fulham were pulling themselves back into the game on the hour, Willie Irvine volleyed Burnley's second from the edge of the area. Fulham seemed to now rely on damage limitation, and although Jack McClelland and George Cohen did enough to preserve their reputations, others were under performing. Fulham appeared to be escaping quite lightly, but with a quarter of an hour left, Stan Brown scooped a header from Irvine away from the goal line with his hand, and Burnley full back Alex Elder put away the resulting penalty. Fulham offered little after this, the match ending in a pretty comprehensive **0−3** defeat.

For the trip to **Stoke City** five days later, Tony Macedo returned in goal after just two games. There was no recording of Jack McClelland being injured, but Macedo had recovered from 'injuries

In the final seconds, Allan Clarke pounces on a rebound from Stoke goalkeeper Farmer to slam in a late winner. The 2–1 win gave Fulham their first points of the season.

and personal problems', and appeared to be 'preferred'. Stoke City had started well, and had won their opening two fixtures. For some unrecorded reason, the game kicked off slightly late, and Fulham were one down early on. The Potters' Tony Allen almost created a goal in the sixteenth minute, when his cross was set up for City's John Ritchie via Roy Vernon, but his shot hit a Fulham defender's legs and was cleared. Two minutes later, however, Stoke did take the lead. Stoke's dangerous George Eastham put in a cross, Ritchie outjumped Macedo to head down, and Roy Vernon pushed the ball in.

Despite this, Fulham looked the more purposeful side. The Fulham defending was tenacious, Macedo looked very safe, and the team were finding large gaps in the uncertain Stoke defence, Johnny Haynes was creating several gilt-edged chances, but the forwards just couldn't apply the final touch.

As the clock ticked on, the game looked like going against Fulham, who had continued to look dangerous, without ever finishing the chances. Allan Clarke was frustrated when, with twenty minutes to go, his super shot was blocked by a brilliant one-handed save from goalkeeper John Farmer. Then, just fifteen minutes from time, Graham Leggat took a superb Johnny Haynes through pass and, as a defender tried to tackle, scored with a lovely shot from the edge of the area just evading the diving Farmer's right hand, and just inside a post.

Fulham carried on searching for the win, and just as the final seconds were approaching, Haynes fired in a magnificent low shot from outside the area through a clutch of Stoke defenders. Stoke's teenage keeper Farmer saw it late, and could only beat out the shot, the ball fell nicely to Clarke following up, and despite a defender attempting a last ditch tackle, Clarke slammed the ball in from close range. The first win of the season was on the board, and away from home. The goal arrived so late in the game that, before the days of super-fast technology, the evening papers reported that the match had finished as a 1–1 draw. In this case Fulham were glad that the media were wrong; it was most definitely a **2–1** win.

Fulham were unchanged on the Bank Holiday Monday evening when facing **Burnley**, and in these times it was often customary to play a particular team twice early in the season. Les Barrett was made substitute to accommodate Johnny Haynes. Burnley were top of the table, and possessed a 100% record with three wins in three games, scoring nine goals in the process. Burnley were still

An unlucky Graham Leggat is foiled once again by Burnley goalkeeper Blacklaw. Despite dominating, Fulham managed only a 0–0 draw at Craven Cottage, a point that ended Burnley's 100% record.

very much a home grown side, but were without dangerous winger Willie Morgan. The first half belonged more to Burnley, with Fulham hanging on at times. Burnley forward Andy Lochhead thankfully had an off day, missing several chances. Tony Macedo was brilliant in his handling, and one diving full length save, when virtually unsighted, was described as 'quite fabulous'. The nearest thing to a goal came in the ninth minute, when Burnley's Les Latcham ran on to a Willie Irvine pass and screwed a shot against the left hand post. A heavy downpour then occurred during the half and seemed to even things up to a degree.

Fulham actually came very close to ending Burnley's winning run, and were in control for the second half, which was played at a furious pace. For long periods the team had the Burnley defence reeling, and just how the ball was kept out of the Burnley net when often just a touch was needed, remained a mystery. Fulham abandoned their approach of playing through the middle and gained far better reward by using the wings. Midway through the half, referee Tommy Dawes added to excitement by breaking down with a twisted left knee, and linesman Ron Challis took over the whistle.

Fulham's best chance arrived near the end, when full back Alex Elder headed Graham Leggat's shot off the line, with goalkeeper Adam Blacklaw stranded. Burnley offered little up front, except for the occasional breakaway threat from Ralph Coates playing in place of Morgan. The game finished **0–0**, a good achievement against a quality side, and a third point was on the board. Tony Macedo had looked sharp on his home return, Johnny Haynes was on song, and on another day, Leggat might have netted at least two goals. The press said that Fulham were 'unfortunate not to win', agreeing that the match had been a thrilling tussle and that 'goals were the only thing missing.'

It was already clear to see that the World Cup was influencing the way teams played, most now opting for a tight defence. The club programme acknowledged this, agreeing that the game was no longer just a case of scoring more goals than the opposition, but rather a 'tactical battle of wits'. There was now regular talk of 'disciplined and packed defences', 'thick ranks', and 'tight at the back with quick breaks'.

September 1966

In this month

* The Queen Mother launched Britain's first nuclear submarine.
* BMC laid off 7,000 workers, and planned a further 11,000 redundancies in November.
* The South African president Hendrick Verwoerd was assassinated.
* The circus owner Billy Smart died.
* Australia's Jack Brabham won the world driver's championship in a car that he built himself.

'All Or Nothing' by The Small Faces topped the charts.

The matches

DESPITE THE fact that **Sheffield United** were a bogey side, Fulham's hopes should have been high. The Blades had lost *all* of their opening four league games, and looked a side in disarray. Fulham replaced Les Barrett as substitute with Fred Callaghan. On another sweltering hot day, Fulham became all hot and bothered trying to break down another packed ten-man Sheffield United defence and, as against Everton previously, they couldn't do it.

Alan Hodgkinson, Len Badger and Reg Matthewson were outstanding for United at the back. United were also dangerous on the break where Alan Woodward and Gil Reece gave George Cohen and Brian Nichols plenty to think about. Tony Macedo also had to be called upon to make several saves, and one was outstanding: Cohen was penalised for pushing, and from the resulting free kick taken by Woodward, Mick Jones put in a thumping header that was superbly tipped over the top one-handed.

The Fulham midfield were performing well, Stan Brown, Bobby Robson and Johnny Haynes desperately prompting the forwards, but the forward line just could not convert. The packed defence meant that Fulham were, in the main, restricted to long-range shots, which goalkeeper Hodgkinson dealt with comfortably. Twice before half time Fulham were unlucky. Graham Leggat cleverly worked himself an opening, beat Hodgkinson but with virtually an open goal, his shot hit the angle of post and bar. Then the hard working Steve Earle forced an opening, but blazed over the bar when it seemed easier to score.

The second half proved to be a real stinker for Fulham, who produced little from midfield, where Haynes was not his usual effective self after taking a heavy knock, and when Earle and Clarke did get service, both looked very out of touch. Leggat seemed to spend most of the second half arguing with referee Harry New. In the fifty-fourth minute, John Dempsey roamed upfield, and full back Badger headed his superb header off the goal line. Typically in a game like this, there was only one goal in it, a fifty-seventh minute effort from blonde Alan Birchenall winning Sheffield the game. He was a threat all afternoon, and in a rare break, Badger took a short corner and found Woodward. Earle failed to block his low cross, and Birchenall stooped low to slip in a fine header. This goal was in addition to the two he had scored to knock Fulham out of the FA Cup

A frustrated Dempsey appears to kick fresh air. It summed up a nightmare afternoon where little went right for Fulham. Bogey side Sheffield United slipped away with a 0–1 win at the Cottage.

in January. Fulham seemed to fold after that. The Fulham attack was at its most frustrating, with near misses, but too many snatched chances.

The nearest Fulham came to equalising, was a close-range 'goal' netted by Mark Pearson that was ruled out for offside. As the Fulham performance deteriorated, and United fell further back with an effective but stifling offside trap, twice the supporters broke out into bouts of slow handclapping, the first time this had been heard at the Cottage for almost a year. Fulham's fragile spirit ebbed slowly away, and many fans left long before the end. United should have then scored at least two further goals, but the match finished **0–1.** It was now three home league games without a goal and the fourth 'blank' in the opening five games. Apart from the back four and Robson, few of the other eleven would wish to be reminded of the second half performance. The press labelled the team's performance as 'unbelievably bad'.

Fulham were without the injured Johnny Haynes for the midweek trip to **Nottingham Forest.** Les Barrett took over the number nine shirt and Fred Callaghan was named as substitute. Even at this early stage of the season, Forest were a far better proposition than last year.

Fulham almost fell behind as early as the sixth minute, when Joe Baker beat Tony Macedo, but Stan Brown anticipated the shot, and running back hooked the ball off the line. Fulham did go a goal down in the twenty-third minute to Ian Storey-Moore, but Steve Earle was on splendid form, taking on the Forest defence almost single-handed. In the first half he hit a cracking cross-shot that beat keeper Grummitt, hit the far post and rebounded into play before being scrambled away.

Despite the close attention of three Nottingham Forest defenders at the City Ground, Steve Earle equalises for Fulham with a fine shot from the edge of the penalty area. An unlucky Fulham succumbed 1–2 to a last minute goal.

It took just six minutes of the second half for Fulham to equalise, when Earle, despite the close attention of three Forest defenders, scored with a shot from the edge of the box that streaked home. Earle experienced more bad luck later with another blaster that brought a desperate full length save from Grummitt. Just as it looked as if Fulham would snatch a point, Storey-Moore netted his second and Forest's winner in the very last minute. Fulham were still not finished, and the team were very unlucky when Forest keeper Peter Grummitt fingertipped a fine shot from Allan Clarke over the bar in the dying seconds. The media thought Fulham were desperately unlucky not to gain a point and conceded that they should have few problems with the season ahead. Fulham had suffered the usual problem of not being able to translate their superior football into goals and had been beaten **1–2.** Fulham's bad luck in the match continued when Brian Nichols was injured, and he had to be replaced by Fred Callaghan, Fulham's first substitution of the season.

Fulham prepared for their trip to the **West Bromwich Albion** with some optimism, as the Midlands side were two places below Fulham in the table. There was almost a hint of what was to come that afternoon from the pre-match preparations, which, compared with football today, appeared to be a complete farce. The injury to Brian Nichols at Nottingham had given a rare opportunity for Bobby Drake to deputise at full back. On the evening prior to the match, Drake became ill with stomach problems, and Fred Callaghan was immediately contacted on Saturday morning in order that he could rush to the team coach to play full back leaving Fulham with *no substitute*. Fortunately, the injured Johnny Haynes had travelled with the party, and had to be named as the emergency substitute! Haynes, kitted up, hobbled over to the bench. Fortunately he was not called upon to play, but it would have been interesting if he had been. The mix up certainly left the travelling Fulham fans perplexed as to why one of their best players was only substitute, until they learned of the full facts surrounding the incident. The reconstructed defence was a possible explanation for the ensuing dismal display.

There wasn't much evidence during the first half as to what was coming in the second half. There was not a great deal between the sides in an untidy first half, and the only goal of the half came in the twenty-seventh minute. Albion's Bobby Cram made a fine run from full back, and crossed. Tony Brown headed the ball down, and Albion winger Clive Clark converted the chance. Little was seen of the Fulham attack, except for a cracker of a shot from Les Barrett well turned aside by Baggies keeper Dick Sheppard. The only other two efforts of note for Fulham came from England back George Cohen, desperately trying to encourage the other forwards to shoot.

Fulham collapsed completely after the interval. Albion striker Jeff Astle added the second just seven minutes after half time, taking a pass from Clark and beating Macedo from close range. Fulham then experienced a disastrous spell, conceding three goals in just four minutes twenty minutes from the end. Firstly, Albion's Bobby Hope took Kaye's pass and his shot looped over Macedo, deflecting in off Stan Brown's shoulder. In the next minute, Albion's Clark surged past three static Fulham defenders, before rounding Macedo and scoring from close range. Finally the Fulham defence allowed Albion's Doug Fraser to steam through before laying on a gem of a pass for Bobby Hope to shoot the fifth.

Macedo was the busiest man on the field, and he made several other fine saves. In an amazing match, Albion also had three 'goals' ruled out, two of these falling to Astle. By this stage Fulham were very fortunate that Albion had not put ten or twelve into the net, halfbacks Bobby Robson and Stan Brown seemingly powerless against the powerful West Bromwich forwards.

With ten minutes to go Albion switched off, and the home defence, probably asleep through boredom, allowed Steve Earle to wriggle through to thump home a consolation. He cleverly ran onto a through ball, and blasted home an unstoppable shot ahead of the advancing keeper. The game finished **1–5**, and Fulham had again lost by a four-goal margin at the Hawthorns, just like the previous year.

After the display at Nottingham, the match had proven to be another Jekyll and Hyde performance. Fulham already seemed on a slippery slope with just three points from the opening seven games.

A brief respite from the league fixtures saw Fulham take on Second Division London rivals **Crystal Palace** in the League Cup midweek. The Palace side were doing well and were near the top of the division. The side included keeper John Jackson, Alan Stephenson, later to play on loan with Fulham, a young seventeen-year-old Steve Kember, and the experienced ex-Wolves centre forward Bobby Woodruff. Also, it was a quick return to the Cottage for Brian O'Connell freed by Fulham in the summer. Allan Clarke was rested from the side, which included Les Barrett in the unusual role of centre forward in the number ten shirt. The now fit Johnny Haynes took the number seven shirt. Jimmy Conway was named as substitute for the first time.

Palace defended bravely for long periods with Alan Stephenson outstanding, and in Kember, the south Londoners possessed the player most likely to make or score a goal. Fulham controlled most of the play, but again seemed reluctant to shoot when faced with a packed defence. Finally, Fulham were given a lucky break when Palace full back John Sewell attempted a back pass, the

In Clarke's absence, Graham Leggat scores Fulham's second goal from the penalty spot past John Jackson in their 2–0 League Cup success over Crystal Palace.

ball was intercepted by the alert Graham Leggat, and as keeper Jackson came out, Leggat guided the ball under him into the far corner. On seventy-five minutes the game was effectively sealed when Palace defender Jack Bannister handled a harmless Les Barrett cross, and in Clarke's absence Leggat made no mistake from the penalty spot. It would be the only game that season where Fulham were awarded a penalty (forty-eight matches!). At **2–0** Fulham progressed smoothly to the third round.

The Fulham programme notes had a rather depressing air as Fulham took on **Leeds United** at the Cottage that weekend. It could not be denied that the team were already just one place off the bottom with just three points. Leeds, in their blue and yellow away strip, were without centre forward Alan Peacock who was replaced by Rod Belfitt. They were lying mid-table in the league. Fulham's programme for the first time showed the team in 4–3–3 formation, which for the older supporters must have been confusing. Left back Fred Callaghan would wear the number five (centre half) shirt, centre midfield Johnny Haynes would wear the number seven (right wing) shirt, and centre forward Allan Clarke would wear the number ten (inside left) shirt. Perhaps the numbers confused Leeds United as well as the teams lined up!

Peter Lorimer gave Leeds United the lead in the twenty-second minute when he took a pass from Johnny Giles, and from the right wing hit a remarkable 'special' twenty-five-yard shot, which swooped and dipped over the arms of the despairing Tony Macedo, who seemed out of position. Fulham equalised when Leeds lost the ball in midfield to Mark Pearson, who fed Bobby Robson. Robson's pass found Allan Clarke lurking out on the right wing. He put in a perfect low centre that eluded Steve Earle and a Leeds defender, but Graham Leggat met the ball just ahead of Paul Reaney and slid the ball in with Leeds keeper Gary Sprake beaten.

Fulham had their best spell immediately after half time. Jack Charlton was having a poor game, looking a shadow of the player that had won the World Cup, and was consistently beaten on the ground by Earle, and in the air by Clarke. Fulham could have won the game during this period, when shots from Haynes, Leggat and Earle were blocked near goal or on the Leeds goal line, there being no one following up to touch the ball home.

Therefore it was a major surprise when Leeds took the lead again with twenty minutes left. The goal was a comedy of errors in the Fulham defence, with Macedo committing the final handling blunder. Bremner and Lorimer combined, and Lorimer put in an accurate uncontested cross that found Albert Johanneson unmarked just three yards out. Johanneson juggled and fussed with the ball, but Macedo failed to move decisively for it, finally diving the wrong way as Johanneson slotted in.

In a midfield tussle, the aggressive Clarke tries to get under the skin of the combative Bremner. Referee Tinkler already looks poised to blow! The match against stylish Leeds finished all square, 2–2.

The Leeds lead lasted for just five minutes and justice was done when Earle ran through the centre with the Leeds defence retreating. With the Leeds midfield expecting a pass, Earle instead unleashed a flashing shot from over thirty yards that deceived everyone, and gave Sprake in the Leeds goal no chance. Fulham, however, were fortunate in the final seconds when Macedo mishandled again and Stan Brown swept the ball away from the empty goalmouth, just before the Leeds forward Paul Madeley could reach it. The final result of **2–2** seemed a point lost, rather than one gained, despite the quality of the opposition.

The match was covered the next day by television's *Star Soccer*, and the pundits agreed that Fulham had been the better side overall and that the team had made enough chances up front to win—but at the end of the day, they hadn't. At least Fulham had scored at home in the league after three 'blank' fixtures. With Leeds driven on by the energetic, rugged and probing pocket-dynamo Billy Bremner, Fulham had struggled defensively again for most of the game, despite George Cohen's manful efforts.

At St James' Park the following week, Fulham were unchanged and playing in the attractive all red away strip. As last week Fulham looked the superior side with Steve Earle maintaining his excellent scoring run. Earle gave Fulham the lead against **Newcastle United** as early as the

Just two minutes in, and Leggat's pass splits open the Newcastle defence for Steve Earle to slot the ball in. Fulham failed to take other chances, and were held 1–1, conceding a late equaliser. Note St James' Park before stands were built!

second minute, when he was set up by Graham Leggat's long through pass, and scored with a low shot into the corner of the net from just inside the box. The Newcastle defence had frozen momentarily, appealing in vain for offside, but referee Peter Rhodes had waved play on. Fulham should have put away at least three more during the game, Leggat narrowly missing two chances created by George Cohen and Allan Clarke heading straight into Marshall's arms.

Fulham were also unlucky; Johnny Haynes put in a cracking drive, well blocked by Marshall, and Leggat netted on the hour only to be wrongly judged offside. Newcastle at last began to rally; Dave Hilley hit the Fulham bar, and Tony Macedo scooped Bryan Robson's effort from the rebound off the line. The Fulham defence were coping easily with the bunching Newcastle forwards, and the home crowd were now assisting Fulham by giving the home side 'the bird' for their poor attacking efforts. Fulham's own poor finishing eventually cost them a point, and the team let Newcastle off the hook when they allowed them to poach an unlikely equaliser inside the last ten minutes. The goal was netted by Peter Noble, playing his first game of the season: Newcastle's Alan Suddick moved out to the right, and lobbed a gentle centre into the middle where Noble headed in from ten yards.

The goal stirred Fulham from their indifference and the team tried to win the match. It looked like they had won the game following an amazing solo run from Allan Clarke, who beat three defenders and then the advancing keeper, only to see his shot hit the post, and bounce away. The **1–1** draw was the same as the result achieved four months previously on the same ground. Fulham had controlled nearly the entire game, but had still not been able to secure maximum points.

Vic Buckingham was frustrated with Fulham's recent performances and despite two good draws commented: 'I honestly feel unhappy with the last two results. It's pointless saying we are the better side, we have to prove it,' then rather obviously adding, 'by getting more goals than our opponents!' Whether or not this was a veiled kick up the pants aimed at centre forward Allan Clarke was unclear, but it *was* clear that the young Clarke was obviously struggling to get to grips with the pace and subtlety of the First Division, and that, to date, his seventeen league games had produced just two goals, both against Stoke City. Questions were being 'asked in the house'.

In some ways Buckingham's comment was unfair, as Clarke had been asked, on several occasions, to play a deep-lying and 'scheming' role behind Earle and Leggat/Barrett, or to replicate Johnny Haynes' role, when Buckingham had dropped the England man from the side. The fact was obviously weighing on Clarke's mind too. The young Black Country man was not finding it easy to fit in and settle into the West End of London, or the easygoing style at Craven Cottage.

October 1966

In this month

* The Government invoked a prices and wages freeze.
* The Jensen Interceptor was launched.
* The GPO announced that houses and businesses would have postcodes.
* Unemployment rose by 25% in one month.
* 130 people, mostly children at a school, were killed by a slagheap slip in Aberfan, Wales.
* The UK army dropped its 'colour bar'.
* Elizabeth Arden died.
* Spy George Blake escaped from Wormwood Scrubs by scaling the outer wall.
* A car strike closed all of the BMC factories.

'Distant Drums' by Jim Reeves topped the charts.

How the league was looking

Chelsea were the early pacesetters, with Stoke City holding a surprise second place. Tottenham were third, and Leicester City and Manchester United held fourth and fifth spots respectively. Just four points covered the top eleven clubs in the table, with champions Liverpool lying only eighth. Blackpool were rock bottom with just two draws from their opening nine matches. Arsenal and West Ham were mid table. Fulham held the other danger spot, but were only two points adrift of five other clubs.

The matches

THE FULHAM programme warned that the team couldn't miss chances against **Tottenham Hotspur** and reminded fans of the previous encounter at White Hart Lane in February which Spurs had won 4–3. It was unlikely that history would repeat itself—or could it? Fulham were again unchanged, and one ray of hope was that Cliff Jones, who had scored a hat trick in the previous encounter, was not in the Spurs starting line-up. Nevertheless, Tottenham arrived in third place, just one point behind the leaders, and playing some quality football. Spurs had added

An angry Mackay and Mullery argue about who should have been marking Steve Earle, after the forward had headed Fulham level against Tottenham. The Fulham team duly celebrate. Despite later taking the lead, the Cottagers finally went down 3–4.

Wales international centre half Mike England to their ranks from relegated Blackburn Rovers for a very large fee of £95,000, and also signed Terry Venables from London rivals Chelsea. The afternoon was beautiful and sunny following earlier rain, and 28,000 were in attendance.

From the first minute, the game on a wet pitch was a defensive nightmare for both managers, the press referring to a 'heavy glut of defensive mistakes'. Indeed it took Tottenham just two minutes to take the lead, when Alan Gilzean had time to chest down Venables' lofted pass, turn, and slide the ball gently past Tony Macedo. Fulham came back strongly and in the tenth minute were awarded a free kick for a mild looking foul by Mike England. Johnny Haynes put in a beautifully weighted cross, and Steve Earle headed in a magnificent goal from six yards; it was his fifth goal in five games. Just a minute later, Fulham were ahead when Allan Clarke received the ball from a miscued Spurs clearance from England, turned and hit a first timer from twenty yards that, despite two Spurs defenders closing in, went in off a post. The goal was an excellent strike, and it showed the trademark Clarke goal celebration for the first time, similar to that of Alan Shearer, with one arm raised in gladiatorial salute.

Fulham's euphoria was short lived as Scottish winger Jimmy Robertson put Spurs level from a free kick taken by Jimmy Greaves just two minutes later. Macedo managed to block Frank Saul's initial shot, but the ball fell to Robertson, who shot home through a ruck of Fulham defenders in a crowded penalty area. This made it four goals in the opening thirteen minutes, similar to the start at White Hart Lane in February. Some defensive sanity then prevailed, and the scoreline remained at two apiece until half time.

Both defences tightened up considerably in the second half, but Spurs began to up the tempo, and the ageing Fulham midfield in Haynes, Pearson and Robson began to tire in the sun with Spurs' Alan Mullery and Dave Mackay dominating in the midfield.

However, the game remained all-square until the last fifteen minutes. Finally, Macedo, remaining on his line, flapped at, and missed, a corner from Jimmy Greaves. England's ensuing effort was blocked by a wall of defenders and Mark Pearson attempted to scramble the ball away. Unfortunately for Fulham it fell kindly for Venables, who put Tottenham ahead with a cracking shot through a crowded goalmouth. Then, almost inevitably, the vigilant Jimmy Greaves darted through with a fourth three minutes later, slotting Gilzean's subtly flicked back header from Robertson's cross into the net via Fred Callaghan's boot.

There was still enough time for Fulham to poach another goal ten minutes from time, when Graham Leggat nodded in a bouncing ball from Pearson's corner with the Spurs defence motionless; this made it another glut of three goals in just six minutes. Finally Fulham's and Earle's luck ran out very late on when he got his head to Johnny Haynes' cross, but the ball flew just inches too high to deny Fulham the draw they had probably merited. In the end, Fulham's efforts just weren't enough; history *had* repeated itself and Spurs had again run out **3–4** winners.

Whilst Fulham's forwards Earle, Clarke and Leggat had each looked impressive, all of them scoring, the defence had experienced a poor day. Macedo had looked slow and at fault with at least two of the goals, possibly following the injury he received to his jaw; Stan Brown had looked edgy at the back, and Robson ponderous. Five of the seven goals had resulted from set pieces, a source of concern for both Buckingham and Bill Nicholson. The press agreed that the match had been a 'splendid spectacle', and that defeat was 'pretty rough justice' on Fulham. Sam Leitch described Fulham as 'luckless' and 'hoped their luck would change soon'.

This, however, cut little ice with Buckingham who replied tersely: 'Praise is no good, it's points that count.' Fulham were still one place off the bottom, had still not won at home in the league and surprisingly the match proved to be Leggat's last appearance in the first team for some time. The match was covered on television for *Star Soccer*, who were full of praise for Clarke's display— ex England player Billy Wright, co-commentating with Peter Lorenzo, saying: 'I bet Vic Buckingham's laughing his head off, he's got so much praise for this young man.'

Whilst Tottenham had hurt us on the pitch, Fulham appeared bizarrely to have upset the Spurs directors off the pitch. In the match programme, there was an 'advert' for a clinic directed at young people of the swinging Sixties 'living for kicks', making brave references to venereal disease and other sexually transmitted diseases, and including the slogan: 'If in doubt, find out.' The Spurs directors questioned why the advert had been included for the Spurs game, and asked whether there had been an inference directed towards the Spurs players and their supporters!

Fulham's reward for beating Crystal Palace in the previous round of the League Cup was another home tie, this time against **Wolverhampton Wanderers**. For the midweek game Fulham made changes; Tony Macedo was axed following his rusty display at the weekend and was replaced by Jack McClelland, Les Barrett replaced Graham Leggat, and there was a home debut for young Irishman Jimmy Conway in midfield, in place of Mark Pearson. Wolves were doing very well in the Second Division under new manager Ronnie Allen, and were re-building; the Midlanders were also unbeaten in nine matches. Ron Flowers had now gone, and had been replaced at right half, and captain, by the tenacious Mike Bailey, signed from Charlton Athletic. The side also included the experienced centre forward Hugh McIlmoyle, an FA Cup finalist, and the skilful young Peter Knowles, the brother of Cyril who had played for Tottenham at the Cottage just four days earlier.

On the night, though, Wolves were never in it. Fulham produced a glorious exhibition of attacking football from start to finish with devastating finishing. Steve Earle scored the first with a rasping volley from ten yards from a sweet Johnny Haynes pass, and Allan Clarke added a second just before half time, the result of an inch-perfect pass from Earle.

The highlight of the evening was still to come. On the hour, debutant Conway picked up the ball in the centre circle and ran fifty yards on a solo run, virtually unchallenged, before blasting the third. The shot was hit so hard that the Wolves keeper Fred Davies barely moved as the ball hit the stanchion at the back of the goal and rebounded into play as far as the edge of the penalty area; fortunately the referee awarded the goal. Earle then turned provider with another great sixty-yard solo run, beating three men before squaring to Clarke to slide in the fourth from six yards. The recalled Barrett then justified his place with the fifth goal, a rocket drive from the edge of the penalty area near the end of the game, which again keeper Davies never saw; Fulham had romped home with an impressive **5−0** scoreline.

The result was just the tonic that Buckingham had needed after the Saturday game, five goals and a clean sheet. The result remains, along with Northampton Town the previous season, Fulham's best ever win margin in the competition. The three forwards had looked classy throughout, feeding off the exact passes supplied by Johnny Haynes, and John Dempsey, improving with every game, had mopped up any rare Wolves breaks. The most positive aspect of the night, however, had been the skilful and hard working display from Jimmy Conway. Eire representatives were at the debut, and left impressed with what they had seen.

The display spurred Fulham on to obtain their best result of the season to date on the following Saturday. Anfield was an unlucky ground for Fulham, but hopes were high and Buckingham named an unchanged side, giving Conway his league debut. The champions **Liverpool** were not at their best and were currently lying seventh, but ominously only three points behind the leading club.

Fulham produced another skilful and tenacious display to secure a draw. They did, however, make the worst possible start, going a goal behind in the first forty-five seconds when Bobby Robson needlessly conceded a corner in Liverpool's first attack. From the flag kick supplied by Peter Thompson, Geoff Strong headed in. Fulham then hit back purposefully, and the match was all about Allan Clarke. Like the previous encounter between the two teams in February, Fulham's first goal caused controversy. In the sixteenth minute, Fred Callaghan put across an accurate centre, and Clarke forcefully challenged Liverpool keeper Tommy Lawrence for the ball in the air, some three or four yards from goal. In the wet and slippery conditions, Lawrence dropped the ball and fell, leaving Clarke to bang the ball into an empty net from a couple of yards, despite the best efforts of Liverpool centre half Ron Yeats on the line to keep the ball out. Liverpool furiously claimed that Clarke had impeded Lawrence in the jump, but referee Harper gave the goal, leading to a chorus of booing for both Clarke and the referee.

However, there was no disputing his second goal just six minutes later, described as stunning. A local reporter claimed the goal had been 'the best *ever seen* by a visiting team at Anfield' and

Drama at Anfield. Left: bottoms up! Liverpool goalkeeper Lawrence sprawls ungainly on the ground, after a hefty 'challenge' from Allan Clarke. Clarke scores despite the efforts of Yeats. The controversial goal was Fulham's first in a creditable 2–2 draw. Right: got it! Goalkeeper McClelland acknowledges his save late in the game. World Cup winner Roger Hunt can't believe that the ball has stayed out. Haynes shows his delight whilst Callaghan and league debutant Conway reveal the anxiety of the moment.

was epitomised as 'sheer grace'. Haynes started the move with a perfect pass out to the wing to Clarke, who cut inside, skilfully beat full back Chris Lawler, Ron Yeats, then Geoff Strong and finally Tommy Smith, before drawing Lawrence from his goal and rolling the ball arrogantly past him; even the diehard Liverpool supporters applauded the strike. Clarke's fortunes had now changed dramatically with five goals in a week.

Fulham held their lead, and the disjointed Liverpool defence were struggling with Johnny Haynes' through passes. Jack McClelland, relishing his recall, showed remarkably quick reactions, and made many spectacular saves. He couldn't have been faulted for the Liverpool equaliser when, ten minutes before half time, Ian St John scored with a fierce drive following a Geoff Strong corner, which Clarke had failed to clear.

The second half was certainly less hectic, and to be fair Liverpool dominated with numerous counter-attacks, but Fulham had their tails up, and fought hard to hold on for the draw. Johnny Haynes still managed to set up opportunities, and Fulham moved the ball about well, as opposed to the Liverpool plan of individual possession. Fulham earned themselves one slice of luck seven minutes from time, when Hunt's shot was deflected off Haynes' boot, but luckily the ball flew straight into the arms of McClelland. The exciting match finished at **2–2**.

Clarke's efforts did not go unnoticed, and the following day's papers gave Clarke rave notices for his all round display. The improved display may have been as a result of swapping the duties of Stan Brown and Bobby Robson. Stan Brown had requested a more attacking role, whilst Robson, now thirty-three, thought that he was now better suited with his experience to a defensive half back role.

The classy display by Clarke gave rise to a call up to the England Under-23 squad as a late replacement for Chelsea's broken leg victim Peter Osgood. Clarke made the team against Wales Under-23s and celebrated in some style, scoring four goals, including two penalties, as the England side romped to an 8–0 rout. Although it wasn't the strongest opposition, it was still a memorable achievement. A delighted Buckingham commented: 'It has been a marvellous week for him.'

Fulham had also made progress in the London Challenge Cup for a change, defeating the now defunct amateur side Leytonstone in the first round. Fulham put out a strong side with eight players with first team experience, including Tony Macedo, Brian Nichols, Terry Dyson, Mark Pearson and Graham Leggat. Fulham cruised to a 5–1 lead at one stage, before surviving a late onslaught to emerge 5–3 winners. The goals came from Ryan (2), Leggat, Dyson and O'Connor.

Fulham faced **West Ham** next at the Cottage, for a second consecutive London derby. By coincidence, the match occurred at much the same time of the season as the previous year. The match featured four World Cup winners on the pitch at once. The worrying fact was that Fulham had yet to secure a home win this season, but they were not alone—West Ham were also without their first home win! The Hammers' form, however, was impressive, having lost just one out of their last eight matches, including four unbeaten away. The Hammers lay a mediocre fourteenth in the league, but four points ahead of Fulham. A goal feast was expected, as West Ham's opening eleven league fixtures had already produced forty-five goals!—World Cup final hero Geoff Hurst already had nine to his name. Apart from the absence of Hammers veteran centre half Ken Brown, both sides were at full strength.

Fulham had an early scare when Jack McClelland held a firm shot from John Sissons, but the team were soon into their stride and took the lead in the tenth minute. Allan Clarke's cross-field ball found Johnny Haynes on the left, who chased and pulled the ball back, and from his tempting low centre Steve Earle casually sidefooted the ball wide of Jim Standen in the Hammers goal. Fulham became a little slack after that, and allowed West Ham a classy nineteenth minute equaliser. Bobby Moore found Hurst running down the right wing, the Fulham defence missed the centre, allowing Johnny Byrne, who had progressed alongside Hurst through the middle, to drive first time past McClelland.

After this, the Fulham defence had some anxious moments as West Ham tried to dominate, Fulham's only reply being a Les Barrett header just wide. But two minutes before half time, Fulham were handed another gift goal, and, exactly like last year, it was another own goal! Haynes' snatched shot looked to be going wide, until Hammers full back Dennis Burnett, running back, stuck out a leg, and turned the ball tidily into his own net.

Fulham wasted no time in getting to grips with the game in the second half either. On fifty-three minutes the effervescent Earle put in a stinging shot that Hammers goalkeeper Standen couldn't hold and Clarke calmly tucked in the rebound. Fulham were unlucky not to go further ahead when the lively Barrett hit a post. The Hammers defence was now looking distinctly nervy, and Bobby Moore was having to do the work of two men to keep the score down. With Byrne pulling the strings, West Ham tried to get back in the game and it looked like they had when Byrne, instead of shooting, played in Hurst to net, only for the Hammers striker to be given offside by the referee.

Whilst West Ham argued the validity of the decision, Fulham took the free kick quickly and broke to the other end of the pitch to seal the game. The persistent Earle turned provider with a great run and the ever-dangerous Clarke sidefooted in his long centre at the far post. It was Clarke's eleventh goal in five games (Fulham and England-Under 23), and he delivered an all round match-winning performance.

Allan Clarke, arm raised in gladiatorial salute, celebrates Fulham's third goal against West Ham; goalkeeper Standen failed to hold Earle's powerful shot and Clarke prodded the rebound into the open goal.

As usual there were plenty of goals in the fixture and nine minutes from the end, Martin Peters' centre set up Hurst for a consolation goal that made the scoreline more respectable. Hurst and Peters had worked hard to keep the Hammers in the game, but overall the east Londoners' general play had been disappointing and they had been outclassed, Robson and Haynes had dominated the midfield, and the game finished **4–2**.

The match was shown on *Star Soccer* the following day and many positive comments came out of Fulham's display, especially the form of Earle, Clarke and Barrett, who were beginning to look capable of giving any defence in the First Division a hard time. Conway had settled immediately into midfield, and Fulham had scored fourteen goals in four games. The move up the table had been a big fillip for the club.

The winning streak continued in the London Challenge Cup as well, with Fulham surprisingly beating a strong Spurs side 4–0. The Tottenham second string were regarded as the best around at the time, and were top of the Combination division. To be fair, Fulham put out another strong side with plenty of first team experience. The Fulham goals came from Leggat, Parmenter, Ryan and young Henry Hill.

Fulham travelled to Hillsborough the following week to meet Vic Buckingham's old club **Sheffield Wednesday**. George Cohen was absent on international duty, giving a start to Bobby Drake, and Jimmy Conway's meteoric rise had meant an early call up to the Eire team. Conway was to make his debut against Spain in the European Championships. All of a sudden, the city of Dublin was becoming *very* interested in Fulham FC! Vic Buckingham restored Graham Leggat to play an unlikely midfield role in the number six shirt.

Both of the game's goals came in the first half. Jim McCalliog put Sheffield Wednesday ahead in the eighth minute: Colin Symm centred, Quinn put in a firm header across the box, and McCalliog dived on his chest to steer the ball in off a post. Fulham however were level just seventeen minutes later. The goal was down to Les Barrett, who set off on a mazy run down the left hand side following Clarke's astute flick on, which culminated in him drawing out the Wednesday keeper. He then unselfishly squared the ball to Johnny Haynes, who hammered it left footed through a crowded penalty area into the net from eighteen yards. Fulham moved from strength to strength, and took control of the game. Allan Clarke, with a new found confidence, was not only taking chances, but also creating others with his stylish footwork and nonchalant first time passes.

The only downside to the accomplished performance was an injury to Man of the Match Haynes ten minutes from time, which caused him to leave the field and be substituted by Mark Pearson

Johnny Haynes finishes off Les Barrett's fine run and cross with a trademark 'rocket' from the edge of the area. The strike earned Fulham a deserved 1–1 draw. Note Graham Leggat wearing an unfamiliar half-back's shirt (no. 6).

playing against his former club. Wednesday upped their game in the last quarter of an hour and peppered the Fulham goal with shots in a somewhat frantic attempt to win the game. McCalliog twice went close, and a good save was required by Jack McClelland to keep out his second effort. In terms of possession, physical effort and territorial advantage, Wednesday probably deserved both points, but a defensively minded Fulham, faced with uncertain Wednesday finishing, held on fairly comfortably to secure a **1—1** draw. Although the team hadn't produced a great deal up front, it proved to be another tenacious performance by Fulham to secure the point, and meant that it was now only one defeat in the last eight games.

With the injuries piling up, now was not a good time to face **Blackpool** at Bloomfield Road in the fourth round of the League Cup. Although Blackpool were struggling in the league, the Tangerines had improved dramatically over recent weeks, scoring six goals against Newcastle United. The Lancashire side had also knocked high-flying Chelsea out of the League Cup after a replay in the previous round, and were confident going into the game. Fulham entered into the match missing Jimmy Conway and Johnny Haynes in midfield and Steve Earle up front, their replacements being Brian Nichols, Mark Pearson and Terry Parmenter. George Cohen returned but Graham Leggat was omitted. It proved to be a very lively game, full of attacking football.

Confident Blackpool had been close twice before Parmenter gave Fulham a surprise lead in the twentieth minute. The lead lasted precisely thirty seconds, when Blackpool's Ian Moir skipped through the Fulham defence to equalise. Before Fulham had recovered, the team were a goal behind to Blackpool's Ray Charnley. This goal meant that three goals had been scored in a four-minute spell. Still Fulham could not hold on, and at the interval were two behind, Blackpool's Jimmy Robson converting close to half time.

The second half continued in the same vein, with Blackpool launching several sorties on the Fulham goal, and there was much desperate Fulham defending. It was a second half of exhilarating pace and non-stop entertainment. A quarter of an hour before the end, Blackpool's Charnley scored his second and Blackpool's fourth to seal the tie. Fulham's sole response was a close-range goal from Fred Callaghan six minutes from the end that had a strong hint of offside about it. The only positive note was that the goal was Callaghan's first for the club. Fulham could have had few complaints, and were eliminated from the competition **2—4**.

At least the result would go down as an excellent Blackpool performance rather than a poor Fulham performance. The match was officiated by a gentleman with an appropriate name for a referee—Maurice Fussey! Graham Leggat, losing patience with the in/out role he was being given, formally requested a transfer after the game.

In the final match in October, Fulham faced **Chelsea** at the Cottage, a third consecutive London derby. Chelsea were playing very well at the time, and were second in the league, just a point behind leaders Stoke City. Their team was packed with young talent, the oldest player being just twenty-six! Fulham were without the injured Jimmy Conway, hurt on his international debut, Johnny Haynes and the omitted Graham Leggat.

The omens were made worse inasmuch as Chelsea were parading their latest big money signing Tony Hateley, signed from Aston Villa for a fee of £100,000. Hateley always seemed to do well against Fulham. Hateley had been signed to supplement the squad following the broken leg sustained by starlet Peter Osgood in the previous round's League Cup tie at Blackpool. A massive 43,000 crowd paying record receipts packed in to see the match, and the atmosphere was electric.

Still, in the first twenty minutes Fulham took the game to Chelsea, and were the better side. The foraging Fred Callaghan, the elegant Bobby Robson and quicksilver Barrett keeping the Chelsea defence at full stretch. Speedy Chelsea full back Eddie McCreadie just about cleared Steve Earle's shot from the line, and Allan Clarke headed onto the Chelsea bar. Although Chelsea were superior technically, Fulham's hard working approach was knocking them out of their stride. The Fulham defence looked very firm, but the team failed to capitalise on the chances that they had created during this purple patch. Fulham were then hit by two hammer blows either side of half time.

In front of a massive 43,000 crowd, Chelsea's Hateley volleys his side in front, past Robson, Cohen and a groggy McClelland, following a highly disputed bounce up in the Fulham area. In an even contest, the Pensioners were fortunate to record a 1–3 win.

The first Chelsea goal, five minutes before half time, was loaded with bitter controversy. Hateley was beaten to a high ball by goalkeeper Jack McClelland, and in the course of the challenge, Hateley appeared to elbow the Fulham custodian in the face and he crashed to the ground, hitting his head hard on the turf—it was obvious that the keeper required immediate treatment. George Cohen complained, 'He was gone,' and added: 'I was yelling at him to release the ball, so I could kick it into touch, but he was gone.'

Typical aggression from Allan Clarke on Chelsea's Peter Bonetti, ably supported by Fred Callaghan—but where's the ball?

McClelland was obviously dazed and confused, but incredibly the referee ordered only a bounce up in the Fulham six-yard area, and from the resulting melee the ball ran loose to Hateley, who promptly volleyed in left footed past Cohen and Bobby Robson and the partially unsighted McClelland. The remaining five minutes of the half were played out in a cacophony of booing from the enraged Fulham supporters.

Early in the second half, and before Fulham could really recover, Chelsea doubled their lead. John Hollins floated in a free kick, John Dempsey made no aerial challenge and McClelland (probably still groggy) stayed rooted to his line, leaving Hateley to steal in like a bulldozer, rise superbly and plant a trademark bullet header into the goal from six yards. It was as good a goal as you could wish to see, a headed goal in the class of Tommy Lawton.

Les Barrett pulled a goal back for Fulham twenty minutes from time, following good approach work. A deflected header bounced out of the box, and Barrett sent in a spanking half volley that even the agile keeper Peter Bonetti hardly saw. In the last ten minutes, with Fulham pressing for the equaliser, Chelsea began to exploit the gaps at the back. The underrated Johnny Boyle started and finished a move that involved Charlie Cooke and Tommy Baldwin that put the game beyond doubt. He brushed past three tired defenders to sweep the ball into the net.

In the absence of midfield partners Haynes and Conway, Stan Brown had put in an exceptional ninety minutes, covering and tackling, and looked totally shattered at the end of the match; Mark Pearson, however, was never an adequate replacement. Les Barrett had also been a constant threat, but Allan Clarke, recently so lethal, had a 'bad day at the office'. Hateley had been ably supported by Tommy Baldwin and had again proved to be a real thorn in Fulham's side. The media agreed it had been an excellent game, and much tighter than the final **1–3** scoreline had suggested, reporting that Fulham had 'deserved a better result'.

During this period, television, trying to capitalise on the popularity of football, put out a show called *Quiz Ball*. Fulham entered, as did a number of other First Division sides; Scottish sides were also represented. The objective was to score 'goals' for your team by answering questions. The team had to accumulate four points to be awarded a goal. The team could try one very difficult question that would score all four points (route one football!), or the team could choose any combination of questions of one, two or three points to 'pass' their way upfield and try to accumulate the necessary four points. An incorrect answer meant surrendering 'possession' to the opposition.

Fulham did very well in the early stages. Fulham's initial team comprising chairman Tommy Trinder, manager Vic Buckingham, and players Johnny Haynes and George Cohen 'beat' Sunderland 4–0 in the first round. Fulham were subsequently edged out 4–3 by Arsenal in the next round. DJ Pete Murray guested for Fulham in place of Trinder in this encounter.

November 1966

In this month

* Ronald Reagan was elected Governor of California.
* James Lovell and Buzz Aldrin splashed down after orbiting five days in *Gemini 12*.
* Spy George Blake emerged in communist East Berlin.
* Unemployment rose by a further 20% in one month.
* J. Edgar Hoover announced that Lee Harvey Oswald acted alone in killing President JF Kennedy.

'Good Vibrations' by The Beach Boys topped the charts.

How the league was looking

Chelsea and Stoke City continued to set the pace. Everton had now roared up to third on the back of a fine run. Manchester United and Leicester City were still holding fourth and fifth respectively. Spurs had dropped to sixth position. Liverpool were making little impression at eighth, and last season's third-placed team Burnley were just seventh. Four points covered the top nine clubs. Arsenal were just sixteenth, only three points off the relegation places. Blackpool were still bottom, but had started to make a little recovery, Fulham still held the other black spot. Three clubs, Newcastle, Manchester City and West Bromwich Albion, had just two more points than Fulham.

The matches

THE FIRST match of November was appropriately on the fifth, and the encounter certainly brought its share of 'fireworks'. Fulham took the short journey to Upton Park having confidently beaten **West Ham** in their last three encounters, scoring ten goals in the process. Fulham were back to full strength, and it had the prospect of a good contest as West Ham were also on very good form.

West Ham started like demons, swarming all over Fulham, and forcing six corners in the opening ten minutes. The Irons should have scored two goals inside the first minute. Jack McClelland then saved shots from John Sissons and Johnny Byrne, both with an outstretched foot.

Against the run of play, however, it was Fulham who took a surprise lead on the half hour. Bobby Moore fouled Stan Brown, and Johnny Haynes tapped a free kick sideways. Jimmy Conway sold the 'dummy' by jumping over the ball, and this set up Fred Callaghan, who blasted in through a gap in the West Ham wall from twenty-five yards, straight into the corner of the net. However, the Hammers replied immediately, and levelled just thirty seconds later. Byrne put winger Sissons away, and from his hard running and cross, Geoff Hurst turned in the leveller. Somehow Fulham managed to hold on to that position until half time.

The second half proved to be a total disaster for Fulham and the team collapsed as West Ham ran riot, scoring *five* goals without reply. West Ham, throwing caution to the wind, pushed Eddie Bovington up front as an extra forward. Soon Peter Brabrook and Sissons were terrorising Fulham on the flanks, and the experienced Byrne was giving John Dempsey a real roasting in the centre. The avalanche started just after the hour, when the unsighted Jack McClelland failed to hold Sissons low centre, allowing Martin Peters time to thump in an easy goal. Then Byrne, playing with England class, weaved his magic, twice leaving Dempsey stranded in the middle and setting up Hurst for his second and hat trick goals.

For the first, Byrne cleverly held up a long goal kick. As the Hammers forward was tackled by Dempsey he fell, but slipped a perfect pass through for the ubiquitous Hurst to race onto and score. Before Fulham could recover, West Ham scored again just three minutes later. This time Byrne nodded the ball through perfectly for Hurst to repeat the exact same run and shot manoeuvre. Then the danger started to come from the other flank, and with ten minutes left, Brabrook mesmerised Callaghan, and from his pinpoint centre, Peters picked his spot for the fifth with a perfectly placed header; this made it four West Ham goals in eighteen minutes.

Fulham were now being dazzled and hopelessly outclassed. McClelland brilliantly turned over another Hurst piledriver, and the killer instinct of Hurst brought his fourth and Hammers sixth, three minutes from the end. Eddie Bovington put in an accurate centre, and Hurst just beat McClelland to the ball by a fraction. In truth, there should even have been a seventh goal, Hurst missing possibly the easiest chance of the afternoon in the final seconds. World Cup star Geoff Hurst had been at his predatory best, controlling the ball well, taking up scoring positions with uncanny skill and scoring four of the goals, whilst his World Cup colleague Martin Peters had been excellent in scoring the other two.

The Hammers manager Ron Greenwood, however, complimented Johnny Byrne as the main threat, saying that he and Hurst together were like 'bacon and eggs'; certainly it had been a 'sizzling' performance from the pair. The media called the Hammers' performance 'poetry in motion'. Fulham had been truly walloped, losing **1−6**.

Even allowing for the dazzling form that West Ham were on, it was an alarming Fulham performance, with the West Ham strikers, Hurst in particular, given far too much room. No one could remember the last time Fulham had conceded five goals in a half, and it hardly seemed possible that Fulham had been beaten by that margin by a team that they had so comprehensively outclassed at the Cottage just three weeks previously.

On the following Monday, however, West Ham proved just how good a side they were, by demolishing a polished Leeds United side 7−0 in the next round of the League Cup, and then putting four past Spurs at White Hart Lane the following Saturday. This was turning out to be a topsy-turvy season for all the clubs in the First Division at the time, full of crazy results and wildly swinging form. Don Revie, the Leeds manager, summed the situation up by saying: 'Anybody can beat anybody, there seem to be no bad sides left in the First Division.' Despite those words, the unpalatable truth for Fulham was that the team were still in one of the two relegation places.

Fulham were, however, still making progress in the London Challenge Cup, and in the semi-final faced Leyton Orient from the Second Division of the Football Combination. In an away game, Fulham threw away a two-goal lead, and were pegged back to 2−2, forcing a replay; Mike Pentecost and John Ryan were the Fulham scorers.

Fulham's chance to redeem themselves began the following week with the visit of **Aston Villa**. Villa arrived at Fulham in seventeenth position, and Tony Hateley was still their leading scorer despite the fact he had been a Chelsea player for almost a month. Villa had brought back ex England and Wolves player Peter Broadbent from the lower divisions (Shrewsbury) to add some craft and experience to the centre of the field. Villa's lack of attacking ambition was identified when the Midlanders lined up with full back Charlie Aitken occupying the inside left position. In the team as Hateley's replacement was reserve local lad Lew Chatterley.

This was surely a chance for Fulham to get back to winning ways. It was uncertain whether McClelland had played that badly at West Ham, but he was again dropped giving Tony Macedo another chance in goal. Stan Brown was relegated to substitute, and Steve Earle was also still not fully fit; Mark Pearson and Terry Parmenter deputised. The first half was a dismal dour affair, with little to report, both sides seemingly reluctant to break out of defence, and neither team gave any indication as to what was to follow.

The encounter exploded into life early in the second half. Mark Pearson, having a good game with plenty of pace, scored the first—his first of the season—with a close in shot. Johnny Haynes bamboozled the Villa defence and pulled them out of position, then stabbed a cross over to Les Barrett, whose quick, return cross was netted by Pearson.

The second goal just a minute later, and Allan Clarke's first, was ranked as one of the best seen at the Cottage for a very long time. Haynes again provided the waist high pass, and Clarke won possession. He hooked the ball over his shoulder, and turned whilst appearing to perform a juggling act with the ball, mesmerising defenders. He finally crashed the ball powerfully home

From Les Barrett's superb run and cross, Allan Clarke scores his second and Fulham's third against Aston Villa. Fulham scored five second-half goals to trounce Villa 5–1. Note the halftime scores glowing brightly in the November gloom.

on the volley past the bewildered Colin Withers in the Villa goal, a truly superb individual effort.

Fulham then became a little careless, allowing Mike Tindall time to run in and chip John MacLeod's free kick over Macedo to pull a goal back. Any hopes Villa entertained of a revival were brushed aside just ten minutes later, when Clarke scored the third after a beautiful run and left wing cross from Les Barrett. The cross beat Villa keeper Colin Withers comprehensively, leaving Clarke to nod powerfully into an empty net. Clarke was then unfortunate not to complete a second half hat trick minutes later, but his headed effort struck a post.

Clarke's second had made it four goals within a fifteen-minute spell. A further ten minutes passed and another Fulham goal arrived. Jimmy Conway scored his first ever league goal when he crashed the ball through a forest of legs from twenty-five yards, and the ball was finally deflected in. Ten minutes later it was Terry Parmenter's turn, and he shot the fifth after the Villa defence had failed to clear a headed effort from the goalmouth. The goal was Parmenter's first ever league goal. Fulham, in the end, strolled out easy winners by a **5–1** margin.

In an excellent all-round performance, Macedo had been secure, with George Cohen dominating at the back. John Dempsey had also impressed snuffing out the remote Villa attacks, springing mainly from MacLeod. Conway was again impressive in midfield, and Clarke had caused havoc in the visitors' defence all afternoon. Only goalkeeper Withers and half backs Tindall and Deakin had stood out, all working overtime saving their team from a far worse savaging.

Having conceded five goals in the second half the previous week, Fulham had promptly *scored* five goals in the second half this week, and the statistic summed up the inconsistent season so far. Nevertheless, the match produced two badly needed points. The match had been officiated by the beautifully named Rex Spittle from Great Yarmouth. The Villa fans were sure that their manager would have been 'spitting mad' with the performance of his side.

The match was doubly important, as it commemorated Fulham's 2,000th League game, and their 1,000th home game; the first-ever home match was against Hull City on 3rd September 1907. The club received a congratulatory letter from the League Secretary, Alan Hardaker. The summary of Fulham's 2,000 matches was as follows:

Played 2,000   Won 773   Drawn 461   Lost 766   Points 2,007

So things had pretty much evened themselves out over sixty years, with Fulham winning just seven more than they had lost over that sixty-year period. Ironically, the statistics pointed out the names of sixteen league clubs who had 'yet to visit Fulham FC' (because they were a great deal further down the league). It could not have been contemplated on this particular day that within two-and-a-half years, *eight* of those clubs mentioned *would* visit Craven Cottage on a league basis in vastly different circumstances.

A week later, Fulham visited Highbury and **Arsenal** in an attempt to break the hoodoo at that ground, having taken just one point there from thirteen visits. Johnny Haynes was out injured, but apart from that it was Fulham at reasonably full strength. Arsenal had not scored in three consecutive league games.

A remarkable first half sequence saw Fulham denied a goal three times in a matter of seconds. This was thanks to a brilliant triple save from Arsenal keeper Jim Furnell. Allan Clarke put Les Barrett clean through the middle; Furnell rushed from his goal to firstly beat out Les Barrett's shot, then, as the ball bounced up, he somehow pushed out Barrett's follow-up header. The ball fell finally to Jimmy Conway, and his second follow-up hammer drive was foiled by a superb full length save. Fulham too had an escape when Colin Addison's whiplash header hit the bar. The first half had been very even, but like the week before, pretty uninspiring. The triple miss, one stinging Clarke effort well tipped over by Furnell, and a weak shot from Conway were the sum total of Fulham's attacking endeavours.

As in the previous year, Fulham were unlucky and were beaten by a second half goal, a twenty-five-yard curved strike from Arsenal captain Frank McLintock in the sixty-fifth minute. The effort was a real right foot rocket that was in the top corner of the net before Tony Macedo really saw it. In the second half, and alien to their normal attacking nature, Fulham switched to a 4−4−2 formation, and tried to play for the draw.

Allan Clarke, possibly playing under orders due to the absence of Haynes, was withdrawn into the midfield, and a lot of Fulham's chances disappeared with him. Stan Brown, Steve Earle and Conway worked like Trojans in a congested midfield, but their tenacity had little effect up front, as Ian Ure, Peter Storey and Terry Neill were in fine form at the back. Arsenal continued to make and waste a number of clear chances, with Addison and George Graham, recently signed from Chelsea, the principal culprits. In one attack, George Cohen cleared a Gordon Neilson effort off the line. Even so, Fulham were unlucky not to steal a goal and to draw this uninspiring game.

Macedo was in brilliant handling form at the back, coping with anything thrown at him and giving the defence a great deal of confidence. In truth, it was just an 'unlucky day at the office', and the final scoreline of **0−1** didn't do the performance justice.

Fulham did however make the London Challenge Cup Final, comprehensively beating Leyton Orient 5−1 in the semi-final replay. Fulham included Steve Earle in the attack, whilst recovering from injury, and he responded with a brace; there were also two goals for Terry Dyson, and one for young Jimmy Dunkley. Earle had a hand in all five Fulham goals, and one set up for Dyson was rated one of the best seen at the Cottage for a long while. This put Fulham on track to win the trophy for the first time since the 1951−52 season!

In the final week of November, Fulham entertained **Manchester City** at the Cottage; it was their first season back in the top flight. Fulham were back to full strength, as were City except for the absence of half back Alan Oakes. In the Manchester City line-up that day was Stan Horne who would join Fulham in just over a year's time. City were finding life tough back in the First Division, and were just three places above Fulham. It was a damp, foggy afternoon, making the bumpy pitch very greasy.

In the first half hour, however, City belied their league position to a degree, playing like a side nearer the top of the table, and it was only the brilliance of Tony Macedo in the Fulham goal denying Mike Summerbee and Neil Young that prevented City going in with a two goal half time lead. Then, in the final seconds of the first half, full back George Cohen showed how it should be done, scoring his first goal for the club for over two years.

A Fulham move was going nowhere, and Johnny Haynes, denied an opening, passed to Jimmy Conway. Conway similarly frustrated passed the ball sideways again to Cohen, sneaking upfield down the right wing. Cohen slashed at the ball, and his long-range ground shot from over thirty

Steve Earle eludes a sliding tackle from Manchester City centre half Heslop to send over a cross which Allan Clarke converts with his head. Three late goals enabled Fulham to finish comfortable 4–1 winners.

yards skidded along the greasy turf and into the net, just inside a post with City goalkeeper Harry Dowd sprawling. The ball crept in through the hands and under the body of the surprised goalkeeper. Dowd should have stopped the shot, but the soft goal gave Fulham the opening they badly wanted. Sadly, the goal would prove to be George's last goal for the club. The 'joke' goal was the only highlight in another dreary and scrappy first half performance.

As in the Aston Villa game a fortnight previously, Fulham were a different side in the second half, but it took a City equaliser six minutes after half time to really rouse them. Young caught the Fulham defence on the hop, and scored with a cracking left foot shot from twenty-five yards, after a Johnny Crossan free kick had bounced back to him from Fulham's defensive wall. Finally, in the last half hour, the Fulham forwards began to click, finding holes in a shaky City defence, with keeper Dowd particularly uncertain.

City began to resort to unnecessary fouls and lost their composure. Allan Clarke, following an anonymous first half, scored the second goal to restore Fulham's lead in the seventy-second minute. Conway's astute pass gave Steve Earle the opportunity to launch an impressive run down the left. Earle beat most of the City defence, dodged George Heslop's last-ditch tackle, and delivered a pinpoint cross that enabled Clarke to soar and head in.

Fulham's third was just as impressive with a flowing move which started from keeper Tony Macedo, and flowed through the midfield to Haynes. The midfielder found Les Barrett on the left wing, and the unmarked Clarke hammered Barrett's accurately placed cross superbly past Dowd. Johnny Haynes, back from injury, completed the scoring with another long-range shot from over thirty yards that whistled in past the despairing Dowd's hands with virtually the last kick of the match. This meant Fulham had scored three goals in an eighteen-minute spell.

Clarke had continued to excel up front, feeding on the supply from Haynes, Earle and Barrett, and Macedo looked to have shaken off his early season rustiness. City, to be fair, did not play that badly, and the **4–1** scoreline certainly flattered Fulham to a degree, but the home side had definitely been worthy of the points. The press were aware that Craven Cottage was now a place that few teams would relish visiting that season, and talked of 'a new militancy'. Allan Clarke's progress was such that he had now been drafted into Alf Ramsey's full England twenty-two for the England v Wales game after winger John Connelly withdrew from the squad.

On the final day of the month Fulham competed in the final of the London Challenge Cup, facing Brentford who were, like Leyton Orient, in the Second Division of the football combination. The Cup final had to be a great opportunity for the club to add some silverware to the bare cupboard. The side that Fulham put out was less experienced than in previous rounds, especially up front, and Fulham just about escaped with a goal-less draw!

December 1966

In this month

* Walt Disney died.
* Rhodesia left the British Commonwealth.

'The Green, Green Grass Of Home' by Tom Jones topped the charts.

How the league was looking

Manchester United's fine form had seen them take top spot, with Chelsea dropping to second. Champions Liverpool were at last finding their form, shooting up to third. Stoke City, now feeling the pace, had dropped down to sixth. Everton's surge had faltered badly, and they had dropped back to seventh. Spurs were dropping to mid-table alongside West Ham. Blackpool were still bottom, three points adrift of Newcastle occupying the other relegation berth. Fulham had moved away, up to eighteenth. Above bottom placed Blackpool, just four points covered the next *ten* teams.

The matches

THE MANCHESTER City win lifted Fulham's confidence further and the team travelled back to Bloomfield Road to meet **Blackpool** again, just five weeks after going out of the League Cup there. Fulham were at full strength, as were Blackpool. Blackpool were now at the bottom of the table with just ten points from eighteen league games. They were, however, still on pretty good form, having beaten Everton at Goodison Park the previous week. Just 13,000 spectators watched the match.

The match produced a dull, cheerless performance from both sides, both teams affected by tricky, windy conditions. Fulham still couldn't really 'click' away from home, and for both sets of forwards it was an untidy match full of missed chances, most spooned high over the bar, again described by the press as 'rugby shooting'. Blackpool really controlled the game, put in a great deal of effort, but just couldn't put the ball in the net. Blackpool missed three chances in the first fifteen minutes, Leslie Lea, when put clean through, Jimmy Robson and Ray Charnley all missing presentable opportunities. Fulham were once again indebted to the on-form Tony Macedo. His cat-like agility and uncanny anticipation depressed the Blackpool forwards as the game progressed,

Steve Earle is foiled this time by a timely tackle from Blackpool's Emlyn Hughes, later to sign for Liverpool. Earle had the last laugh, however, scoring the only goal in Fulham's 1–0 win at Bloomfield Road.

not providing a single chance. One tip-over save from a long-range shot from Jimmy Robson in the first half was straight out of the top drawer.

Fulham were being bruised and battered in defence, caused by Blackpool's all out assault tactics, and Charnley was again unlucky when John Dempsey kicked his shot off the line. Fulham's attack seemed to have totally disappeared from view, but the team finally broke away and won the game with their first real attack of the second half and a goal from Steve Earle. Twelve minutes from time, Johnny Haynes split the Blackpool defence with a telling through pass, Earle took the ball in his stride before swerving to the left and the right, finally planting a perfectly placed shot past Tony Waiters in the Seasiders' goal. In the last seconds Jimmy Conway just managed to deflect Jimmy Robson's shot to safety with the studs of his boot. The final **1–0** result was more important than the mediocre performance, and it was another very important two points in the bag.

The result meant that it was the first time Fulham had won consecutive league matches that season. The most important fact of the game was that it was George Cohen's 400th for the club, and he was still only twenty-seven. Continuing the subject of full backs, Fulham's forgotten full back Barry Mealand had received permission to start training again, nearly fourteen months after breaking his ankle at Highbury.

The next home match at Fulham saw the visit of the other promoted side **Southampton**. The Saints had made a solid start and were lying in twelfth position, but just two points ahead of Fulham; the south coast side had already created a reputation for playing quality, attacking football. The Saints line-up contained a twenty-year-old defender David Webb, but it was in attack where Southampton held a number of aces, England right winger Terry Paine being complemented by the young Martin Chivers and bustling Welsh centre forward Ron Davies, signed from Norwich City in the close season for £55,000. Pulling the strings in the inside forward position was veteran schemer Jimmy Melia, formerly of Liverpool and England. *Star Soccer* chose to show this match the following day.

On a heavy pitch Fulham won convincingly, attacking from the start, and establishing a superiority that they were never going to lose. They played 'killer' football, holding possession of the ball for long periods, and creating several chances against a creaky defence. The Southampton team had a lop-sided look, full of running and panache in attack, but looking out of their depth in defence. Fulham were already marauding down both wings with George Cohen and Fred Callaghan giving the attack excellent support, whilst John Dempsey, virtually on his own, kept things tight at the back. Southampton made the mistake of letting Fulham dictate the midfield and retreating whenever the home side were in possession. This often led to overcrowding in their penalty area, and to some degree this was their undoing.

Fulham took the lead in the twentieth minute in rather fortunate fashion. Johnny Haynes, always given too much space, struck a long shot from a free kick into a crowded goalmouth that was deflected in by Allan Clarke. Fulham's lead lasted just ten minutes when winger Terry Paine equalised. Macedo failed to hold a cross, and the ball fell loose to Paine, who volleyed splendidly into the roof of the net.

Southampton dropped their concentration after this, and just two minutes later Fulham were in front again. Jimmy Conway burst into the penalty area, resisted three tackles and had his initial shot charged down. The Saints defence was slow to clear, and from the rebound, and by sheer persistence, Conway did score with his second effort, ending up flat on his face in the mud, as the ball spun into the net off Saints keeper Dave MacLaren's fingers.

In the second half Fulham were totally in control, Steve Earle, Clarke and Leggat, when he came on, having a field day. The Saints defence was reduced to total panic every time Fulham were in possession around the box. Only spectacular saves from MacLaren, and some incredible near misses kept the Saints in the game. Clarke completed the scoring for Fulham fifteen minutes from the end, and it was a gem. Graham Leggat started the move, Earle ran across the field with the ball, before producing a stunningly accurate reverse pass to Clarke. Clarke brought the ball quickly under control, before beating MacLaren with a low drive. The only worrying point in the match

Les Barrett spins away after scoring Fulham's second goal at Goodison Park, leaving Everton goalkeeper Gordon West on his knees. Despite this late fightback, Fulham went down narrowly 2–3.

was a late injury to Bobby Robson. Southampton on the whole, apart from the effervescent Webb and the unsupported Chivers, played poorly. The final **3–1** score had produced Fulham's third successive victory.

Man of the Match Robson was moved to quote: 'I think our present side is one of the best we have had in a long time. It is a fine blend of youth and experience, and with luck, we could go higher up the table.' Clarke's scoring run was now becoming quite remarkable as this was his fifth two-goal haul in the last six home matches, and overall it meant thirteen goals in the last thirteen matches for the young star.

John Dempsey's consistent displays at centre half had not gone un-noticed either, and he had been selected to play for Eire. Dempsey was a Londoner from Hampstead, but possessed a 'dual nationality qualification' as both his parents were Irish. John 'renounced' his English right and agreed to play for Eire. He made his debut in a 0–2 defeat against Spain in Valencia. He had become Fulham's second Irish debutant in the last three months.

On the debit side, a youngish Fulham side competed in the replay of the London Challenge Cup Final that week at Fulham. Fulham, on paper, should have won, but in true Fulhamish style, the team just about held on in the first ninety minutes thanks to a Terry Dyson goal, but lost the cup 1–2 in extra time. The chance for some silverware, however small, had gone!

Fulham's first team were now brimming with confidence and visited one of their unluckiest grounds, Goodison Park, to face **Everton**. Bobby Robson's injury forced him to miss his only league game that season, with Brian Nichols substituting. Everton were on poor form, and had only secured one goal and two points from their last four league games. Robson's absence, for some reason, seemed to upset the balance of the defence.

Everton made a dream start. After just three minutes, the classy Alex Young put Alan Ball clear through the middle and he was quicker to pounce on the ball than Tony Macedo. Ball whipped the ball past him to score from close range, despite Fred Callaghan's efforts to clear the ball off the line. The second goal had an element of luck about it; Everton's winger Alex Scott badly mis-hit a first time shot, the ball thudded against teammate Derek Temple and landed right at his feet, giving him a chance he could hardly miss. Everton's third, eight minutes before the interval, was, however, was a classy affair. Everton's Man of the Match Young played a beautiful lofted pass over the Fulham defence, leaving the path clear for Temple to run thirty yards, and beat Macedo for his second and Everton's third goal. Fulham were reeling at three behind at the interval. Macedo had also made three magnificent saves, and it could have been a substantial deficit at half time. Everton were playing vintage soccer, and showing delightful class.

The second half, however, was a real transformation, and Fulham, showing themselves to be a 'second half' side, were excellent. Everton appeared to lose the incentive to go for more goals, and Fulham initially did not seem to have the firepower to reduce the deficit. Everton were trying to play possession football and to slow the game down, but Fulham were beginning to make the running, and now it was Everton's turn to be in complete panic. Twelve minutes from time, Jimmy Conway started a move, Johnny Haynes worked the ball on, and the move culminated with the unmarked Allan Clarke heading Les Barrett's precise centre into the top corner. Then, just a couple of minutes later, Everton's Jimmy Gabriel made a last ditch tackle to prevent Clarke scoring again.

Clarke then turned provider seven minutes from the end, linking up with Johnny Haynes to put Les Barrett through with a glorious pass to squeeze a super shot just inside the post, giving Everton keeper Gordon West no chance. Fulham came close yet again, but just couldn't quite pull the game back, and their winning run had come to an end, with a **2–3** scoreline.

Fulham's forwards and Haynes had all looked dangerous in the second half, and the whole team earned merited applause for their 'never say die' fighting display. Vic Buckingham had praise for Everton's first half onslaught, and admitted: 'They deserved their one goal winning margin.' The win gave Everton the double over Fulham.

Over Christmas, Fulham again, as last year, took on **Leicester City,** initially on Boxing Day at Filbert Street. It was a very cold day, and the pitch was pretty treacherous. The match looked a tough fixture on paper, as Leicester had won seven out of their nine league fixtures at home that season. Fulham took the lead in the first half, when Haynes' corner was headed out, and the ball fell nicely to Fred Callaghan, who returned it venomously into the top corner.

With the 'frozen' Leicester defence caught off guard, Fred Callaghan volleys in Haynes' corner for Fulham's first at Filbert Street. The 2–0 win at a wintry Leicester on Boxing Day was Fulham's fourth in their last five games. John Dempsey's breath gives away the temperature of the day!

Fulham on the day were the masters of the conditions, and wrapped up the win in the second half when Les Barrett picked up a Jimmy Conway pass and angled a cross-shot past Gordon Banks. The **2–0** result reflected a fine victory, and was ample revenge for the 0–5 drubbing received in the Midlands over Christmas the previous year! Due to the lack of Christmas match coverage by the media, there is very little written recorded information about the game to be found.

The excellent performance was marred, however, by a serious injury to skipper George Cohen, who was carried off with a suspected broken leg. Graham Leggat came on as substitute and the re-shuffle, which had to occur, made Fulham's win even the more impressive. After a tense review, the injury was thankfully confirmed as just a badly sprained ankle and torn ligaments. The next

Surrounded by Leicester defenders, Leggat is thwarted at the last by the onrushing Gordon Banks. Despite being halted this time, Leggat completed a superb hat trick to help Fulham to an impressive 4–2 win at a foggy Craven Cottage.

day George turned up at the ground on crutches and encased in plaster from ankle to knee, to watch the return fixture. Cohen said: 'It might be a three-week job, it might be six, I'm just grateful it wasn't something worse.'

The following day, **Leicester City** visited Craven Cottage. Leicester were in sixth place in the division and already had forty-six goals to their credit, the second best in the league. The Foxes were, however, slightly vulnerable away from home. Leicester were at full strength, and Buckingham selected Bobby Drake at full back to replace the injured George Cohen. Steve Earle, despite playing well, had only scored once in the last two and a half months, and was dropped down to substitute, Graham Leggat coming in wearing the number nine shirt.

Fulham missed two early chances, and received a nasty shock when Jackie Sinclair put Leicester ahead in the tenth minute, scoring nicely after a slick one-two with the dangerous Derek Dougan. Fulham, however, were quickly level, Johnny Haynes won a tackle with Leicester's Peter Rodrigues, and before he could be tackled again, put in an exquisite centre allowing Graham Leggat to equalise with a trademark jack-knife header.

Fulham then wasted no time in going ahead and the second was a carbon copy headed goal from Leggat again, following a perfectly flighted corner from Haynes. The header possessed such power that, although Gordon Banks got his hand to the ball, he could not stop it. It was now Leicester's turn to come back strongly, and Davie Gibson netted Leicester's equaliser just before half time.

The second half saw Leggat complete a 'real' hat trick (three consecutive goals). Ten minutes after half time, he slotted into an open goal after a fantastic and persistent, mazy run by Les Barrett had beaten Graham Cross, John Sjoberg, other City defenders and finally goalkeeper Gordon Banks. Leicester again pressed hard for another equaliser. Leicester's Mike Stringfellow put in a stinging shot that Tony Macedo did miraculously well to save. So good was the save that England keeper Banks joined in the applause at the other end; the game could have gone either way at this point.

Johnny Haynes, however, had the last word and sealed the win with a tremendous shot in the last minute. He was surrounded by Leicester defenders, and threw them all off balance by feigning a pass. He moved the other way instead, found himself a yard of space, and hit a swerving shot from twenty-five yards, which gave Banks no chance at all. The result gave Fulham their first double of the season. Leggat showed just what an asset an experienced goal scorer was when you decided to shuffle the pack, or freshen up the forwards. The **4–2** score reflected another excellent performance and thrilling encounter. The papers were suitably impressed saying: 'It was the perfect climax to an almost perfect game. Leicester will often play much, much worse and still win!'

The only sad part of this Christmas bonanza was that Fulham recorded the death of former player and trainer Frank Penn, who had joined the club as a winger in 1915 and had remained at the club in various capacities, mainly as trainer, for the next fifty years. He had retired just the previous summer, and had given Fulham a lifetime of service. The Fulham players wore black armbands against Leicester as a mark of respect.

For the final match of the year on New Year's Eve, Fulham entertained dark horses **Stoke City**, who had sustained a good start, and were currently flying high at third in the table. Fulham, unsurprisingly, announced an unchanged side. Apart from the experienced Dennis Violett, Stoke were also at full strength. It was an interesting match in prospect, with Stoke City's experience being matched against Fulham's cut and thrust young side.

It was another cold and windy day, and the pitch was not at its best. Fulham started arrogantly, Graham Leggat hit a post, and then missed another chance, but the home defence were soon in

Two England warhorses battle it out for dominance of the midfield. In this particular encounter, a heavily bandaged Haynes gets the better of Stoke midfield general Eastham. Played on a muddy New Year's Eve, the game saw Fulham race to a 4–1 victory over Stoke City, and their best position in the division that season, in sight of the top six.

trouble. George Eastham was at his England best, and was supplying the ammunition for Peter Dobing and Gerry Bridgwood. Bobby Robson soon retreated from the forward role to help stem the tide. It was no surprise when Stoke took the lead after twenty minutes. Stoke's Alan Bloor broke down the left, and his accurate cross was headed home delightfully by veteran Roy Vernon. Another Stoke veteran Maurice Setters was blunting most of Fulham's attacking responses. Fulham were lucky not to go further behind, and it looked as if Stoke had doubled their lead when Dobing fired in an effort from Bridgwood's centre. Fortunately for Fulham the ball hit the bar and was cleared. This forced Fulham to finally shake off any Christmas cobwebs, and the home side levelled after thirty-two minutes.

Leggat forced a corner off Setters, and from Les Barrett's short corner, Johnny Haynes floated in a centre to the near post. Leggat powered a typical head on it, and the ball headed goalwards only to rebound off Setters. However, before any Stoke defender could react, the alert Leggat whipped the rebound into the net. This inspired Fulham, and Fred Callaghan's marauding runs from defence were causing Stoke no end of problems.

It was from another of these dangerous overlapping runs that Fulham took the lead shortly before half time, and again Leggat was involved. Callaghan's hard cross was steered back by Allan Clarke into the path of Leggat. His first time shot looked to be going wide, but it cannoned against Stoke defender Eric Skeels, who had been running back to assist his goalkeeper John Farmer. He was powerless to get out of the way of Leggat's shot, and the ball flew off his thigh and hip and into the net for an own goal.

In the second half City, with the wind, came at Fulham strongly, but they were vulnerable to the counter-attack. Barrett anticipating a back pass from Setters swept past the keeper, but slipped at the final moment, and from yet another Callaghan cross, Clarke fed Barrett again, who, under pressure from Setters, mis-hit his shot just wide. Midway through the second half, however, Fulham scored a third, and the goal was a real peach. Stan Brown put in an excellent corner, John Dempsey headed the ball on at the near post, and Clarke coolly chested it down before firing a sidefoot shot past Farmer, just inside a post.

Stoke were now beginning to be rattled by the quality of Fulham's play, and Potteries defender Calvin Palmer was involved in a flare up with Leggat for which Palmer was rightly booked. Then Fulham were angered again when Barrett robbed a Stoke defender, and was clearly fouled in the penalty area. Barrett staggered but remained on his feet, and went through to 'score'. Amazingly, referee Wallis disallowed the goal and gave Fulham a free kick *outside* the box, which came to nothing.

Minutes later it was Stoke's turn to be fuming. In a breakaway, a shot by winger Harry Burrows hit the bar, rebounded onto goalkeeper Macedo and rolled over the goal line. The referee immediately awarded a goal, but Haynes persuaded the referee to consult his linesman, after which he disallowed the goal and gave Fulham a free kick, much to the disgust of the Stoke team.

The match, however, was over as a contest a minute from time when Leggat scored his second, sliding in late to meet a cross at the far post, crashing home a shot high into the net from close range. In was Leggat's fifth in two games. The match had been a superb spectacle in front of a 25,000 crowd who had witnessed Fulham's sixth win in seven games. The **4−1** win gave Fulham the double over Stoke.

Fulham had now netted twenty-five goals in their last nine league games. Fred Callaghan deserved the Man of the Match award, and was singled out as Fulham's most improved player. The win, the seventh in nine games, pushed Fulham up to fourteenth in the table, *but just a mere six points below third-placed Stoke*! The match retained all its glory when it was the main match shown on *Match of the Day* that evening. It was well worth missing some of the New Year celebrations to watch.

It was very hard not to be impressed with Fulham's current form, and the Fulham supporters were really buzzing with anticipation as to what 1967 would bring. Even the cynical press admitted: 'Fulham have a great chance of jumping into the talent money for the first four places.'

Vic Buckingham, in his summary of 1966, was happy with the team's performances, but pointed out that George Cohen, Bobby Robson and Johnny Haynes had played more league games than

Oof! Reserve full back Bobby Drake takes a clattering from Stoke goalkeeper Farmer when coming up to support the attack; Allan Clarke is poised for any mistake. On the six-yard line, and in the thick of the action as always, is Graham Leggat, playing his final game for the club. In typical fashion, one of Fulham's greatest ever forwards responded with two opportunist goals. Buckingham controversially sold Leggat just a few days later to Birmingham City for a giveaway fee.

the other team members, and still thought that the side lacked the necessary experience, making it clear that he wanted competition for places. He stressed that Fulham would still not be in a position to compete and pay out fees in the £100,000 bracket for players, and that he and the Fulham board were committed to finding their own 'stars'.

Unfortunately, December's position would prove to be the highest that Fulham would achieve that season, and January would start with yet another controversial Buckingham decision.

January 1967

In this month

* Alf Ramsey was knighted, and Bobby Moore was awarded the OBE
* Jack Ruby, the killer of Lee Harvey Oswald, died.
* *The Forsyte Saga* was shown on television.
* The Society for the Protection of the Unborn Child was formed.
* Britain's largest new town of 22,000 acres was to be built in Buckinghamshire. It was to be known as Milton Keynes.
* Jo Grimmond resigned as leader of the Liberals, and Jeremy Thorpe took over.
* The lone yachtsman Francis Chichester was awarded a knighthood.
* A flash fire killed three American astronauts on a launch pad rehearsal.
* Donald Campbell died when *Bluebird* overturned at 300 mph on Coniston water.
* The *Boys Own Paper* closed on its eighty-eighth anniversary.

'I'm A Believer' by The Monkees topped the charts.

How the league was looking

Champions Liverpool had taken over at the top, level on points with Manchester United. Nottingham Forest had become the team of the moment, with five wins and a draw from their last six games propelling them from mid-table to third. Stoke City were hanging on to fourth. Chelsea had experienced a poor month dropping to fifth. Leicester City had dropped right down to mid table. Blackpool were at last off the bottom, but still in the relegation zone, Newcastle taking over the bottom place. West Bromwich Albion were struggling just above the bottom two, alongside Aston Villa.

The matches

THE NEW year was welcomed in with the shock news of goalscorer Graham Leggat's sudden departure. Leggat had been sold to Second Division Birmingham City for a paltry £15,000, and the move ended an eight-year association with the club. Leggat had been transfer listed at his own request earlier in the season, following his latest omission from the team. Although Buckingham's first choice was obviously the younger Earle, Clarke and Barrett, having an experienced back-up forward was invaluable in case of suspensions or injury, and Leggat was just thirty-two.

Leggat had scored 135 goals for Fulham in 254 games, (an average of a goal every other game), an amazing record. Over 100 of these goals had been scored in the First Division; he had secured six hat tricks and two four-goal hauls in that tally. He held the record of the fastest ever First Division hat trick, three goals in four minutes during the 10–1 demolition of Ipswich Town on Boxing Day 1963. He had been Fulham's leading scorer in four of the last seven seasons, including the previous season, and had scored ten in just fourteen appearances in the current season. He had also just returned to the side and scored five goals in the last two games! The commending feature of Graham Leggat's game was that he could play in any of the five forward positions with grace; he could shoot accurately with either foot, and was a master in the air.

He was also a modest and very popular player at Fulham, and would be greatly missed. Many in the game questioned Buckingham's judgement in selling Leggat, and it was not immediately obvious as to who would be the 'fourth' forward. The Fulham programme afforded Graham Leggat a single scrappy paragraph, which did no justice to his heroic efforts for the club. In true Leggat style, he had contacted the club after settling in at Birmingham, passing on best wishes to his teammates and supporters.

Leggat's time at Birmingham was not a particularly happy one, as he was asked to play behind the two main forwards, which was quite alien to him. He made just thirteen (plus three substitute) league appearances for the Blues in an eighteen-month spell, scoring just three league goals. Leggat's position was hampered by the other signings at Birmingham such as Fred Pickering (£50,000) from Everton, Barry Bridges from Chelsea and Trevor Hockey. Leggat would still perform well, as early in the next season (1967–68), he would score eight goals in four reserve fixtures, including five in one game, but even these heroics would not be enough to earn him a guaranteed first team place.

Finally, Leggat left the Blues to join Rotherham United linking up for the first time with his Scottish international teammate Tommy Docherty who was then manager. He stayed at Millmoor for just one season making thirteen (plus three substitute) league appearances and scoring seven league goals for the Millers. He finally hung up his playing boots in 1969, initially taking a coaching position at Aston Villa. At Villa he linked up for the second time with Tommy Docherty, who had then moved to Villa Park as manager. On completion, Leggat emigrated to Canada and made an exceptional career for himself in sports commentary and television. George Cohen would often remark: 'Leggat was the finest winger ever to come out of Scotland.'

The whirlwind transfer appeared to cast a shadow over the club, and may have affected the team's first performance of the year. Fulham travelled to Yorkshire to play their bogey side **Sheffield United**. Steve Earle came in to replace the departed Leggat; Fulham's performance was awful. Sheffield United were on a very bad run, with just one win in their last ten games, and there would never be a better time to beat them. Club photographer Ken Coton took just five photographs during the entire game, vividly reflecting the side's dismal performance. The pitch was difficult, the weather conditions poor, and there was little atmosphere as the ground was part of a cricket ground that was empty on one side.

Sheffield United were in control from the start, and, despite one early opportunity for Allan Clarke, the Fulham team, especially in defence, were looking utterly bewildered at times. United took their chances clinically, Mick Jones opened the scoring with a low drive from fifteen yards, and then Alan Birchenall nipped in front of a hesitant defence to add the second.

The second half was no better, and Fulham conceded a third straight after half time. Tony Macedo managed to block United's Bill Punton's fierce shot, but the rebound fell straight to Jones, who made no mistake for his second; United's winger Alan Woodward then hit a post. The Fulham goal was under almost constant siege, and nothing was seen of Johnny Haynes or the Fulham attack. Fulham survived until the last five minutes. Finally, Bobby Drake's slow, wayward back-pass to Macedo was easily intercepted by Birchenall, and he advanced to score his second goal into an empty net. Only the usual heroics from Macedo saved Fulham from a far heavier pasting, and Birchenall had done it again—he had scored five against Fulham in the last three encounters

In a rare attack, Les Barrett's shot is charged down by United's Len Badger. It was a rare goal attempt on a gloomy afternoon in Sheffield. Fulham lost 0–4, their performance at Bramall Lane as grey as the weather.

between the clubs. Fulham lost **0–4**, and the Sheffield side had done the double over Fulham. In the last four league matches between the sides, Fulham had not managed to score a single goal!

The only piece of good news that emerged from the bad week was that injured skipper George Cohen was already back in training, and progressing rapidly. Fulham had been drawn away against Fourth Division side Bradford Park Avenue in the third round of the FA Cup.

The following week Fulham took on **West Bromwich Albion** at the Cottage. Despite the dismal performance the previous week, Buckingham announced an unchanged side. Albion now possessed another ex-Chesterfield goalkeeper, John Osborne, in goal, and had signed John Talbut from Burnley at centre half. Veteran Bobby Cram was in for the injured full back Dennis Clarke. Since beating Fulham 5–1 earlier in the season, the Baggies had not fared that well in the league, dropping dramatically to just above the two relegation places. The Throstles had lost seven out of the last ten matches. The match was officiated by the renowned Welshman Clive Thomas of Treorchy; Albion played in a changed strip of red and white.

Conway, Robson and Drake keep a watchful eye on goalkeeper Macedo as he intercepts an Albion attack. Fulham fought back on this occasion from a two-goal deficit to claim a 2–2 draw. Full back Drake (right) was making a rare appearance, deputising for George Cohen, who was injured.

Again, Fulham were quick out of the starting blocks, and dominated the first twenty minutes. All three forwards tested the Albion goalkeeper Osborne, who was equal to the shots with three point blank saves; he then drew an ovation for one save from Les Barrett. The forwards were not accurate enough, however; Les Barrett missed two further chances, and Allan Clarke overran a further opportunity. Then, for some inexplicable reason, the team fell away badly and Albion's controlled football put them on top. Half back Ian Collard put Albion ahead, following a simple breakaway, Albion's first real attacking move of the match. He took a right wing pass, cut inside and scored with a swerving drive off Tony Macedo's right hand.

In the second half, Fulham continued with their profligacy, and Steve Earle skied an easy chance. It proved a costly miss, as minutes later the hard working Albion full back Bobby Cram, a high scoring defender, sneaked upfield to score a second with a fierce twenty-yard drive, delivered from the right wing. Fulham's halfbacks were again struggling to keep the aggressive Albion forwards at bay, and Bobby Drake was being given the run-around by able winger Clive Clark. Fulham looked down and out, and Clarke was now limping badly following a tackle and contributing little.

Whilst Johnny Haynes was unusually subdued, the rest of the Fulham team finally began to get their game going, and eventually made a great recovery. The team attacked non-stop, and in one raid Bobby Robson had a shot charged down and full back Fred Callaghan, supporting the attack, rammed home the rebound from close range. The goal was the full back's fourth in the last two months. Fulham's spirits were raised, and Robson was in the thick of things. He put in one tremendous first time volley that flew past the post with Osborne motionless in the Albion goal. Fulham were rewarded again when, fifteen minutes from time, Barrett, in fine form throughout, ran down the left wing, cut in, and with everyone expecting a cross slammed a shot into the roof of the net from the tightest of angles. The goal was tough on the Albion keeper who had, up to then, saved virtually everything thrown at him. Fulham went for the jugular and seemed the more likely side to win the game.

However, as the home team charged forward once more, the floodlights failed, and the game came to an immediate halt as players and spectators were plunged into total darkness. It took some time for power to be restored, some seven minutes, and during that hiatus Fulham's attacking impetus was lost. The game in the end petered out as a tame **2−2** draw. Fred Callaghan was named again as Man of the Match, and looked at times to be Fulham's sixth forward. He had come on in leaps and bounds in the last six months and his aggressive style had won him many admirers.

When Fulham met **Leeds United** the following week, it was again another poor away performance. Fulham were changed only inasmuch as George Cohen made a welcome return from injury; Fulham were again in their changed strip. Leeds had Paul Madeley deputising for the England centre half Jack Charlton. It was Madeley who assisted in the first Leeds goal; he slipped a perfect through pass to Jimmy Greenhoff and he beat Tony Macedo with a perfectly placed drive. Johnny Haynes was doing his best to inspire the forwards, but to little effect. Only twice in the first half did Fulham seriously threaten, when Les Barrett moved smartly onto two Haynes' passes but both times drove very narrowly wide.

Fulham had no chance to settle after the interval, and again conceded a preventable goal immediately after the re-start. Greenhoff put in a teasing cross, and Macedo moved for the ball too late, allowing pint-sized midfielder Johnny Giles to slip in front of him to score with a neat header. The only positive emerging from the game was Cohen's duel with the Leeds speedy winger Albert Johanneson, the Leeds man coming out second best on nearly every occasion. Johanneson escaped from Cohen's clutches just once on the hour, but that was enough to see him score a cracking goal that had the Elland Road faithful on their feet; the goal virtually sealed the match.

Fulham's only consolation was Barrett's second half goal just four minutes from time. The goal was a carbon copy of the goal he had scored the previous week against West Bromwich Albion, a shot into the net from a very narrow angle. It was one of those games where Allan Clarke had again played very deep in a 'provider' role, and again it hadn't come off. Fulham had been well-beaten **1−3**, and after the very bright Christmas period, the team had picked up just one point out of six. The seven goals conceded in the two away games were serious causes of concern for Buckingham.

Fulham returned to Yorkshire for the third time in four weeks the following Saturday to play their next fixture against **Bradford PA** in the third round of the FA Cup, whilst definitely not looking in the best of form away from home. Fulham, despite their poor form, were unchanged. They again played in their changed strip to avoid a colour clash, their opponents playing in an all white strip. The game had drawn a large crowd of 15,000. Bradford's form was poor, and they were lying second from bottom in division four, and had won just two of their twelve home league games; the FA Cup was, however, a great leveller! The match was officiated by portly 'Pickwickian' referee Roger Kirkpatrick.

Fortunately, Fulham had the fillip of a goal in the first minute. George Cohen made ground upfield, and from his cross Steve Earle fired in a fierce shot, which was only parried by Hardie, the Bradford goalkeeper. The Bradford defence got in a bit of a muddle with the loose ball, and Allan Clarke was quickest to put away the rebound. Fulham doubled their lead in the twentieth minute, and again the goal was scored by Clarke who netted from close in following further defensive blunders by the Bradford rearguard. Panic began to set in, however, when right-winger Phil

Allan Clarke, hidden beyond Stan Brown, scores his, and Fulham's, second goal at Bradford in the FA Cup. Fulham eased through the third round tie 3–1 after surviving a determined second-half Bradford fightback.

Robinson reduced the arrears and scored for Bradford nine minutes before half time, skilfully lobbing the advancing Tony Macedo for a peach of a goal.

In truth, Bradford had the better of the second half, and threatened many times to equalise; the Fulham goalmouth lived a charmed life on occasions, and was saved only by the lack of composure from the Bradford forwards. It was touch-and-go and end-to-end stuff, with an injury to Cohen, who had to limp off midway through the second half, certainly not helping Fulham's cause. Finally, two minutes from time, Bradford at last succumbed when Johnny Haynes fired in another of his characteristic rocket shots from the edge of the box, and Fulham were relieved to have survived **3–1**.

Fulham could hardly have been happy with their performance. Despite showing all of the class the team had been clearly rattled by Bradford's fiery response, and the defence had looked unhappy throughout, resorting to many last ditch clearances, and no-one had looked shakier than keeper Macedo who had dropped a number of shots and crosses.

Despite the win, there was trouble on the train on the way home from the game, when a seat was slashed, and the communication cord was pulled *eight* times, causing almost a two hour delay returning to King's Cross. At one stage, police and dogs boarded the train, but couldn't identify individual troublemakers. This was rare behaviour from Fulham supporters, and the committee of the supporters' club responded decisively by suspending all of the 1,000 club members, until the club could be 're-formed' with the 'undesirables' rooted out.

February 1967

In this month

* Teenagers ran wild at Heathrow Airport trying to get a glimpse of the Monkees.
* *Georgie Girl* and *Alfie* won top honours at the Golden Globe awards.
* The underground magazine *Oz* was launched.
* Vyella closed two Lancashire cotton mills.
* Dougal Haston and Mike Burke became the first Britons to scale the north face of the Matterhorn in winter.

'This Is My Song' by Petula Clark topped the charts.

How the league was looking

There was little change with Liverpool still on top, leading Manchester United by one point, with Nottingham Forest just one point behind. West Ham had risen to ninth. Everton had dropped back into mid table alongside Arsenal. Blackpool had returned to the bottom slot, but Newcastle were still in the danger zone. There was some daylight now between the bottom two clubs and the next six.

The matches

NEWCASTLE UNITED visited the Cottage the following week and, like West Bromwich a fortnight before, the Geordies came to Craven Cottage in deep trouble, lying in twenty-first place, having lost ten of their last fourteen games; the northeast side had, however, won impressively at Coventry in the FA Cup the previous weekend. Newcastle put out a much-changed side from the one that visited Fulham the previous season. Gordon Marshall had replaced Dave Hollins in goal, and there were three other significant signings—Dave Elliott from Sunderland, debutant centre half John McNamee from Hibernian and former Bolton Wanderers Welsh centre forward Wyn Davies, whom the Magpies had signed for £90,000. There was a major surprise at the start. Newcastle had forgotten about the colour clash, and had arrived with only their customary black and white kit (it was the responsibility of the away side to change colours). Without any back-up strip, Newcastle could not change, and so Fulham took to the field in their 'blood red' away kit.

The lack of coordination between Marshall, McNamee and Elliott was evident from the start. In the opening seconds, Jimmy Conway and Stan Brown combined to send Fred Callaghan streaking away down the left, and from his curling cross, Allan Clarke's header was only inches too high. In the next five minutes, Fulham had three further chances; Les Barrett just failed to connect with a Clarke cross, Steve Earle shot weakly at Marshall with the goal at his mercy, then the agile Newcastle keeper was forced to rush out to save at Barrett's feet.

Clarke finally put Fulham ahead in the sixteenth minute after a defensive mix up, and Earle doubled the lead five minutes before half time. Newcastle's Dave Hilley tripped the raiding George Cohen, playing as an extra winger, and from Johnny Haynes' floating free kick, Earle lost his marker to score with a corking header. Clarke had 'roughed up' keeper Marshall during the first half, causing him to receive treatment for several minutes.

Newcastle were allowed no time to recover from the half time deficit, and were five goals down just after the hour mark. Clarke made the score three just two minutes into the second half with an audacious overhead kick, his back to goal, casually flicking the ball up and spectacularly beating Marshall. This type of effort would become Clarke's trademark in future weeks. Earle then grazed a post before Haynes added the fourth in the fiftieth minute when he arrowed a low twenty-yard drive into the corner of the net from a narrow angle. After Newcastle's Elliott had limped off, Clarke completed his hat trick eight minutes later after a very sweet move involving Haynes, Callaghan and Earle. It was Clarke's first league hat trick in Fulham colours. Fulham had netted five goals in just under fifty minutes.

Steve Earle eludes his marker to head Fulham's second goal against Newcastle, in a classic Ken Coton goal picture. Fulham, playing in their away kit at home, romped to an easy 5–1 victory, thanks to an Allan Clarke hat trick.

Mark Pearson came on for the slightly injured Earle, and Fulham took their foot of the gas a little, allowing Newcastle into the game in the final fifteen minutes. It was a lack of concentration that allowed Bryan 'Pop' Robson to poach a consolation close-range goal ten minutes from time. Even so, Fulham ran out easy **5–1** winners.

Clarke had looked aggressive and top drawer from the start, always unsettling the Newcastle defence; he could have scored more goals. Fulham defensively had looked very sound and the expensive Wyn Davies was hardly seen, totally shackled by John Dempsey. It had been an excellent all round performance from Fulham, with the forwards ably supported by the outstanding Bobby Robson, and prompted by the graft of Conway and Brown.

Fulham, however, would rarely meet such poor opposition bereft of ideas and punch. The press said, 'Fulham dazzle', some going so far as to suggest that this was 'the best side to represent Fulham since the war'. Vic Buckingham was pleased with the comments, but was realistic enough to say, 'Frankly, the goals came a bit easy'. Sportingly, Wyn Davies said of Clarke: 'What a tremendous performance, he is going to be a great player.' Fulham at this stage had scored more goals at home than any other First Division club.

The following week Fulham played **Tottenham Hotspur**, a match regarded by many supporters and players as *the* game of the season. The previous two encounters between the sides had produced fourteen goals, and this game was to prove to be no exception, with plenty of action and controversy. Tottenham were on fine form, fourth in the table, and had conceded just two goals in their previous eight games. A crowd of nearly 44,000, including England manager Ramsey, packed into White Hart Lane for the game. The Fulham team played as usual in a change red strip. The game was officiated by Harry New, who was renowned for being a fussy referee and had already sent off Spurs' Alan Gilzean for swearing in a League Cup tie at West Ham earlier in the season.

Like the previous year's encounter, there were plenty of early goals. Johnny Haynes supplied a range of passes to Steve Earle, Allan Clarke and Les Barrett, whilst Jimmy Greaves and Alan Gilzean had the Fulham defence at full stretch. In the seventh minute, Tony Macedo totally misjudged Spurs' Dave Mackay's soft cross-cum-shot, the ball hit the foot of the post, and Gilzean easily swept home the rebound. Fulham immediately went on the offensive and were rewarded for their pressure in the seventeenth minute. Haynes swept out a fine pass to George Cohen. Cohen's low cross was controlled well by Clarke, who turned the ball neatly back to Haynes, who had supported the move. Haynes hit a beauty, a first time shot from well outside the box, rising only a couple of feet from the ground, that gave Jennings in the Spurs goal no chance at all. Fulham were level for only two minutes, when Jimmy Greaves put Tottenham ahead again; it was an even better goal. A three man move involving Mackay, Cliff Jones and Jimmy Robertson led to Gilzean flicking the ball in to the blind side of the Fulham defence, leaving Greaves to slot home, with two Fulham defenders trailing. It was *déjà vu*, three goals arriving in the opening nineteen minutes.

Fulham pressed forward and equalised with the goal of the game six minutes before the interval. Cohen, defending, was accidentally kicked in the face by teammate Conway, but recovered swiftly and weighted a beautiful high pass downfield to Clarke who controlled the ball perfectly with his chest, and without pausing in his run, and despite the close attention of Alan Mullery and Cyril Knowles, put a fierce first-time shot past Jennings.

Close to half time the game exploded into a brawl out of the blue when Terry Venables was the victim of a late tackle from Fred Callaghan. As the ball was cleared upfield, both players squared up to each other and soon both were exchanging blows. The 'blow up' was pretty much handbags stuff and would have been over in seconds if Allan Clarke had not joined in. This led to a melee with at least a dozen players pushing and jostling, with Mullery trying to act as peacemaker.

Referee New appears to be conducting his own dance ensemble. In truth, Steve Earle had his shot charged down by Spurs full back Cyril Knowles. In a fiery match played in a charged atmosphere, Fulham were very unfortunate to leave White Hart Lane without a point, finally going down 2–4.

After the fracas had died down, referee New, with little alternative, dismissed both Venables and Callaghan; Clarke fortunately got off with just a booking. John Dempsey initially thought that only teammate Callaghan had gone off, and was almost berserk. He had to be forcibly restrained and almost wrestled to the ground by other Fulham and Spurs players to stop him protesting; he was also lucky to stay on the field.

The incident had completely marred an otherwise excellent match. What was sad was that Venables and Callaghan were old friends, and had been chatting together at length before the game. Both had very good disciplinary records, Venables had only been cautioned once, and Callaghan possessed a completely clean record; both were extremely downcast after the match.

The ten-a-side second half was obviously an anti-climax as the tension dropped. The game was still pretty evenly matched, but Stan Brown was looking uneasy as a makeshift left back. Tottenham turned up the pressure, and in a flowing move Greaves beat Robson and Dempsey and hit a fierce shot that Macedo parried, Alan Gilzean turned the rebound across the face of the goal, and Greaves side-footed against the post when it looked easier to score. The Fulham nemesis, Cliff Jones, then put Tottenham ahead again just before the hour. A Greaves corner was headed back into the goalmouth by centre half Mike England to Jones, who, despite falling backwards, smashed the ball home on the volley. In a further escape, Macedo turned a centre from Gilzean against the bar, but fortunately caught the rebound.

In search of a third equaliser, Robson and Haynes slowed the pace of the game down. A pass from midfield to Clarke allowed him to obtain possession of the ball in the penalty box and weave through. He looked certain to score, but as he was about to shoot, ex Fulham player Mullery took his leg. The incident looked a clear-cut penalty, but referee New waved play on. Encouraged by this, Fulham continued to press and impress. In one attack Barrett flicked in a shot that struck the bar with Jennings well beaten and, moments later, Cyril Knowles desperately kicked a goal-bound shot from Cohen off his own line.

With the minutes ticking away and with Fulham still pressing, Tottenham broke away and in the last minute Jones ran clear onto a pass from Greaves and galloped through the Fulham defence to make the game safe for Tottenham.

Fulham's only consolation in a **2–4** defeat was that they had taken part in an excellent game, repeated on television the following day. Skipper Cohen bemoaned Fulham's fortunes stating: 'At times we tore Spurs apart, but they still ran out the winners.' Johnny Haynes had been outstanding, and Les Barrett had Spurs on the back foot when Fulham pushed forward, but the defence had looked jittery, with Macedo again looking particularly slow and hesitant. The newspaper summed it up with the headline 'All pals at White *Hot* Lane', and conceded that Fulham were 'desperately unlucky to lose'! Manager Vic Buckingham had missed the match, as he had been in Ireland attempting to sign Glentoran forward Terry Conroy.

A rueful Venables commented after the game:

> It was all so silly. I feel choked, but I think it would have been over quickly if a second Fulham player had not joined in. Then I was forced to defend myself. [...] Fred and me had a bit of a flare-up. I was kicked and retaliated. We were grappling and it would have been all over if this other Fulham bloke hadn't come rushing. Then I saw red with two of them having a bang at me. I threw a right hander after that!

Fulham would need to knock out their bogey team **Sheffield United** in order to progress into the fifth round of the FA Cup; the draw paired them at the Cottage. Fulham were keen to get revenge for the previous year's FA Cup exit and the two defeats in the league in the current season. With Fulham's good form, especially at home, the FA Cup was the only remaining hope for the season. For Johnny Haynes and Bobby Robson the cup-tie was probably their last chance for glory. The match took place on Robson's thirty-fourth birthday. With Fulham's recent good performances, the club decided to again break with tradition and retain their blood red kit at

In a frustrating second half at home to Sheffield United, even the Fulham defenders venture forward in search of an elusive first goal in the fourth round cup-tie. Here full back George Cohen finds time to send a fierce shot against the bar. Despite dominating the half completely, Fulham were forced to settle for a 1–1 draw, scoring a last minute equaliser.

home. Sheffield United also changed from their customary red and white stripes to all white; there was an expectant crowd of 33,000 in attendance.

Fulham's hopes were increased as United were without forwards Alan Birchenall, who always scored against Fulham, and Wales international winger Gil Reece, replaced by veteran Bill ('Old Bill') Punton, recently signed from Norwich City for £7,000, who despite being thirty-one looked nearer fifty-one! For Fulham, whether Macedo was injured or dropped was unsure, but the recalled Jack McClelland replaced him. Referee Ray Tinkler would officiate an amazing encounter.

The first half was fairly lacklustre; Bobby Robson dominated the centre of the field and Fulham were in complete control, but the ball refused to run in the box, and when it did, the finishing was erratic. Robson was ably supported by Stan Brown and John Dempsey, who restricted the United attack. In the fourteenth minute, Allan Clarke just failed to control a bobbling ball and Hodgkinson advanced, charging down the shot, and minutes later Les Barrett hit a rising shot just too high.

In a rare chance, a Fred Callaghan slip let in United danger man Alan Woodward, but he shot over with just McClelland to beat. The veteran winger Punton was causing England star Cohen unusual problems. Twice he pushed past him on the outside causing McClelland to make two fine catches from his accurate centres. The first half closed scoreless, but it was followed by an amazing second half.

Strangely, it was Sheffield who started the onslaught when, three minutes after half time, McClelland made the save of the match. Ken Mallender's fierce drive from twenty-five yards caused McClelland to move at least ten feet and dive full length to push the ball round for a corner. From then on, the match was *all* Fulham. What followed was forty minutes of pure attacking football, against United's dogged man-to-man marking.

In the fifty-third minute, Clarke had a goal disallowed for a marginal offside decision. Then on the hour Barrett crashed in a shot that hit the underside of the bar and bounced clear. Five minutes later, Clarke cleverly headed in Steve Earle's cross, but again the effort was mysteriously disallowed for offside. Then, in the seventy-second minute George Cohen struck the bar with a raking shot.

Clarke also experienced a string of near misses; in one he planted in a header that hit keeper Hodgkinson's legs as he dived the wrong way, then in the space of a couple of minutes he had two further shots kicked off the line, one by Reg Matthewson and one by Ken Mallender. On top of all this, Johnny Haynes hit the post, and in the seventy-sixth minute, Barrett just failed to get a touch to Earle's centre in front of an open goal.

Then, with just nine minutes left, the inevitable happened; with their only attack of the second half Sheffield United scored. A ball rammed out of the massed Sheffield defence found Tony Wagstaff, who put winger Woodward away on the right; he squared the ball accurately for Mick Jones to beat McClelland at the angle of post and bar with a shot from the edge of the penalty area. The Fulham players could not believe it. Seasoned professionals like Robson almost wept when the goal went in, but Fulham kept going. The United goalkeeper Hodgkinson appeared to have a charmed life, with defenders Matthewson and Len Badger outstanding in a 'backs to the wall' battle.

Fulham seemed to be heading out of the Cup, but with just ninety seconds remaining, Barrett picked up the ball on the right hand side, and touched in a low cross to the near post where Earle picked it up. Earle immediately cut it back across the tired Sheffield defence to Clarke, whose low first-time shot hit the back of the net from six yards to scenes of absolute jubilation; a **1–1** draw had been salvaged. Vic Buckingham was proud of the way his Fulham had kept going and never given up hope.

The club programme described the match as 'an overdose of drama with an extra helping of frustration'. If the game had finished 10–1, it would have been a fair scoreline and reflection of the game. The press said: 'Sheffield United had enough luck to last them the whole season.' Buckingham said: 'Thank heavens that's over, I was beginning to think we would *never* score against that lot, we can now move in for the kill at Bramall Lane; we feel we have slain the United bogey at last!' Proof of the one-sided battle was not needed, as it was the main match shown that evening on *Match of the Day*.

The Fulham players, however, were seemingly less confident; the team knew that they rarely beat Sheffield United or played well against them. Fulham had failed to score against them in the last four league encounters and had been knocked out of the Cup there the previous year. Some voiced exactly those opinions after the Cup game: 'We'll never beat them', but Bobby Robson shouted them down: 'The whole point is we have already laid the ghost, we pulverised them at times, and came back.' No one was sure how the replay would turn out. John Dempsey and Jimmy Conway would have to withdraw from the Eire squad because of the replay, which was now all the more important as victory would secure a lucrative and exciting fifth round tie with neighbours Chelsea at Stamford Bridge.

The Fulham players settle down to an evening meal instead of an evening match at Sheffield. They—and supporters—had a wet and wasted journey.

Fulham took two trains and five coaches to **Sheffield** for the replay on the following Wednesday. The weather had been appalling all day with non-stop heavy rain. The Fulham team and their supporters had already arrived at Sheffield when referee Ray Tinkler made a decision to **postpone** the game due to a waterlogged pitch. The decision infuriated Buckingham, as it was a waste of a journey and the supporters had wasted a great deal of money.

Fulham could have been forgiven for being tired after the Sheffield debacle, but the **Liverpool** encounter on the Saturday showed how far the club had progressed in what was another classic encounter. Fulham's changes were Stan Brown coming in to replace Callaghan at left back, not his favourite position, with Mark Pearson coming into midfield. Jack McClelland continued in preference to Macedo in goal. Like the previous season, Liverpool arrived again as league leaders, having gained real momentum since Christmas and having lost only two out of their last seventeen league fixtures. Liverpool were without World Cup forward Roger Hunt on the day and Liverpool's defensive strategy was emphasised inasmuch as Hunt's replacement at number eight was full back Gerry Byrne. On a very blustery day, over 37,500 turned up at Fulham to watch the game.

Fulham played well from the start, Steve Earle, Allan Clarke and Les Barrett ripping at the Liverpool defence, and it took all of Tommy Smith's rugged play to subdue Barrett, who was on top form and showing what a prospect he was. It took a last gasp tackle by Yeats to force a corner from Barrett after a flowing move from Johnny Haynes and Bobby Robson. From the corner, Clarke headed just over. Then again after a Haynes and Jimmy Conway move, Barrett broke away on the right wing, slipped Ron Yeats and set up Earle, who was a little too slow to accept the chance and the ball was gone.

Tommy Lawrence, the Liverpool keeper, gets close enough to have his fingernails clipped, but cannot prevent Les Barrett from putting Fulham ahead. The thriller at the Cottage ended all square at 2–2, thanks to an own goal by Liverpool captain Yeats in the last few seconds.

In an isolated Liverpool attack, John Dempsey gave away a disputed free kick twenty yards out. A fierce shot was put in that hit the unsighted McClelland straight in the chest, the rebound was seized upon by Geoff Strong, who steered the ball back goalwards where McClelland threw up an instinctive hand to divert the ball onto the bar and over.

Barrett finally gave Fulham the lead on the half hour against the tightest defence in the league. Following a bout of Fulham pressure, Liverpool were pushed back, and from a cross, Haynes' headed flick found Barrett in the penalty area. Barrett showed beautiful control, picked the ball up and flicked it into the air, swivelled quickly in the area, and put in a shot on the volley that the Reds goalkeeper Tommy Lawrence got close to, but couldn't stop; this was despite the close attention of four Liverpool defenders. Liverpool started to come forward more often, with Strong looking very dangerous in the air, but it was fair to say that both defences were solidly on top.

The second half belonged mostly to Liverpool, but Fulham made a bright start with George Cohen frequently joining in the attack. Haynes made an interception and set up Earle, but again the ball was scrambled away. Liverpool were, like the previous season, beginning to become rattled by Fulham's determination and their own lack of scoring chances, and renowned referee Bill Gow gave Ian St John (sent off at the Cottage the previous year) a very stern lecture after successive fouls on Clarke and Cohen, and then a third 'irrational' foul on Cohen that injured him.

With Fulham still in the driving seat, and against the run of play, Liverpool equalised midway through the second half. Strong headed Ian Callaghan's cross into the penalty area. St John rose with McClelland to challenge for the free ball almost underneath the crossbar. McClelland somehow completely missed his punch, and the ball hit St John on the head and shoulder and slowly rolled over the goal line, hardly having the strength to hit the back of the net, both players finishing in the goal. McClelland half-heartedly claimed a foul, but the referee waved aside his protests, and awarded the goal.

Fulham were now rattled, and thirteen minutes later, Liverpool scored again. In a Liverpool attack, Cohen panicked and conceded a needless corner. Callaghan took the flag kick, and Strong lost his marker Dempsey to put in a firm header. McClelland appeared rooted to his line, and made no challenge as the ball flew into the net directly over his hands and just underneath the bar. Liverpool were buoyant now and could have gone further ahead, but Willie Stevenson was unlucky.

Clarke was not getting any room and was being heavily tackled by the Liverpool defence, causing him to react petulantly at the lack of protection. Fulham knew they had aided the Liverpool cause by donating them two sloppy, preventable goals.

Fulham raised their game, but it looked as if it was not going to be their day until deep into injury time. With the referee looking at his watch, Fulham were awarded a corner. Barrett took a low in-swinger from the left to the near post. The ball was helped on, Dempsey distracted the defence and the ball hit the shins of the unsighted Liverpool centre half and captain Yeats as he tried to get out of the way, deflecting sweetly into the net. Yeats bemoaned his luck: 'I didn't even see it until it struck me.' In the nick of time, Fulham had salvaged a deserved **2−2** draw.

The quality of the game shone through when it was shown again on television's *Star Soccer*. The media hailed the game as fast, intriguing and exciting and gave Fulham credit for having 'guts at sticking to the task'. The Man of the Match was unquestionably Stan Brown who the press agreed had made 'a big contribution in both attack and defence'. Fulham were now unbeaten in nine home matches.

Vic Buckingham had missed this game as well, still in Ireland chasing Glentoran's Conroy and also inside forward Eric Ross. Neither of the deals would come to fruition; Conroy signed for Stoke City the following month, and enjoyed significant success in the First Division and internationally, whilst Ross joined Newcastle at the end of the season, but failed to make a significant impact in the First Division. Buckingham saw the match replayed on television, and whilst not openly blaming the goalkeeper for the goals, had privately made a decision to restore Macedo immediately to the line-up for the Cup replay, insisting that: 'Macedo was the first choice goalkeeper, and mistakes can happen to anyone.'

Fulham took the journey to **Sheffield** again on the subsequent Monday; the weather was worse than the previous week and again the team's worst fears were confirmed on arriving at Sheffield, that the replay had been **postponed** by referee Mr Tinkler yet again—pitch unplayable. Buckingham was incandescent with rage, stating: 'I knew as soon as we arrived that we'd had another wasted journey, the weather was worse than last week, by five o'clock the pitch was a lake!'

It was almost believable that this had been part of a conspiracy to tire out the Fulham team. Fulham supporters branded Sheffield United 'a disgrace to the First Division, who had made little attempt to protect the pitch or to make it playable'. The travellers also slammed the Sheffield club's 'lack of communication'. Hundreds of supporters at Kings Cross had been told that the match was definitely on, many had lost two days' wages, and already this was 800 wasted miles.

After much haggling, Fulham declined an offer to stay in Sheffield overnight and play on Tuesday, opting instead to return to London. Buckingham was adamant that the pitch would take at least a full day to dry. Fulham also refused to put back the league game with Chelsea scheduled for the following Saturday. Fulham insisted they would return on Wednesday and if the tie could not be played at the third attempt, the team would stay overnight and play the tie on the Thursday.

March 1967

In this month

- * The decimal currency bill was published.
- * QPR became the first Third Division club ever to win a Wembley final, the Football League Cup, beating First Division side West Bromwich Albion 3-2.
- * The police began the trial use of helicopters.
- * Mrs Gandhi was re-elected as Prime Minister of India.
- * The 'star' grading of petrol was introduced.
- * The tanker *Torrey Canyon* ran aground off Land's End, polluting 100 miles of Cornwall's shores with 100,000 tonnes of oil.
- * De Gaulle launched France's first nuclear submarine.
- * The thalidomide drug firm Chemie Gruementhal was charged with a series of offences.
- * Stalin's daughter defected to the West.

'Release Me' by Engelbert Humperdinck topped the charts.

How the league was looking

With two-thirds of the season gone, it was neck and neck at the top between Liverpool and Manchester United, with Forest slightly adrift in third. Chelsea and Tottenham were handily placed in the top five. Stoke had dropped right down into mid-table, and the West Ham run had also faltered back down to fourteenth. Blackpool were still bottom, with Newcastle four points better off in twenty-first place. West Bromwich Albion were also in deep trouble now, just one point above Newcastle.

The matches

AMAZINGLY, FULHAM travelled up the motorway again just forty-eight hours later, and the third time in a week, to attempt to resolve the FA Cup tie. This time the game went ahead, and ironically the pitch looked perfect. Fulham again stuck with their lucky red strip, and again **Sheffield United** played in all white. Jack McClelland was dropped after his shaky display against Liverpool and Tony Macedo returned. Despite the postponements, the game attracted a crowd of 33,000.

Within fifteen minutes Fulham probably wished the tie *had been* postponed again; the team had given away two bad goals, and the epic fifth round tie with Chelsea had seemed to vanish. It was ironic that Macedo had been recalled, as he was clearly nervous and rusty, and was either wholly or partially responsible for all three of the goals on the night.

Macedo was recalled by Buckingham due to McClelland's 'suspect skill' in the air, but the first goal, scored by centre forward Mick Jones after just four minutes, came from just that route. Winger Bill Punton forced his way through, but had a short centre easily cut out. Referee Tinkler's view amazingly was that Punton had been impeded. United's Tony Wagstaff floated in the disputed free kick, Macedo made a half-hearted attempt at the ball, but Jones headed over the keeper's hands, and in the ensuing melee still had time and space to follow up and touch the ball into goal on the first bounce.

Worse was to follow. Tinkler awarded another dubious free kick, which found Punton who immediately chipped inside to Alan Woodward, who returned the compliment back to the winger. Punton received it and scored with a brilliantly taken volley that flew between Macedo and his near post from a narrow angle. The goal was well taken, but Macedo had looked very slow getting down. Fulham fought back to dominate virtually all of the rest of the game, pounding incessantly at the Sheffield United goal, but they managed nothing before half time.

Fulham came out all guns blazing, and following a three-man move involving Les Barrett, Stan Brown and Jimmy Conway, the ball was inched back to full back Fred Callaghan, who brought

'Oi, you lot—OFF!' During a light-hearted break in training for the Sheffield United cup-tie replay, Fulham players bring a new meaning to the term 'the swinging Sixties'. Left to right: Barrett and Earle, Clarke, and Haynes and Brown.

Fulham back into the game with a tremendous first time twenty-five-yard shot, which thudded into the net off a post. The goal was awarded, despite a linesman's flag against another player apparently offside. There followed several near misses, and the Blades were hardly ever out of their own half. In one move, Johnny Haynes hit a tremendous shot that beat Hodgkinson all the way, but fizzed inches wide of a post. The equaliser could and should have arrived; it was nothing less than Fulham deserved on this display. Fulham experienced one stroke of good fortune when Tony Wagstaff was sent sprawling by John Dempsey. The incident looked a penalty, but referee Tinkler ignored the claims.

After Fulham had thrown everything forward, Sheffield United again broke away out of defence twelve minutes from time and Punton, virtually anonymous until then, scored his second, and United's third; it was another messy goal. A low cross from the right was side-footed by Mallender straight at Macedo, the ball spun unluckily away from the keeper straight to Punton, who lobbed it back over Macedo's head and into the net off a post. The game ended **1–3** and Fulham had thrown away a cup-tie they should easily have won; a very good chance to progress 'all the way' in the Cup was gone—the team had given everything yet still lost.

The press were wholly sympathetic, one saying: 'Fulham showed skill and ambition way beyond that of their opponents. Haynes, Robson and Conway ruled midfield, and Clarke and Barrett alone carried more threat than the entire United attack.' Another said: 'Fulham were beaten in a match they had travelled 1,000 miles to throw away.' And another stated: 'Fulham played all the better football, made all the better chances, and weathered all the decisions of a haphazard referee to emerge only with real proof that mistakes count dear in the Cup.'

The views on Punton's contribution were polarised. One journalist commented: 'Fulham will wince that two of United's goals were scored by balding veteran Punton. A player so feeble last night that Cohen had time to mark him and yet remain Fulham's most consistent sixth forward.' Another remarked: 'Punton gave World Cup star Cohen a chasing he won't quickly forget.' George Cohen remarked after the match: 'It seemed Bill could not put a foot wrong, it was just one of those games.'

The game broke the hearts of the players and supporters, and would have a dramatic effect on the remainder of the season. Fred Callaghan said afterwards: 'It was a real shaker, the team were confident, I *still* think we deserved to win.' Later in the season Cohen admitted that the result had 'drained a lot of confidence and resolve from the team.' The result was made worse by the fact that Sheffield United were meekly eliminated from the competition by Chelsea at Stamford Bridge just

From an early flurry of corners, John Dempsey, later to join Chelsea, gets the better of the Chelsea defence. Despite plenty of chances for both sides, the derby game ended as a 0–0 draw.

ten days later on their way to the final. Without any doubt the Sheffield United hoodoo was still well and truly with Fulham.

Despite the trauma of the Cup defeat, Fulham and **Chelsea** played out an entertaining encounter at Stamford Bridge on the Saturday. Fulham played as if the team needed to exorcise the Cup disappointment from their systems. Chelsea were still flying high, and in with a chance for the championship. The day attracted another excellent west London attendance of 47,000. Fulham switched back to their normal colours, but retained the red socks to avoid clashing with Chelsea. Fulham were without Fred Callaghan, a victim of tonsillitis.

Fulham poured forward from the start in a first half that they dominated. At one stage the team forced seven corners in three minutes. Chelsea had eight men back and were defending desperately. Again George Cohen was in fine form as Fulham's sixth attacker. Chelsea produced nothing of note for twenty minutes, except when Stan Brown cleared from Chelsea's John Thomson after a Tony Macedo error.

After twenty-seven minutes, Chelsea should have scored. A mis-placed back-pass from John Dempsey only found centre forward Tony Hateley. As Macedo advanced, he slipped on his back and was helpless in the penalty area. Instead of shooting, Hateley elected instead to chip the ball inside to the un-marked Charlie Cooke, who ballooned over the bar. At the other end, Eddie McCreadie kicked an Allan Clarke header off the line following a Johnny Haynes free kick. Bobby Robson and Haynes were dominating the midfield and it was only over-elaboration and some hesitancy by Steve Earle and Clarke that kept the scoreline blank at half time.

The second half was also mainly Fulham, and the team enjoyed long periods of possession. Two minutes after half time, Les Barrett cut in but Peter Bonetti saved his snap shot. Later, Cohen threaded a beautiful through ball to Clarke, who netted, only to be the victim of a marginal offside decision. Hateley looked more dangerous in this half and it looked as if he had continued with his hoodoo on Fulham when he 'scored', but fortunately he was well offside.

In another raid, Bonetti parried Earle's fierce drive and Cohen, still enthusiastically supporting the attack, just failed to turn the ball into an unguarded net. From another excellent Cohen run, it was Mark Pearson's turn to crack a shot against the Chelsea post; this appeared to rouse Chelsea from their slumbers. Tommy Baldwin then hit a post, and Macedo made the save of the match, acrobatically turning over a shot from Bobby Tambling. At the death, Fulham were still trying to win both points, and only desperate tackling from Chelsea's Ron Harris and Marvin Hinton prevented Fulham's eager forwards from getting through. The game ended **0–0**. Some were demeaning about Fulham's performance, suggesting that Chelsea had one eye on the following week's fifth round FA Cup tie.

Buckingham said, 'We're happy', but Tommy Docherty was less so. 'The least said the better,' he growled. The press were again generous in their praise, describing Fulham as 'the First Division's most improved side since Christmas'. Like the Liverpool game, most neutrals agreed Fulham had been the better side. Most of the individual praise was reserved for Les Barrett, who was described by the media as 'England class'. One reporter commented: 'He has guts, speed, reads the game like a veteran, finds space and takes on defenders.' Another headline relating to Barrett left no doubt as to its meaning: 'Here's your boy, Sir Alf.' Strangely, it was the same day that a Rodney Marsh-inspired QPR disposed of First Division West Bromwich Albion 3–2 in the League Cup final at Wembley. How good would this Fulham team have been with a more mature Rodney in the squad?

The following week was a blank one for Fulham as it was the fifth round of the FA Cup, so the squad had a deserved fortnight's rest from competitive football. When the campaign resumed at home to **Sheffield Wednesday**, however, the team's performance looked very jaded indeed in a frustrating game. The club programme remarked: 'Our aim is to finish as high as possible. We aim for a *top ten* finish to prove we are improving by results, not just favourable press reports.' The programme also challenged the team to 'fight for every point to the end of the season'.

Fred Callaghan was out as a result of a seven-day suspension imposed for the Spurs dismissal, Stan Brown deputising again at left back. Wednesday arrived in twelfth place, but just two points above Fulham. It was a very similar Wednesday line-up to the previous season, but the Owls had made one significant addition to their squad in the form of centre forward John Ritchie. Wednesday had paid Stoke £70,000 for his signature earlier in the season. Sheffield Wednesday gave notice of their attacking intentions by replacing inside forward David Ford with left back Colin Symm and by including midfield player Peter Eustace as a 'winger'.

In an early raid, Sheffield Wednesday's centre half Vic Mobley deflects Barrett's cross just over the bar with goalkeeper Springett poised to collect the ball. In a frustrating game a below-par Fulham lost 1–2.

To be fair, Wednesday gave a very solid performance. Driven on by John Quinn, and with forwards Jim McCalliog, John Ritchie and Johnny Fantham all looking dangerous, Fulham found it difficult to break forward and to start moves going. Each of the three mentioned forwards missed chances in the first half to give Wednesday the lead. There was a possible excuse for Wednesday, as they were struggling with a difficult wind against them, but the Yorkshire side failed to make the most of John Dempsey's unusual unease. From Fantham's cross, Ritchie headed into the goalmouth, and with Tony Macedo on the ground, McCalliog headed wide. An even worse miss followed this, when Dempsey slipped and the error left Fantham with an open goal, but he sliced the ball horribly wide.

At the other end, George Cohen had tried to start moves going down the right, and Les Barrett tried to do the same from the other flank. In one raid, Barrett beat three defenders, but Mobley cut out the centre, and in another Allan Clarke robbed a defender, but sent a twenty-five-yard drive just over. But the game looked, in a very congested midfield, like a stalemate. In one rare raid, Springett pushed Cohen's long-range shot round the post, and in the final seconds of the half, Springett saved well from Haynes.

Thanks to some frustrating decisions by referee Peter Bye, the game became an increasingly stop start affair in a stuttering second half. When attacking, the powerful Vic Mobley cut out most of Fulham's attacks, and when he didn't, Springett's handling was confident. Johnny Haynes was having one of those games where nothing was going right or coming off, and it summed up Fulham's performance. Early in the second half Haynes put in a shot that looked in, but Springett diverted the ball around the post. Fulham's off-colour and stale performance looked as if it could concede goals, and it did—the team didn't learn from Wednesday's first half near misses. The Fulham defence was creaking, and when Macedo totally missed a corner, Stan Brown gratefully put the ball behind. A further Dempsey slip then gave Ritchie a clear run on goal, but he waited too long and Macedo came out to block. Bobby Robson was also continually losing the ball in the middle of the pitch.

Twice in the second half, and thanks to some slack marking, two goals by veteran forward Fantham in the space of thirteen minutes secured the points, and from then on it was effectively game over. On the hour, Wednesday scored a lucky goal; a clearance in midfield by Wilf Smith hit Ritchie on the shoulder, but the deflection turned out to be the ideal 'pass' to Fantham. Macedo came out in a futile attempt to save, but Fantham beat him with a soft shot that rolled into the net off a post. Then, fifteen minutes from time, Fantham received Symm's pass, and again beat Macedo with a firm twenty-yard cross-shot. Fulham carved out one chance when Mark Pearson, up with the attack, lashed a shot through a packed penalty area; the effort beat Ron Springett, but flashed just wide.

It was not until four minutes from time that Fulham managed to breach the Wednesday defence, when Les Barrett, Fulham's only effective forward, finished a strong run with his trademark kind of finish. The defence expected a cross, and instead Barrett shot low firmly home between the near post and the goalkeeper, the shot deflecting in off keeper Springett's hand. The game finished **1−2**, and it was easily Fulham's worst performance of the year. Buckingham was diplomatic about the game, saying, 'Not at our best.'

The match continued Fulham's jinxed run against the Sheffield clubs that season—six matches played against them, and not one of them won. It certainly hadn't been a good match for John Dempsey to celebrate his twenty-first birthday. Only Jimmy Conway emerged with much credit with a classy attacking display, and marking McCalliog out of the game, in a match that many considered unworthy of First Division status.

The one spark of good news that emerged from the week was Allan Clarke's first major inclusion in the England squad. He made his debut in the 'Football league v Scottish League' match at Hampden Park. In appalling conditions of snow, hail and rain, England won 3−0. Clarke scored twice in the game, once early in the game and once late on. He gave an excellent performance, and was now widely tipped for full honours in the very near future. Clarke was going from strength to strength, and the England goals took his total to twenty-five for the season in all competitions, virtually a year to the day after signing for Fulham.

Les Barrett watches his shot slide the wrong side of a post, as the Southampton goalkeeper and defenders look on anxiously. Despite the impetus of an early goal, an off-colour Fulham lost 2–4.

Fulham attempted to repair the damage of the previous week when the team visited the Dell the following week on Easter Saturday, against relegation-haunted **Southampton**. Fred Callaghan returned, with Brown moving back to midfield. The team did suffer a blow, however, when Johnny Haynes was ruled out through a groin injury.

Fulham were gifted an ideal start after just fifty-five seconds. Eric Martin, making his home debut in the Southampton goal following a transfer from Dunfermline, fluffed a goal kick straight to Les Barrett; he squared the ball unselfishly to Steve Earle, who netted from ten yards despite the close attention of two defenders. Jimmy Melia then began to exert pressure on Fulham with a range of precision passes that kept the Cottagers' defence at full stretch.

Fulham were then rocked by a controversial penalty decision on the half hour, when John Dempsey was adjudged to have handled a Ron Davies header from Terry Paine's cross. Dempsey protested vociferously that the ball had just hit the arm, and the decision seemed a very harsh one. Terry Paine took the penalty kick, Tony Macedo dived full length to his left to punch out the penalty, but unfortunately the ball rebounded straight to Paine following up, and he touched the ball home. Macedo was then called upon to turn a rushed back pass from Jimmy Conway over the bar.

The second half was all action. Allan Clarke missed a sitter after being set up by Conway immediately after half time and Saints Ron Davies netted, only to be ruled offside. Fulham received their second dose of ill fortune on the hour, when Paine shot, and Stan Brown, unable to get out of the way, deflected the shot past Macedo and into his own net; from that point Fulham capitulated. Twenty minutes from time, Paine was fouled on the edge of the penalty area, and with all eyes on Martin Chivers, Paine and Dave Webb set up a chance instead for Ron Davies, who lashed the ball home. Southampton were now well on top, and after a great move involving Paine and Davies, Chivers scored the fourth in the seventy-eighth minute.

Showing the more petulant side of his nature, Clarke was booked after persistently arguing with the referee. Clarke did at least make the scoreline slightly more respectable when he scored a consolation goal seven minutes from time, a super twenty-yard shot that left goalkeeper Martin helpless. Haynes had been sorely missed, and only Fred Callaghan had really stood out, although Davies and Chivers had been a real handful up front. Fulham slumped to defeat **2–4**, and there was little to suggest that this Fulham team would put up much of a fight against Manchester United on the Monday.

Buckingham was starting to become angry at the team's current form, and was furious with Fulham's second consecutive poor display, admitting publicly: 'We were a shambles, and turned in some dreadful stuff.'

Allan Clarke puts in an unstoppable header to open the scoring against Manchester United. In a brilliant encounter, Fulham twice held the lead, before United levelled with a late Nobby Stiles goal in a 2–2 draw.

The Bank Holiday Monday brought **Manchester United** to the Cottage. The match attracted a post-war attendance record of just under 47,300. It was a very cold Monday, with a sharp wind, but it was also very sunny. The crowd were packed so tightly inside the ground that it felt like being in a sauna. That season Fulham had always seemed to face teams in tip top form—Chelsea, Stoke, Spurs and Liverpool were examples—and United arrived having taken over at the top of the table, unbeaten in ten matches. Alex Stepney now owned the goalkeeper's jersey, and England Youth international Bobby Noble was keeping Shay Brennan out. Apart from that, The Red Devils brought down the standard array of glittering stars. A late change was that of David Sadler playing up front to replace the experienced centre forward David Herd, who had broken his leg the previous week scoring against Leicester. A seventeen-year-old Brian Kidd was the United substitute.

Former Busby Babe Mark Pearson faced his former club in place of Steve Earle, who reverted to substitute. The programme stressed, 'We need points to make ourselves safe', emphasising that Northampton had been relegated last year on thirty-three points, and Fulham were currently on twenty-eight points. *The 'R' word* was being used for the first time that season.

A classic encounter followed and Fulham turned in a very spirited performance, transformed from the previous Saturday. Fulham immediately took the game to United, giving United's slightly fragile defence a torrid time in the first fifteen minutes. The team produced a series of quick and clever moves, which left United in panic and bewildered, Fulham just failing with the final pass. Fulham took the lead as early as the eighteenth minute, when Noble fouled Mark Pearson. Johnny Haynes floated a free kick perfectly into the goalmouth, and Allan Clarke, judging his run perfectly, slipped in front of and out-jumped the United veteran Bill Foulkes to plant in a perfectly headed goal.

Play then swung from end to end, before George Best equalised before half time. Denis Law set up the equaliser, starting the move. Law fed Best, who swerved beautifully away from John Dempsey, looked to go the other way, but suddenly unleashed a stroked shot out of Tony Macedo's reach into the far corner. Fulham's heads were suddenly down; a Bobby Charlton cross caused problems and United winger John Aston hit the Fulham bar.

Fulham re-asserted themselves at the beginning of the second half, and again the game ebbed and flowed. Fulham took the lead again with the goal of the match, possibly the goal of the season, in the seventy-third minute. George Cohen raced upfield, took a flicked pass from Les Barrett, and smashed a tremendous volley against the United post. The ball was hit so hard, that it rebounded over Cohen's head to winger Aston, who hared off with a free run towards the Fulham goal, with Cohen in hot pursuit. Cohen chased back, and successfully harassed Aston into a poor cross-cum-shot and regained possession. Cohen then started an attack with a pass to Haynes on the right. He ran through and slid a perfect pass out to Pearson, who in turn flicked a perfect fourth pass to

Barrett in the penalty area. Barrett hesitated briefly and then drove the ball into the roof of the net; United did not know what had hit them.

It took all of United's resilience to fight back, but they pressed and showed their true championship quality. Pat Crerand and Nobby Stiles ventured upfield to add their weight to the attack, and with just six minutes remaining, Nobby Stiles, of all people, equalised, popping up to beat Macedo to a deflected Charlton cross. In those last few minutes, United could have actually won the game; the match finished **2–2**.

The press were effusive in their reporting of the game, and said: 'It had been punch for punch, and Fulham gave United one of their toughest matches of the season.' Another report said: 'It fell just short of a classic, due to a couple of mistakes and lulls.' A third said: 'Fulham put United's leadership credentials to the sternest test; although United created more chances, it would have been unfair if Fulham had not at least drawn.' The headlines confirmed 'Fulham up with the greatest'—and it was true.

It had been a tremendous game that neither side had deserved to lose. Fred Callaghan had excelled in defence and midfield and Clarke had posed numerous problems for the United defence. Internationals Charlton and Crerand had been hard pressed to contain the vibrant Fulham midfield. Buckingham conceded: 'United are a hell of a side, they always had players ready to switch to attack.' Apart from the attendance, the match set records inasmuch as the gate receipts of over £9,000 were the highest ever, and 32,500 matchday programmes were sold.

To complete the Easter programme, Fulham played the reciprocal match against **Manchester United** at Old Trafford the following, bitterly cold, evening. Tony Macedo had injured himself the previous day and hobbled into Craven Cottage with a damaged thigh, and with Jack McClelland out of favour and now transfer listed, Fulham turned to eighteen-year-old Ian Seymour and told him he would make a daunting debut against the champions elect. The headline read: 'You play—Fulham tell kid Seymour.' It is amazing to recall that only a few months previously, Seymour had been playing in front of a couple of hundred people rather than 51,000! He had played only fourteen reserve games to date. A Fulham spokesman played down any concerns with this vote of confidence: 'We have no worries, he is one of the most courageous around, and one of our brightest prospects.'

Again Fulham ran the champions elect all the way and the game remained goalless at half time. United, as expected, made most of the running with John Aston heading wide from a Charlton cross, and then Seymour had to dive at Aston's feet to prevent an opening goal. David Sadler withdrew into the defence in the second half, allowing Nobby Stiles an unaccustomed role in attack. The game remained very much a defensive stalemate, with a great deal of tip-tap football and sideways passing on view. Seymour made two great saves early on, and then continued to show tremendous composure and sound judgement.

United were, at this point, suggesting only rarely that they would breach Fulham's well-organised defence. One good move between Denis Law and Aston ended with Bobby Charlton's shot rebounding from Seymour's chest, and then George Best robbed Fred Callaghan and looked clear, but dribbled into trouble with colleagues better placed. Finally a shot by Stiles drifted well wide to ironic cheers from the Old Trafford faithful.

The game remained goalless until well into the second half, when Nobby Stiles, who very rarely scored, again put United ahead with a glancing header. The goal arrived in the sixty-eighth minute following a cross by Pat Crerand. Fulham brought on substitute Steve Earle for Mark Pearson in the seventy-sixth minute, and within six minutes he had equalised; it was a tremendous solo goal. Earle collected a long pass, rounded David Sadler, and, despite the close attention of Tony Dunne, scored with a tremendous twenty-yard shot. By doing so, Earle made history by becoming Fulham's first-ever scoring substitute.

Fulham were robbed of a deserved point in the last forty seconds of the match. After holding firm against all of United's star-studded forwards, it was yet another defender, veteran centre half Bill Foulkes, who netted the winner. Stiles provided the cross, and Foulkes, up with the forwards by inspired forethought, nodded the ball to the left of Seymour, just out of reach. All the talk after

Well protected by Dempsey and Cohen, debutant goalkeeper Ian Seymour confidently makes another stop as United's John Aston closes in. Despite a brave defensive display, Fulham lost 1–2 at Old Trafford to a rare goal from Bill Foulkes in the last seconds.

the match, however, was about the performance and the saves of the young goalkeeper, rather than the fact that Fulham had unluckily lost **1–2**.

The Fulham players had recently been complaining that the state of the Craven Cottage pitch was contributing to recent poor performances. The Cottage surface had become one of the worst pitches in the First Division. The drying weather had left the pitch lumpy and bumpy, and one Fulham player commented: 'We are a team of runners, but we cannot run with the ball on this pitch, you never know what the pitch is going to do, at times it makes you look foolish.' Following these complaints, the club confirmed that the pitch would be dug up and re-turfed during the close season.

April 1967

In this month

* Britain's first ombudsman was appointed.
* The Government backed 'the pill', saying thrombosis risks were 'slight'.
* A Picasso was sold for $532,000, a record for a living artist.
* Konrad Adenaur, the first Chancellor of the GDR, died aged 91.
* Consideration was given to strengthen the race relation laws.
* Muhammed Ali was stripped of his boxing title for 'draft dodging'.
* The 100/1 outsider *Foinavon* won the Grand National.
* Sandie Shaw won the Eurovision song contest for the UK with 'Puppet on a String'.

'Something Stupid' by Frank and Nancy Sinatra topped the charts.

How the league was looking

Manchester United still held top spot, two points ahead of Nottingham Forest, now offering a sustained challenge in second place. The pressure had told on Liverpool, who had dropped down to third. Leeds United were now in fourth place, with Chelsea and Tottenham a couple of points behind. Arsenal had pushed up to ninth and West Ham had re-discovered their form to be tenth. Blackpool now looked doomed, six points adrift. West Bromwich Albion were now in real danger after slipping into the other relegation spot. Newcastle, Aston Villa and Southampton were just a couple of points clear of the drop zone.

The matches

IN THE cold light of day, Fulham's Easter programme had yielded just one point from three games. The following club programme repeated the 'R' word again, warning the team that 'a string of defeats, and we could be in trouble.' Buckingham said a minimum of thirty-four points was required, and Fulham currently held twenty-nine. As if to push the message home, the programme repeated the fact that Northampton were relegated the previous season on thirty-three points, and this time ominously added the final line: *'Time is running out.'* The programme pointed out that those clubs around Fulham—Southampton, Newcastle and West Bromwich Albion—had all picked up points recently; a good performance was desperately needed.

Thankfully, the next fixture, on April Fools' Day, was against lowly **Sunderland**. The visitors arrived just one place and two points better off than Fulham, and their current form was not very good—just one win in eight matches.

There was no Charlie Hurley or George Kinnell in the Sunderland back four that season, but instead one player, Colin Todd, was emerging as 'one for the future'. Sunderland gave a debut to England Schoolboy international Colin Suggett deputising for George Herd. Fulham brought back Tony Macedo in goal, and Mark Pearson was still preferred to Steve Earle, again named as substitute.

Fulham were very lax early on, and Sunderland's Neil Martin and Alan Gauden put in early, unchecked shots that flashed just wide. Suggett put Sunderland ahead in the seventeenth minute; it was a move created by Jim Baxter that gave John O'Hare the chance to shoot. His shot was blocked, and in the ensuing goalmouth scramble Fulham gave the young debutant too much room and he scored easily.

From then on Sunderland looked ominously in control. Baxter was again superb in defence and midfield, and keeper Jim Montgomery was handling well. Despite excellent promptings from George Cohen and Fred Callaghan, the midfield was creating little, and the forwards even less. Johnny Haynes, however, went close when he hit the bar with a header from Jimmy Conway's accurate cross.

Photographer Ken Coton catches the moment for one of the goals of the season. Allan Clarke has just rolled the ball away from the groping Sunderland keeper Jim Montgomery with the sole of his boot. He then flicks it up and into the net in one movement. Haynes, Conway and Barrett look on expectantly. The goal was the equaliser in Fulham's 3–1 victory over Sunderland.

It finally took a wonder goal from Allan Clarke just three minutes before half time to put Fulham back on the right road. Les Barrett crossed low from the left, and as Montgomery dived to grab the ball in a goalmouth melee, Clarke nonchalantly rolled the ball away from his groping hands with the sole of his boot, and with the keeper still on the ground, and in one movement, flicked the ball high into the open net; it was a goal good enough to win any game.

In the second half, Fulham initially did not look the superior side, but gradually got their game together. Bobby Robson, Haynes and Conway were putting in a great deal of spadework in midfield and the team began to raise the tempo of the game. Clarke was well wide with a header, and Conway forced Montgomery to make a full-length save from a thirty-yard drive. Haynes was starting to cause chaos and brought another super save from Montgomery.

Fulham's nerves were finally steadied when Mark Pearson, after an extended run in the side, put Fulham ahead for the first time just before the hour. He took a pass from Clarke and cracked home a left footer from the edge of the penalty area. Montgomery was partially at fault, as the ball passed him into the corner of the net. Sunderland roared back, full back Cecil Irwin shot over, Neil Martin missed an open goal sitter, and Gauden hit the foot of a post.

When the injured Les Barrett was substituted with five minutes to go, Steve Earle came on again, and repeated his feat of Monday night within sixty seconds, taking George Cohen's pass and scoring Fulham's third goal to seal the win four minutes from the end; it was just his second touch of the ball. Earle was beginning to be tarred with the 'supersub' tag and joked with Buckingham: 'Do I *really* have to train for this?'

The **3–1** win brought huge relief and took Fulham over the thirty-point mark. The match was also televised, and Clarke's wonder goal was repeated in all its glory; the result was Fulham's first win in ten outings. The Sunderland manager Ian McColl was far less charitable stating angrily: 'We were in command, and just threw it away.'

In the following game, Fulham travelled to Villa Park, where **Aston Villa** had slipped into serious relegation danger. Thanks to his two appearances as a scoring substitute, Earle was awarded the injured Barrett's coveted number eleven shirt. The match was Johnny Haynes' 500th league match, and he characteristically turned in a Man of the Match performance.

Haynes put Fulham ahead as early as the ninth minute with a twenty-yard strike through a ruck of players. The goal followed a sparkling move between Fred Callaghan and Allan Clarke

George Cohen adds his weight to the attack with another upfield surge! On this occasion Aitken and goalkeeper Withers just manage to stop him getting the ball. Despite an early goal from Haynes in his 500th league game, a dominant Fulham were forced to settle for a 1–1 draw at Villa Park.

and from Callaghan's centre Haynes had hit a first-time shot. Fulham continued to look like scoring, and Callaghan had a tremendous thirty-yard shot turned over by goalkeeper Colin Withers.

It was a complete surprise when Barry Stobart levelled for Villa after twenty-four minutes. He took Broadbent's pass, swerved around Bobby Robson, cut inside and, from an acute angle, put a drive past Tony Macedo. These few minutes were Villa's only real spell of domination; George Cohen immediately re-marshalled the Cottagers' defence.

Fulham remained on top in the second half and Steve Earle hit the bar with Withers again helpless. Then Clarke, with a gaping goal, headed Earle's centre straight at Withers; the goalkeeper could not hold the ball, but the rebound was scrambled away. Haynes shot into the side netting, and Earle wasted two further opportunities with a wayward final pass. The **1–1** draw and point took Fulham nearer to Buckingham's target.

Although Villa had put in a fighting performance, Fulham had shown all the class. The midfield of Conway, Haynes and Robson had carved the Villa defence open on a number of occasions, but lax finishing had prevented the win, so all in all it had to be seen as a point lost rather than one gained. By way of coincidence, the score and goalscorers were exactly the same as those in the League Cup tie against Villa at the Cottage the previous season.

Within the club, there was a major change in the boardroom that week, with the appointment of Eric Miller (JP) as a board director. Miller, who also supported Arsenal, was chairman of the Peachey Property Corporation. Eric Miller would have a significant effect on Fulham's affairs over the next decade.

The following week was a blank one for Fulham because of the England international match, and Buckingham took the opportunity to bring down senior Scottish side **Kilmarnock** for a **friendly** on the Friday evening. The friendly attracted over 8,000 spectators. The Kilmarnock squad contained Bobby Ferguson who would become West Ham's goalkeeper the following season, and ex St Mirren forward Gerry Queen who had been a Fulham transfer target the previous season.

With George Cohen on international duty, Buckingham gave the first first-team start for almost eighteen months to full back Barry Mealand, now seemingly recovered from his broken ankle. Bobby Robson was rested and Stan Brown wore the number four shirt. Buckingham also gave a first team debut to eighteen year-old youth team forward Bobby Moss. The match was officiated by local Fulham referee Mr Christie, and Kilmarnock wore all blue instead of their normal blue and white stripes. The match was very entertaining and Craig Watson gave Kilmarnock a first half lead.

In the second half Allan Clarke headed a fine equaliser, and, following a through ball from debutant Moss, Steve Earle ran half the length of the field to score the winner for Fulham. Kilmarnock were a little unlucky to lose 2–1, Buckingham described the friendly as 'a good even game'.

Eleven days later, Fulham played London rivals **Arsenal** in what *should* have been a fairly mundane end of season evening affair; Arsenal in mid table had little to play for. However, whilst the quality of the play in the match achieved the mundane billing, the fireworks that surrounded it certainly did not. The Arsenal transitional phase was now nearing completion: George Eastham and Joe Baker had gone, and new faces were full back Bob McNab signed from Huddersfield Town and midfield ball player George Graham signed from Chelsea. Young Jon Sammels was also making an impact.

There had been a lot of rain before the match, making the surface unpredictable and greasy, and it was also a very windy night. For this particular match, half back Peter Simpson replaced David Court on the wing. Skipper George Cohen had been injured on the right knee during England's shock defeat by Scotland at Wembley, but said: 'This [the Arsenal game] is one I do not want to miss. There is bruising and stiffness in the knee, but we are only four points above twenty-first place, we must win tonight.' The media reported that Les Barrett was also far from 100% fit. The programme uncannily predicted 'Derby matches have a needle all of their own' and 'Local rivalry should be enough to spur both teams on.'

From the kick off, the Arsenal Scottish centre half Ian Ure and Fulham's Allan Clarke began a niggling feud. What started with petty fouls escalated into shirt pulling, elbowing, tripping and verbal intimidation. Arsenal's Terry Neill had also marked out Clarke as a target for various assaults. The game had started at a fast pace, but was already littered with mistakes. Clarke had already put in two great headers, but the underlying tension was quickly beginning to destroy the game.

Fulham were unlucky not to have been awarded an early penalty. Clarke set off on a great run, and danced around three Arsenal defenders before being savagely chopped down by Neill. Referee

Fifteen players rush in to separate the brawling Ian Ure (far left) from Fulham's Allan Clarke (fifth from right). Other fights take place whilst referee Osborne tries to distance himself. In a violent derby, with little at stake for either side, Fulham and Arsenal drew 0–0. Clarke and Ure were both sent off; others were lucky to stay on the field.

John Osborne amazingly awarded a free kick just *outside* the penalty area; the decision seemed to upset the Fulham team. With regard to the appropriately named referee, Clarke certainly appeared to 'look back in anger'!

In the last minute of the first half, Clarke was the victim of yet another late tackle by Ure on the halfway line and reacted angrily. Referee Osborne warned both players, but lectured Ure severely. The Haynes free kick was floated downfield into the Arsenal goalmouth and bounced into touch totally unheeded, ignored by both teams! Clarke appeared to lash out, and Ure grabbed Clarke round the neck. Soon, both Ure and Clarke stood toe to toe trading blows in the penalty area. A dozen players were soon involved, trading punches and kicks. Fred Callaghan and Frank McLintock squared up to one another, whilst Clarke appeared to be kneed in the stomach by another Arsenal player. Clarke was lifted off the ground in a bear hug by Bob McNab, and was calmed by Jimmy Conway. A berserk Ure was surrounded by McLintock, Jim Furnell and other senior Fulham players. Still jerseys were pulled and fists were raised.

White haired Suffolk referee Osborne waited for what seemed an age for tempers to subside, before dismissing both Ure and Clarke to the dressing room. As the half time whistle blew, the Arsenal team were pelted with fruit and coins thrown from the Fulham crowd as they left the field.

The second half was just as ill mannered and ruthless as the first, descending into kicks and blows. Other minor feuds followed, as both sides appeared to blame the other. Referee Osborne would have been justified in taking at least two more names. No player seemed to want the ball for long, in fear of being badly tackled on the wet surface, and predictably not much constructive football ensued.

There were few chances of note, the main talking points being that Arsenal's John Radford hit a post, and that Tony Macedo saved full length from Armstrong. For Fulham, Furnell made one excellent save from Conway, who had looked the best player on the pitch. Generally, Arsenal's shooting had been a disgrace, chances sent spinning and ballooning into the crowd. All the players looked as if they wanted to get off the pitch as soon as possible and the game stuttered to a **0–0** draw.

The only positive aspect to come out of the game was that it was another point secured towards the safety zone. In the second half, Terry Dyson, who had not played in the first team for well over a year, made a cameo second half appearance as a substitute for Mark Pearson. He made little impact, except for one shot acrobatically saved by Furnell, and the match proved to be his final appearance for Fulham in a first team shirt. It was a coincidence that both Fulham dismissals that season had occurred against both the north London clubs.

Clarke watched the remainder of the match from the stands, whilst Ure cut an isolated figure drinking tea at the refreshment bar. After the game, Clarke diplomatically made no comment about the sending off, whereas Buckingham said: ' I thought it was a harsh decision.' Ultimately Clarke was suspended for seven days, whilst Ure, the main miscreant, received fourteen days. Clarke's record was clean, whereas Ure had already been sent off three times in his career. One reporter said: 'It was the worst display of 'football' I have seen for many a year. If Arsenal had dropped some of their strong-arm tactics, they might have won.'

Clarke was now becoming a regular target for the rough and tough tacklers, and was often illegally tackled from behind. With his lean, gangling frame, it was a common sight to see him lying prostrate on the ground clasping his ankles. He was also no angel himself, but he was far more sinned against than sinner.

Fulham travelled to Maine Road to vie with **Manchester City** in the quest for the point that would virtually secure safety. Brian Nichols replaced George Cohen and Les Barrett came in for Mark Pearson.

Fulham could have taken the lead early on, when Steve Earle's header from John Dempsey's cross beat the keeper, but passed just wide. Then Earle was again through, but City keeper Harry Dowd thwarted the winger by diving at his feet. In the tenth minute, Tony Book kicked Haynes' shot off the line with Dowd well beaten.

Having unluckily failed to go ahead, Fulham then conceded two quick goals. In the twelfth minute, City's Glyn Pardoe turned the ball to Mike Summerbee, who crossed for Alan Oakes, who scored with a bouncing volley that deceived a slow-moving Tony Macedo. Six minutes later City scored again. City's David Connor centred, Summerbee pushed the ball on and City captain Johnny Crossan crashed the ball past Macedo into the roof of the net from close range with the Fulham defence caught in two minds.

In the second half, Fulham competed far better in midfield, but the City defence was giving nothing away, and Allan Clarke remained an isolated figure. Colin Bell, Summerbee and Neil Young were now completely dominant up front. Macedo subsequently redeemed himself with several fine saves; two in particular stood out. In the sixty-fourth minute he showed incredible reflexes to turn over a shot from City's Mike Doyle and then made the save of the match from City winger Tony Coleman, diving five yards to turn the ball away. Bobby Robson fought manfully in midfield, but Fulham were overrun.

The third goal arrived six minutes from the end. City pivot George Heslop won a crunching tackle with Dempsey, and played the ball out wide to Crossan, Doyle missed Crossan's centre, but Bell met the ball with a full-blooded volley. It turned out to be a poor performance all round and only Macedo emerged with much credit, Fulham going down **0−3**. Fulham were very lucky that it was only the inadequacies of other teams below them that was preventing them from being sucked into yet another relegation struggle.

After the Manchester game, the Fulham team, still not totally safe from relegation, amazingly flew all the way to the United States to play in an exhibition match against **Vasas** of Budapest. The visit would earn the Fulham club £5,000, and had been approved by the Football League. West Ham were also making the trip to play an exhibition match against Real Madrid. A crowd of over 14,000 arrived in San Francisco to see the match on the Wednesday. The purpose of the match was for top European clubs to promote soccer in the States. Fulham played well in the first half, with the Vasas keeper saving on many occasions. As Fulham tired, Vasas won the game 0−2 with two second-half goals from Hungarian World Cup stars, Meszoly and Farkas. The Vasas side won the Hungarian First Division league that season, and so the defeat was no disgrace.

On a hot Saturday at the Cottage, **Blackpool** arrived in their famous tangerine strip, already relegated. Their ageing side had just not been strong enough to survive. The bottom side had lost thirteen out of the last sixteen games. Kevin Thomas replaced the experienced Tony Waiters in goal and Alan Suddick, signed from Newcastle, played on the wing. Blackpool, now managed by ex-player Stan Mortensen, had been hit hard by the loss of their three young stars Alan Ball (to Everton), Emlyn Hughes (to Liverpool) and Hugh Fisher (to Southampton). The total sum received for the three was £210,000, a massive amount in the Sixties. Fulham gave a league debut to nineteen-year-old Mike Pentecost signed from Sutton United in the close season in midfield, in place of the rested Stan Brown. Fulham also rested George Cohen, Brian Nichols deputising.

Despite not being 100% safe, it was a very dreary match, and Blackpool dragged Fulham down to their level. Fulham should have won easily, but with the pressure of relegation lifted from their shoulders, Blackpool kept possession well and played some fast open football, forcing Fulham back on the defensive. Fulham also looked very jaded following their midweek trip, as the team had only arrived back in the country *the day before!*

Fulham had a lucky let off early on, when Jimmy Armfield hit a forty-yard pass, and Tony Macedo had to dive full length to save from Leslie Lea. In the fourteenth minute, Clarke caused havoc, with three shots blocked on the line in rapid succession. Fulham finally took the lead just after the half hour, when Allan Clarke executed another of his specialist overhead kicks from the corner of the six-yard box; the ball floated over everyone's head, deceived the goalkeeper and bounced into the net. He then headed just wide from Johnny Haynes' free kick.

In the second half, Haynes made an inch-perfect pass to Steve Earle, but Thompson tackled him quickly as he was about to shoot. Clarke then shot wide again. Fulham then lost impetus and started to retreat, looking ponderous in midfield, and slow in the tackle. Then a fine move involving Blackpool's Graham Oates, Alan Skirton and Ray Charnley ended with Blackpool equalising

Allan Clarke executes a tremendous overhead kick to give Fulham the lead over relegated Blackpool. A jaded Fulham twice held the lead, but in the end had to settle for an unsatisfactory 2–2 draw. The point gained, however, was sufficient to secure Fulham's status in the First Division for another season.

through Oates, when he cracked in a low drive; Blackpool then increased the tempo. The lively Blackpool wingers were worrying both Fred Callaghan and Nichols, and Macedo was frequently called upon.

Clarke then scored his second goal of the game to give Fulham the lead again, and it was a gem. A cross field pass was missed by centre half Glyn James, Haynes nodded the ball forward into the path of Clarke, and Clarke put in a strong cross-shot into the corner of the net. However, a sleepy Fulham defence allowed Blackpool in for a second equaliser just three minutes from time. A neat through ball from James found veteran Charnley, who scored easily. The match petered out as a very disappointing **2–2** draw.

Only Clarke and Callaghan had shown much enthusiasm, and Fulham's performance had been so poor in the second half that a slow handclap had started. It was a game with 'end of season feel' written all over it, and the only positive aspect to emerge from it was the securing of a point which guaranteed First Division football for Fulham the following season. The press were equally scathing about the display stating, 'Fulham safe, but that's all.'

May 1967

In this month

* £700,000 was stolen in Britain's biggest ever bullion robbery.
* Harold Wilson declared that Britain would apply for membership of the EEC
* The Road Safety Bill became law.
* Enoch Powell declared that Britain was the 'sick man of Europe'.
* The poet laureate John Masefield died.
* Three members of the Rolling Stones faced drugs charges.
* Elvis Presley married Priscilla Beaulieu.
* Francis Chichester completed his round the world solo voyage.
* Celtic beat Inter Milan 2–1 in Lisbon to win the European Cup.

'Puppet On A String' by Sandie Shaw topped the charts.

How the league was looking

Manchester United were now three points clear at the top from Nottingham Forest, and looked likely champions. Tottenham had made determined strides to leap into third spot. The Liverpool challenge was gone, and they had dropped to fifth, with Chelsea now a distant sixth. Blackpool were already relegated, but West Bromwich Albion had made a tremendous surge out of the bottom two, and looked safe in seventeenth place. Newcastle had dropped back into the bottom two, with Aston Villa and Southampton both a long way from safety.

The matches

FULHAM TRAVELLED to Roker Park for the final away match of the season, safe from any worries, but again failed to provide any kind of inspired performance. They played a full strength side. Buckingham surprisingly took the safe option and failed to blood any youngsters or try any new experiments now that Fulham were safe. Fulham had advantages on paper; **Sunderland** were without main stars Jim Baxter and Colin Todd, with George Herd playing an unfamiliar wing half role.

Fulham were never really in it. Early on, both Alan Gauden and John O'Hare fluffed easy scoring chances for the home side. In the nineteenth minute, however, the Wearsiders did take the lead. A cross from Gauden was returned to him out of the Fulham defence, but this time he slipped a pass through to Neil Martin who took the ball round Tony Macedo, before planting it into an empty net. In the next minute, Martin could have scored again, a fine shot going just wide.

Six minutes before half time, Martin did score again. This time George Mulhall made a fine run down the right and centred unchallenged. Martin rose majestically and scored with a fine header via the underside of the bar. Fulham were slightly roused, and Allan Clarke's powerful header was tipped over by Jim Montgomery close to half time.

After a half time rocket, Fulham emerged and reduced the arrears just five minutes into the second half. Clarke crossed, and after good work by Steve Earle, Jimmy Conway scored with a powerful cross-shot from twelve yards through a ruck of Sunderland players and into the corner of the net. That was as good as it became. Macedo was forced to leave his line to save at Mulhall's feet when through, and Martin almost completed his hat trick with a header from a cross by George Kinnell, which went a fraction wide.

The miss only delayed the inevitable, however, and Sunderland sealed the result six minutes from time, when a George Kinnell free kick was headed down by Man of the Match Martin, and Mulhall scrambled the loose ball over the line; the match finished **1–3**.

Stan Brown had worked extremely hard and, as usual, Johnny Haynes had tried everything to scheme and feed Earle and Clarke with accurate passes, but neither forward could position themselves or finish moves; Bobby Robson, however, had looked very out of touch. The Sunderland goalkeeper Montgomery had been given nothing to do except to collect back passes and take goal kicks.

Fulham had no excuses, and the press confirmed that it had been another poor game, stating: 'It was hard to choose a good team from all twenty-two players, no bite, little punch and even less skill.' Whilst another stated: 'Without Neil Martin, this match would have been flatter than a cold Yorkshire pudding!'

Bobby Robson had been playing recently as if his mind was elsewhere, which of course it was. At thirty-four, the former England star had decided to hang up his playing boots in England. Rumours had been rife for about a month that Robson would retire and move to Canada, but only in the last week had he weighed up all of the factors involved, and decide to accept an offer to become player/coach of the Canadian side Vancouver Royals in the newly formed North American Soccer League (NASL). Fulham had been formally approached, and had agreed to terms of his 'transfer', effective 13 May. Whilst in America for the recent exhibition match, the Canadians had visited Robson personally and asked again that he join them. Robson had also visited, and played in, Vancouver in his youth.

The last match of the season, at home to Nottingham Forest would be his final Fulham performance. Despite his age, Robson had missed only one league game all season and had performed admirably. The cultured wing half had served Fulham in two spells and would be sorely missed. He would leave Fulham fans with many happy memories. Robson had always insisted that he would retire whilst still a 'decent' player, and had always maintained that he wanted to remain in football in a management capacity.

The programme said: 'He [Robson] has always given his best, and has been a consistent and dedicated person, both on and off the pitch.' In two spells, Robson had played almost 350 games for Fulham, and had scored almost eighty goals. If his games with West Bromwich Albion were also taken into account, it totalled a career of just under 600 league games, and over 130 goals. Bobby Robson was made captain for the day in his final match.

The match should have been a great occasion; **Nottingham Forest** had been the team of the season and had been chasing Manchester United all the way to the championship. The Cottage was again a sea of red and white, as Forest had brought thousands of fans to the match. Forest needed to obtain a better result than Tottenham to grab the runners-up spot. Forest had been 'on' for a League and FA Cup double, but had faded at the very last minute, being edged out in the FA Cup semi-final by Tottenham. For this game Ian Storey-Moore had moved out to the wing, and reserve Sammy Chapman replaced star Alan Hinton; Fulham were at full strength.

The match ignited as early as the eighth minute, when stand-in Chapman put Forest ahead. The twenty-one-year-old rose brilliantly to head across and past a poorly positioned Tony Macedo for his first goal of the season. Allan Clarke, almost inevitably, equalised for Fulham just three minutes later. Grummitt could only push out a Fred Callaghan centre, and Clarke, with his back to goal, returned another superb bicycle/overhead kick over a crowded penalty area into the net, his second overhead goal in successive home games.

Forest continued to look the more lively side, and John Barnwell put Forest in front again just eight minutes later. This time the goal was controversial, as Chapman blatantly obstructed Robson before setting up John Barnwell, who began a solo run before putting Forest ahead again. Sadly, Macedo looked to be at fault again, diving far too late to save the ground shot.

In the second half Fulham raised their game. Clarke was outstanding up front, but lacked support; despite the attention of two or three defenders he was regularly winning balls in the air. He was presented with two early chances as the Fulham pressure increased. This pressure paid off, and Steve Earle put Fulham level five minutes after the re-start with a swerving shot that Forest keeper Peter Grummitt got a hand to, but could not stop. Grummitt was in excellent form, saving from the speedy Les Barrett, and then twice magnificently from Earle. Fulham's attack was causing great concern to the Forest defence, but the Fulham rearguard were also handing out chances as if it were Christmas.

Surrounded by Forest defenders, Allan Clarke plants another overhead kick into the net. The equaliser wasn't enough to prevent Fulham falling to a 2–3 defeat on the final day of the season, Bobby Robson's final game before retirement.

Forest, with the more urgent need, pushed forward, and Chapman scored his second and Forest's winner twelve minutes from time, when he again rose excellently to steer Barry Lyon's free kick past Macedo, the Fulham marking non-existent. The result really summed up Fulham's season; the team had outplayed Forest for eighty out of the ninety minutes, had deserved at least a draw, but had still lost **2–3**. The match was shown on television's *Star Soccer* the next day.

Man of the Match Jimmy Conway, Clarke and Barrett had looked the part, but the zestful Forest side had outfought and outrun the ageing Fulham team. The Forest fans invaded the pitch to celebrate the runners-up spot with their side, whilst the Fulham team trudged off the pitch, and the Fulham supporters filed slowly away, aptly reflecting the differences between the two sides' fortunes.

To bring down the curtain on the season, Fulham played two more competitive matches, one against a Southern League (east Kent) XI (3–2), and one against Irish club Bohemians, honouring a pledge as part of the transfer of Jimmy Conway and Turlough O'Connor.

Bobby Robson was not the only person retiring at the end of the season. Sixty-eight year-old groundsman Albert Purdy was also retiring. Albert had been a permanent fixture at the club as groundsman for thirty-eight years, after ten years as a player. He had seen many changes of manager, players and staff. During his tenure, Fulham had provided Albert with accommodation, a flat 'on-site' above the dressing rooms. On his retirement, the club provided him with a pension, and found him somewhere to live. Everyone at the club had wished him a long and happy retirement. He added: 'I'll still see the lads on match days, *there is no team like Fulham.*' Albert would be replaced as groundsman at the club by Henry ('Fred') Hall.

1966–67 Season Summary

IT WAS difficult to describe this enigmatic Fulham side. By the middle of February both team and fans were looking toward a top ten finish in the league, and a very good FA Cup run. In the end, the team ended up scrambling for a couple of draws to, once again, save themselves from the jaws of relegation. In fact the season had been a complete reversal of the previous season, where the post-Christmas had been far better than pre-Christmas.

This Fulham side had taken the champions Manchester United to the wire twice on successive days, outplayed both Forest and Spurs on their own ground, drawn with Leeds, and drawn twice with Liverpool, *all teams in the top five*. Yet this same side had floundered woefully against struggling West Bromwich, Southampton, Sunderland, West Ham and Manchester City on their own grounds, conceding twenty-one goals, *all of these teams in the bottom seven*!

The worst statistic was that the team actually ended up with fewer points than the previous 'Great Escape' season, and had won three games fewer! Fulham managed Buckingham's bare minimum of thirty-four points. The team had scored seventy-one goals in the league, as many as third-placed Spurs, and seven more than runners-up Forest. At home, Fulham had scored forty-nine goals, equal second in the league, and just two goals behind champions Manchester United.

The four principal forwards had contributed over sixty goals between them. However, on the other side of the ledger, the team were probably too attack minded. Fulham had conceded eighty-three, the fourth worst in the division. Successful teams in the top five, like Forest and Leeds, had conceded just half that number, and even relegated Blackpool had conceded fewer! Fulham kept just five clean sheets in forty-two league matches. One interesting statistic (in comparison to the modern Premiership) was that Fulham were not awarded a single penalty kick in the league all season!

Fulham had finished eighteenth, just ahead of Southampton, on goal average. Since Graham Leggat's departure at Christmas, Fulham had won just *two* out of eighteen league fixtures, both of these at home to struggling sides, and the team had picked up just eleven points in total since the New Year. 'Top drawer' performances had been rare. At Craven Cottage, Fulham had looked pretty formidable all season, but once again the team had struggled on their travels.

Since Christmas, without including the Cup exit, they had picked up just two draws and had suffered seven defeats, scoring just eight and conceding twenty-four. One of the away victories had been against a relegated side, and one of the draws was against another relegated side. Fulham after Christmas seemed to concede early goals in almost every away match.

Yet it was hard to fathom why Fulham had again finished in such a lowly position. On paper, this probably *was* the best Fulham side since the war, and for most of the season Vic Buckingham could call on ten international players—Macedo, McClelland, Cohen, Dempsey, Robson, Conway, Haynes, Clarke, Leggat and also Barrett—and on the whole they had all played reasonably well.

Also, it could not be denied that individual players had progressed significantly: George Cohen had delivered another superb season in both attack and defence, John Dempsey had emerged as a tough quality international centre half, Fred Callaghan had won the respect and admiration of many clubs with his tenacious and aggressive style, Jimmy Conway had been the find of the season, a real diamond, and already an established international, Steve Earle had become a stylish and mature forward, and both Allan Clarke and Les Barrett had made headlines all round the country with their play. Barrett's speed and eye for goal had won many headlines and he had deservedly gained international recognition.

Clarke's rapid progress had been the most phenomenal. After a sticky start, he had shot to prominence and now looked a certainty for the full England side. Including the England games, his first full season in the top flight had produced thirty-five goals from forty-nine matches. Buckingham had been impressed by Clarke and said: 'The first time I saw him, I was impressed enormously, he had something that Greaves and Law had, a finely attuned sense of positioning in the box.'

All of these players were fortunate to have had 'Mr reliable' Stan Brown, the man with three lungs, buzzing around them all season, and the maestro Johnny Haynes cementing the team together. George Cohen correctly pointed out: 'For five of these players it has been their first full season in the First Division, so we lacked some experience.'

There seemed to be two major factors to account for Fulham's position, and one was the lack of 'hard edge'. In a number of games it was apparent that the team needed someone, probably in midfield, who was a hell-raiser, a player who could turn defeats into draws, and draws into wins. Fulham were too 'nice' a side, a bit of a soft touch on occasions, and were madly inconsistent.

The second factor was the paper-thin depth of the Fulham squad. In the current era of Premiership football, it seems incredible that Fulham played, and relied on, the same eleven players virtually all season: Macedo, Cohen, Dempsey, Robson, Callaghan, Conway, Haynes, Brown, Earle, Clarke and Barrett. The only other players to make any significant contribution were Pearson, Leggat and McClelland.

These fourteen players carried Fulham through their entire exhausting season of forty-nine games, and so some tiredness and staleness must have crept in. Both Allan Clarke and John Dempsey were ever present in the league (all forty-two games), Bobby Robson missed just one match, and Stan Brown two. Eleven players played in thirty league games or more.

The key issue was that there were no significant replacements at the club who could come in when injury, tiredness or suspension came around. In defence, neither Bobby Drake nor Brian Nichols had really established themselves at full back, whilst Barry Mealand had not played a first team league game for a season and a half. There was also no established centre half replacement for Dempsey since Bobby Keetch's departure. Mike Pentecost had played just one game in midfield, and international star Graham Leggat had not been replaced. Terry Parmenter was not looking, as yet, much like a First Division player, so there were very few alternatives up front either. This whole scenario was very worrying.

Amongst Buckingham's reflections were the following: 'There is no way of disguising the fact that it has been a very disappointing season.' He added: 'There are far too many teams between Fulham and the top.' Then with maybe a hint to the board he continued: 'We should not be looking at survival as a success, we should have secured a much higher place in the league.' On the plus side he added: 'Youth has gained experience.' He stated, with possibly another hint to the board: 'It has been difficult recruiting.' That was an understatement. Fulham had signed not one new face all season, and had lost out on transfers to rival First Division sides. How much of this was due to the transfer kitty Buckingham held at his disposal may never be known, but he was still hoping for 'at least one new face for the new season.'

Buckingham then turned his attention to the reserve (Football Combination) side, and said: 'The combination side has struggled.' This again was an understatement. The reserves had finished next to bottom and had been relegated, and faced next season competing against reserve sides like Oxford United and Reading. Buckingham stated: 'There are a couple of youngsters ready to come in.' Despite this pessimism, Buckingham closed by saying: 'I have very high hopes for the future.'

Examining his comments on the combination side more closely, it was hard to see where Buckingham's optimism was coming from. Five players had been the mainstay of the combination side, and yet not one of them had yet figured in a first team performance, even as a substitute! They were: Hugh Cunningham, Jimmy Houliston, Turlough O'Connor, Dave Loveridge and Henry Hill. Buckingham had already made up his mind that ex Spurs veteran Terry Dyson was no longer up to the rigours of top-flight football.

Henry Hill would not make it to the next season anyway. He was one of Bobby Robson's first signings for his new Vancouver club, along with West Bromwich Albion full back Bobby Cram. In O'Connor's case, it was somewhat surprising, as he had done well since his arrival with Jimmy Conway. This left just four players, other than junior players occasionally plucked from the South East Counties League, that Buckingham could have been banking on: Ian Seymour, Mike Pentecost, John Ryan and young, diminutive forward Bobby Moss. These four players had played a total of just four First Division games between them, and it seemed an extremely long shot indeed to hope that these four would all 'hit the ground running' in an extremely high quality First Division.

This was clearly a Fulham team at the crossroads and most supporters knew that the club would have to buy just to stand still, and buy significantly if they were to make progress. Johnny Haynes would be thirty-three the following season, the experienced internationals Robson and Leggat were both gone, and Macedo and McClelland had both looked fragile in goal. The next three months would be critical in determining whether the board would choose to invest, build on its nucleus of fine young players and push up the league, or choose not to, and pin their hopes instead on the inexperienced and unproven reserve team players—**only time would tell**.

League Division One - Season 1966-67 - Final Table

		P	W	D	L	F	A	W	D	L	F	A	Pts
1	Manchester United	42	17	4	0	51	13	7	8	6	33	32	60
2	Nottingham Forest	42	16	4	1	41	13	7	6	8	23	28	56
3	Tottenham Hotspur	42	15	3	3	44	21	9	5	7	27	27	56
4	Leeds United	42	15	4	2	41	17	7	7	7	21	25	55
5	Liverpool	42	12	7	2	36	17	7	6	8	28	30	51
6	Everton	42	11	4	6	39	22	8	6	7	26	24	48
7	Arsenal	42	11	6	4	32	20	5	8	8	26	27	46
8	Leicester City	42	12	4	5	47	28	6	4	11	31	43	44
9	Chelsea	42	7	9	5	33	29	8	5	8	34	33	44
10	Sheffield United	42	11	5	5	34	22	5	5	11	18	37	42
11	Sheffield Wednesday	42	9	7	5	39	19	5	6	10	17	28	41
12	Stoke City	42	11	5	5	40	21	6	2	13	23	37	41
13	West Bromwich Albion	42	11	1	9	40	28	5	6	10	37	45	39
14	Burnley	42	11	4	6	43	28	4	5	12	23	48	39
15	Manchester City	42	8	9	4	27	25	4	6	11	16	27	39
16	West Ham United	42	8	6	7	40	31	6	2	13	40	53	36
17	Sunderland	42	12	3	6	39	26	2	5	14	19	46	36
18	**Fulham**	**42**	**8**	**7**	**6**	**49**	**34**	**3**	**5**	**13**	**22**	**49**	**34**
19	Southampton	42	10	3	8	49	41	4	3	14	25	51	34
20	Newcastle United	42	9	5	7	24	27	3	4	14	15	54	33
21	Aston Villa	42	7	5	9	30	33	4	2	15	24	52	29
22	Blackpool	42	1	5	15	18	36	5	4	12	23	40	21

Allan Clarke—a rising star.

1966–67 Season

	Date	H/A	Opponent	Result	Score	Scorers	Attendance
	Sat, August 20	H	Everton	L	0–1		21,634
	Tues, August 23	A	Burnley	L	0–3		18,340
	Sat, August 27	A	Stoke City	W	2–1	Leggat, Clarke	26,333
	Mon, August 29	H	Burnley	D	0–0		15,027
	Sat, September 3	H	Sheffield United	L	0–1		14,887
	Tues, September 6	A	Nottingham Forest	L	1–2	Earle	22,125
	Sat, September 10	A	West Bromwich Albion	L	1–5	Earle	18,000
FL Cup 2	Tues, September 13	H	Crystal Palace	W	2–0	Leggat 2 (1 pen)	9,906
	Sat, September 17	H	Leeds United	D	2–2	Leggat, Earle	19,915
	Sat, September 24	A	Newcastle United	D	1–1	Earle	20,330
	Sat, October 1	H	Tottenham Hotspur	L	3–4	Earle, Clarke, Leggat	28,628
FL Cup 3	Wed, October 5	H	Wolverhampton W	W	5–0	Clarke 2, Barrett, Earle, Conway	14,321
	Sat, October 8	A	Liverpool	D	2–2	Clarke 2	44,025
	Sat, October 15	H	West Ham United	W	4–2	Clarke 2, Earle, og	34,826
	Sat, October 22	A	Sheffield Wednesday	D	1–1	Haynes	20,044
FL Cup 4	Wed, October 26	A	Blackpool	L	2–4	Callaghan, Parmenter	15,349
	Sat, October 29	H	Chelsea	L	1–3	Barrett	43,149
	Sat, November 5	A	West Ham United	L	1–6	Callaghan	22,260
	Sat, November 12	H	Aston Villa	W	5–1	Clarke 2, Conway, Pearson, Parmenter	16,072
	Sat, November 19	A	Arsenal	L	0–1		25,755
	Sat, November 26	H	Manchester City	W	4–1	Clarke 2, Haynes, Cohen	14,570
	Sat, December 3	A	Blackpool	W	1–0	Earle	13,518
	Sat, December 10	H	Southampton	W	3–1	Clarke 2, Conway	19,874
	Sat, December 17	A	Everton	L	2–3	Clarke, Barrett	31,396
	Mon, December 26	A	Leicester City	W	2–0	Callaghan, Barrett	26,936
	Tues, December 27	H	Leicester City	W	4–2	Leggat 3, Haynes	25,174
	Sat, December 31	H	Stoke City	W	4–1	Leggat 2, Clarke, og	24,851
	Sat, January 7	A	Sheffield United	L	0–4		15,008
	Sat, January 14	H	West Bromwich Albion	D	2–2	Callaghan, Barrett	20,680
	Sat, January 21	A	Leeds United	L	1–3	Barrett	32,015
FA Cup 3	Sat, January 28	A	Bradford Park Avenue	W	3–1	Clarke 2, Haynes	14,710
	Sat, February 4	H	Newcastle United	W	5–1	Clarke 3, Haynes, Earle	21,612
	Sat, February 11	A	Tottenham Hotspur	L	2–4	Haynes, Clarke	43,961
FA Cup 4	Sat, February 18	H	Sheffield United	D	1–1	Clarke	32,659
	Sat, February 25	H	Liverpool	D	2–2	Barrett, og	37,481
FA Cup 4R	Wed, March 1	A	Sheffield United	L	1–3	Callaghan	33,279
	Sat, March 4	A	Chelsea	D	0–0		46,784
	Sat, March 18	H	Sheffield Wednesday	L	1–2	Barrett	21,771
	Sat, March 25	A	Southampton	L	2–4	Earle, Clarke	27,945
	Mon, March 27	H	Manchester United	D	2–2	Clarke, Barrett	47,290
	Tues, March 28	A	Manchester United	L	1–2	Earle	51,673
	Sat, April 1	H	Sunderland	W	3–1	Clarke, Pearson, Earle	22,724
	Sat, April 8	A	Aston Villa	D	1–1	Haynes	13,714
	Wed, April 19	H	Arsenal	D	0–0		27,490
	Sat, April 22	A	Manchester City	L	0–3		22,752
	Sat, April 29	H	Blackpool	D	2–2	Clarke 2	14,867
	Sat, May 6	A	Sunderland	L	1–3	Conway	18,604
	Sat, May 13	H	Nottingham Forest	L	2–3	Clarke, Earle	20,417

1966–67 Season

APPEARANCES *(maximum 48):*

Football League Division 1: Clarke 42, Dempsey 42, Robson 41, Brown 40, Earle 36 (+2), Haynes 36, Cohen 35, Callaghan 34 (+1), Barrett 33, Macedo 33, Conway 30, Pearson 20 (+2), Leggat 13 (+2), Nichols 10, McClelland 8, Drake 5, Parmenter 2, Pentecost 1, Seymour 1, Dyson (1 sub).

FA Cup: Barrett 3, Brown 3, Callaghan 3, Clarke 3, Cohen 3, Conway 3, Dempsey 3, Earle 3, Haynes 3, Robson 3, Macedo 2, McClelland 1, Pearson (1 sub).

FL Cup: Barrett 3, Brown 3, Callaghan 3, Cohen 3, Dempsey 3, Robson 3, Clarke 2, Earle 2, Haynes 2, McClelland 2, Pearson 2, Conway 1, Leggat 1, Macedo 1, Nichols 1, Parmenter 1.

TOTAL: Dempsey 48, Clarke 47, Robson 47, Brown 46, Earle 41 (+2), Cohen 41, Haynes 41, Callaghan 40 (+1), Barrett 39, Macedo 36, Conway 34, Pearson 22 (+3), Leggat 14 (+2), McClelland 11, Nichols 11, Drake 5, Parmenter 3, Pentecost 1, Seymour 1, Dyson (1 sub).

GOALSCORERS *(all competitions):*

Clarke 29, Earle 13, Leggat 10, Barrett 9, Haynes 7, Callaghan 5, Conway 4, Pearson 2, Parmenter 2, Cohen 1, og 3.

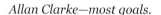

John Dempsey—most appearances. *Allan Clarke—most goals.*

June 1967

In this month

- * Morshe Dayon was appointed Israel's defence minister.
- * The Beatles' 'Sergeant Pepper' album was released.
- * Eighty-eight died as a British airliner crashed in the Pyrenees.
- * China's first 'H-Bomb' was detonated.
- * The Stones' Richards and Jagger were found guilty of drugs offences and convicted.
- * Israel was triumphant in the 'six day war' with the Arabs.
- * Glamour star Jayne Mansfield was killed in a car crash.
- * Spencer Tracy died.

'Silence Is Golden' by The Tremoloes topped the charts.

How the league was won

Manchester United eventually won the title by a clear four points from Nottingham Forest, who finished above Spurs on goal average. Leeds United were a close fourth, just one point behind. Liverpool finished fifth. Arsenal hauled themselves up to seventh, ahead of a hapless Chelsea who dropped to ninth. Blackpool were relegated nearly a month before the end of the season, but Aston Villa with a disastrous run of just four points from their last twelve games, slid down the glass mountain into the other relegation spot. Newcastle United and Southampton survived quite comfortably in the end, thanks to Villa's misfortunes.

The events

A MAJOR shock occurred during the close season when a sudden headline emerged: 'Unhappy Clarke seeks transfer.' Allan Clarke, after an inauspicious start, had worked exceptionally hard on his game and had achieved, for his efforts, a very successful season. Clarke obviously knew his worth, and this was the first sign of a stubborn, opinionated and hard-nosed player wanting more. He had asked for an increase in his wages, and the club had refused.

Clarke was not afraid of ruffling a few feathers, and wanted the dispute resolved before his twenty-first birthday; immediately there was a locking of horns. Clarke promptly upped the ante, by threatening to put in a transfer request. Again, this was met with a cool response from the club; finally Clarke went public. He said: 'I will hand in a request when we assemble for our pre-season tour of Germany. I have told the club the wages I want' and added, 'Their offer comes close, but not close enough.' In a more conciliatory tone he added: 'Meanwhile I'll continue to play my best for the club as always.'

Fulham were bound to refuse a transfer request from one of their biggest assets, even though the club knew that they could already triple their original investment. Clarke kept to his word and handed in the request, and the board met immediately to discuss the issue. The situation was worrying as Clarke was already part of the England set up, and was already in high demand; Chelsea and Manchester United were immediately waiting in the wings. Chelsea had cash burning a hole in their pocket following the sale of misfit Tony Hateley to Liverpool and were desperate for another striker to team up with the classy Peter Osgood. For cash-rich Manchester United, money was no object. This was surely at the forefront of the directors' minds when the board met. Fortunately, the dispute was resolved; Clarke got what he wanted, and withdrew his request.

Les Barrett was rewarded for his fine season by playing in the England versus Young England game on the eve of the Cup Final. He then toured, during the close season, with the England Under-23 squad, winning an England Under-23 cap against Greece on that tour. So good had been his form, that it was rumoured that Manchester United were about to make an offer for Barrett as well as Clarke.

There were plenty of rumours and speculation, but fortunately for the Fulham faithful nothing came of them. Barrett, true to his Fulham and London roots, said: 'I could probably earn twice as much money if I went to one of the top northern clubs, but I would like to get to the top as a Fulham player, and I'd hate to leave everything behind in London.' The chances of hearing phrases like that repeated today are probably remote!

Bobby Robson. The Fulham team would be all the poorer for the absence of the England international who had decided to 'hang up his boots' at the end of the 1966-67 season.

The Close Season 1967

At this time

July

* BBC2 began regular colour broadcasting.
* ATV launched a new regular daily news programme, *News at Ten*.
* Billie Jean King beat Britain's Ann Jones in the Wimbledon ladies singles final.
* It was announced that the seventy mph speed limit was to be retained.
* 5,000 people attended a 'legalise pot' rally at Hyde Park.
* The 'Keep Britain Tidy' group launched Britain's first anti-litter week.
* The Sexual Offences Bill became law.
* The British Steel Corporation was founded.
* Vivien Leigh and Basil Rathbone both died.
* Tommy Simpson (twenty-nine), Britain's most successful road race cyclist, died on the unlucky thirteenth stage of the Tour de France.
* The bill to legalise homosexual acts between adult men was passed.

'A Whiter Shade Of Pale' by Procul Harum topped the charts.

Early August

* The Bill to legalise abortion cleared its third reading, and was expected to become law later in the year.
* The Dartford Tunnel opened.
* The Aberfan disaster was blamed on the coal board.
* Most pirate radio stations closed in advance of the Marine Broadcasting Act.
* The surrealist painter Rene Magritte died.

'All You Need Is Love' by The Beatles topped the charts.

The events

The Fulham board, management, team and supporters took a deserved holiday and it was the summer. The current affairs are included here to retain the 'feel' of the 1967 period!